The World Economy and National Finance
in Historical Perspective

The World Economy and National Finance in Historical Perspective

by Charles P. Kindleberger

Ann Arbor

THE UNIVERSITY OF MICHIGAN PRESS

Copyright © by the University of Michigan 1995
All rights reserved
Published in the United States of America by
The University of Michigan Press
Manufactured in the United States of America
⊗ Printed on acid-free paper

1998   1997   1996   1995   4   3   2   1

A CIP catalog record for this book is available from the British Library.

Library of Congress Cataloging-in-Publication Data

Kindleberger, Charles Poor, 1910–
    The world economy and national finance in historical perspective /
by Charles P. Kindleberger.
        p.   cm.
    Includes bibliographical references.
    ISBN 0-472-10642-2 (alk. paper)
    1. International finance—History. 2. International economic
relations—History. 3. Finance, Public—History. 4. Economic
history.   I. Title.
HG3881.K5323   1995
332'.042—dc20   95-11280
                                                              CIP

Contents

Introduction

In writing books and papers on economics and economic history over sixty years my focus has successively widened and narrowed, but always within the confines of international economics and finance. Starting in the 1930s on capital movements and foreign exchange, it moved to international trade, balances of payments, and, about 1950, to economic and financial history, dealing for the most part with Western Europe. The economics has not been high theory, nor has it involved econometric testing.[1] In the 1930s, requirements for the doctorate included two foreign languages, long since abandoned to make room for more technical economics and especially mathematics. Economic history, too, is losing its place in the graduate curriculum, although of late one can detect the beginnings of a counterrevolution.[2] I am uncertain whether I should be ashamed of being regarded as a literary economist. I am one; if that be shameful, make the most of it.

The present collection of papers is one of several assembled in the past, packaged by-products or hors d'oeuvres, of monographic research and preparation for teaching. They appear more or less simultaneously with a longer work on *World Economic Primacy, 1500–1900,* for which chapter 3 on economic growth and decline can be said to have been an *esquisse.* One who has been in the academy a long time gets calls from time to time to give lectures, contribute to symposia, write in Festschriften for retiring friends and colleagues—and some still a distance away from retirement—all short papers. Lectures are less scholarly than those papers written directly for publication, but it would be tedious to dress them up in academic garb. The two book reviews and the review article,

---

1. These branches of the profession can, on occasion, approach inanity. I recall hearing a young colleague address an older one, saying, "I have just worked out a beautiful model and wonder if you can help me find a use for it." On another occasion, at a consultants' meeting in the U.S. Treasury, a staff member said, "We do not know what to think about the U.S. dollar; all the R^2s in our regression are less than 0.5."

2. See, for example, William N. Parker, ed., *Economic History and the Modern Economist* (Oxford: Blackwell, 1986), and note that the Nobel Prize in economics in 1993 was awarded to two economic historians, Robert W. Fogel and Douglass C. North.

perhaps not on the same intellectual level as the essays, are included from among a larger number of reviews as exhibits of a continuing preoccupation with financial history, especially European.

I am bound to confess that it is not possible for some of us to have a new thought on each page of each exercise. The pages in this volume involve a certain amount, perhaps a considerable amount, of repetition, an affliction, I am told, that increases with age. But again to prune the excess would be tedious for the writer and unrewarding for the reader; the essays are not meant to be read at one sitting, but rather one at a time, short stories with overlapping characters, if you will, rather than a long novel.

The subject running through the essays is the world economy and the place in it occupied by Europe, the United States, and Japan, for the most part in the recent past, rather than earlier centuries—chapter 14 is an exception—the present, and to a very limited extent the future. I regard myself as a historical economist, rather than an economic historian, interested in applying relatively simple economic theory to history, exploring historical episodes to test economic theories for their generality, and, with luck, to turn up some complex reality that calls for a theory beyond those found in the toolbox of the average economist. There are doubtless fewer new theories or insights in these papers than repetition, insistence on and, in rare cases, extension of old views: the need for responsible world leadership in economic and financial crises; the international, rather than national, character of the Great Depression of the 1930s; the close linkages among world capital markets; the need on occasion to depart from mainstream economic rules, despite the cost in creating new precedents.

In particular, I take exception to strongly held views of those whom I call, perhaps ungenerously, "true believers," those with strong prior commitments to monetarism, or for that matter to Keynesianism; who think that markets always work efficiently and that market participants are uniformly rational, informed, and independent minded so that market failure is precluded. In an earlier collection I took the view that both monetarism and Keynesianism were right as approaches to macroeconomic policy, each in its time and place, and sometimes together—a wishy-washy position perhaps, but one that fits the real world better than either pure doctrine alone.[3]

Honest differences of opinion and dilemmas abound in economic policy: if and when to break the rules (rarely, I would hope); whether

---

3. *Keynesianism vs. Monetarism and Other Essays in Financial History* (London: Allen and Unwin, 1985).

a given situation calls for Keynesian or monetarist remedies; whether internal or external equilibrium should have pride of place as a macro-economic target; whether last-resort lending in financial crisis is more or less important than the encouragement that a safety net gives economic actors to take undue risks in the future. Another choice is between centralization and decentralization, an issue faced by corporations as well as by countries in their political organization. Decentralization gives opportunities for the exercise of creative energy. In time of crisis, however, there needs to be some place, institution, or individual that takes charge and accepts responsibility. One would like to be able to shift back and forth as conditions alternate between smooth sailing and storms (and the captain stays below or comes on the bridge), but institutions in a country are not that readily altered, so that the dilemma remains.

Dilemma is sometimes a polite euphemism for sharp division of understanding about how economies, or a particular economy, work. During the 1930s depression, Andrew Mellon, the secretary of the treasury under President Hoover, thought it would be wise to let the purging fires of deflation burn out the excesses of the 1920s, and his advice to the president, not taken, was applauded by the conservative economist Murray Rothbard, and by the popular historian Paul Johnson. Contemporaneously, the policy discussion was echoed in Germany, as discussed in chapter 13, "Rules vs. Men," in the debate on whether Heinrich Brüning, the German chancellor in 1930–31, had alternatives to his policy of swingeing deflation in an effort to demonstrate to the Allies that Germany was unable to pay reparations. I regard these views as aligned with Charles Lamb's recipe for roast pig: Bring the pig into the house; lock the doors and windows; set the place on fire.

I have recently encountered another dilemma, old but infrequently recognized explicitly, which I hope will engage attention in due course when present chores lighten up: whether monetary policy should be focused exclusively on national income and the commodity price level, whether on wholesale or the consumers' price index, or whether some attention should be paid to asset prices—those of equities, perhaps bonds, but certainly real estate. Modern economic discussion of asset prices runs in terms of the technical question of how markets determine asset prices, with a model that calculates expected return and risk of an asset with a stochastic discount factor. My interest is rather policy oriented: when should a central bank pay attention to the course of asset prices and when should it ignore it? Milton Friedman and Anna Jacobson Schwartz took the view that the Federal Reserve made a serious mistake in 1928 and 1929 in worrying about the New York stock market boom and tightening interest rates to slow it down.[4] On the other hand, Koichi Hamada asserts in a new paper that the Bank of Japan erred at the end of the 1980s in keeping interest rates low and the money supply expanding because goods prices were stable and in letting the bubble in stocks and real estate proceed merrily on its way to collapse in 1990.[5] The late Jan Tinbergen's theory of economic policy[6] held that one needed as many instrumental variables as one had targets—in my youth this was summed up in saying that it was impossible to kill two birds with one stone. The monetary authorities then become faced with a trilemma, as opposed to a dilemma: give up caring about asset price bubbles; give up worrying about monetary policy and commodity prices; or find another instrumental variable for dealing with asset prices, while monetary policy copes with commodities, perhaps tougher debt restrictions (margin requirements) for asset buyers, including among assets such derivatives as options, swaps, and futures.

While the research has been mainly on recent European economic and financial history and policy, some has been devoted to the glory days of United States leadership in the world economy, beginning sometime late in the 1930s and continuing until the end of the 1960s or the early 1970s, and to the putative decline of the United States in the last quarter of this century, vigorously questioned, especially by political scientists.

Mild interest in our global village may attach to the fact that many of these talks appeared or were given in papers presented abroad, in Berlin, Rome, Tokyo, Paris, and London, as well as in that other financial capital, New York, and in less eminent foreign cities, such as Copenhagen and Glasgow. Two essays—chapter 10 on the economic crisis of the Thirty Years' War in the seventeenth century and chapter 15 on the German inflation after World War I—were not commissioned or invited, but volunteered. Publication in refereed journals is the scholarly test of personhood (formerly manhood), but if one gets enough assignments there is little time or heart left to compete in the more demanding arena.

The chapter on the seventeenth-century episode reflects a gradual extension of interest in economic history backward in time. My first paper in the field dealt with the varied responses of European countries

4. Milton Friedman and Anna Jacobson Schwartz, *The Monetary History of the United States, 1867–1960* (Princeton, N.J.: Princeton University Press, 1963), 291–92.

5. Koichi Hamada, "Bubbles, Bursts and Bailouts: A Comparison of Three Episodes of Financial Crises in Japan," in *The Structure of the Japanese Economy* (London: Macmillan, forthcoming).

6. Jan Tinbergen, *Economic Policy: Principles and Design* (Amsterdam: North-Holland, 1967).

to the fall in the price of grain in Europe in the 1880s as newly constructed railroads brought grain to the ports and steamships carried it
cheaply and quickly across oceans. Next was a book on economic growth
in France and Britain over the century from 1851 to 1950 (inclusive). For
a time I came forward to the 1930s world depression, then back to the
nineteenth century as a whole. A study of financial manias and panics
regressed further to the Mississippi and South Sea bubbles that burst in
Paris and London, respectively, both in 1720. For lack of the Dutch
language I skipped the tulip mania in Holland that imploded in 1637,
though read about it in English and remain profoundly skeptical of
recent studies by Peter Garber, who believes in rational expectations,
market efficiency, and fundamentals and disbelieves in bubbles. He
seeks to explain the high price of such tulip bulbs as the Semper Augus-
tus as owing to the difficulties of Mendellian breeding.[7] From time to
time, interest turned to the nineteenth century, fulfilling invitations to
write on this and that, and produced separate studies of the 1873 crash in
Austria, Germany, and the United States and the 1890–93 crises in
London, Argentina, New York, and Australia, each included in other
collections. In both, attention is paid especially to the international
aspects.

The division of the chapters into those dealing with the world economy and those with national finance is arbitrary and to some extent
misleading. All are to some degree international in reach. Moreover the
word *world* in the book title is something of a misnomer as coverage is
limited to industrial countries—the world of the Organization of Economic Cooperation and Development (O.E.C.D.)—and leaves out Africa, Latin America, the Middle East, and the Far East, apart from
Japan. Emphasis in part 1 is on the relationships of the United States and
Europe in the world economy, with Japan given less attention except in
the keynote lecture at a March 1990 conference in Tokyo (chap. 3 in this
volume). In that lecture, by the way, I said that I was made uneasy by
the height of the Tokyo stock market, but lost points as a forecaster by
saying preliminarily that I lacked confidence in such judgments and
urged listeners not to bet the store on any prediction that smacked of a
market tip.

Chapter 1, on the United States and the world economy, grew out
of a book on *The World in Depression, 1929–1939.*[8] President Hoover

---

7. Peter M. Garber, "Tulipmania," *Journal of Political Economy* 97 (June 1989),
535–60, and idem, "The Dollar as a Bubble," in *The Economics of the Dollar Cycle,* ed.
Stefan Gerlach and Peter A. Petri (Cambridge, Mass.: MIT Press, 1990), 129–47.

8. *The World in Depression, 1929–1939,* rev. ed (Berkeley, Calif.: University of
California Press, 1986).

thought the depression had its origin in Europe; Europeans and many American economists lay the onus entirely on the United States. In my judgment, echoing one of Robin Matthews of Cambridge University in discussion of the depression of 1836–39, a century earlier, there was no one country that could be squarely blamed, rather than complex interaction. But chapter 1 deals with a different theme, the need in crisis for effective national leadership. Political scientists took up the issue more often than did economists and economic historians, discussing it with stronger rhetoric than leadership, namely in terms of dominance and hegemony. To hegemonic stability, political science offered two alternatives: *regimes,* or principles and habits of cooperation, perhaps developed under the sway of a benign hegemon, and the balance-of-power system. A strong possibility exists that any and all systems of international relations in the economic field, and perhaps in the politico-military as well, are subject to entropy or breakdown over time, and the basic question is not which system is best in and of itself, but which has the best prospect for lasting.

This first chapter ranges the changes in the U.S. roles in the twentieth century, first as follower, then isolationist, then gradually accepting responsibility for world economic leadership, and now possibly fretting as it contemplates a less stellar role than that it played in the Golden Age after 1950. Written for a Festschrift for Professor Wolfram Fischer of the Free University of Berlin, the editor of the series in which the book on the depression appeared, the paper was on a subject of my choice. The second and third chapters represent keynote lectures delivered before large audiences at conferences, each on an assigned topic. The Rome conference was on "Building the New Europe," that in Tokyo on "The World Economy of the 1990s." Chapter 4, an essay rather than a lecture and for a popular financial journal rather than a scholarly periodical, was also on an assigned topic for an issue around a single topic. Assignments have an advantage in stimulating thought on a subject at the same time that they relieve one of the necessity to think of a topic of one's own.

The chapters on Europe in the world economy (chap. 2) and on the evolving organization of the world economy (chap. 7), both on topics picked out for me, were flattering because of the strong impression that the invitations originated with former students, Mario Baldassari of the University "Sapienza" in Rome and Robert Mundell of Columbia University in the first instance, Mundell alone in the second. The two were different. The Rome meeting was a huge conference over three days, the proceedings published in two fat volumes, one set in English, one in

Italian, of six hundred pages each for the English. In New York, the talk was to a private seminar, chaired by the conservative editor of the *Wall Street Journal,* Robert Bartley. There were perhaps twenty people present, many of them right-wing observers of the economic scene, such as Lewis Lehrman and Jude Wanniski. The occasion had slight overtones of bearbaiting, but it was stimulating.

Chapter 5 is a short paper delivered at a National Bureau of Economic Research Conference in Cambridge, Massachusetts, in October 1989, as a member of a panel of four discussing international aspects of financial crises, following a long paper on the subject. I confess to some satisfaction that international aspects of financial crises, which I had been extolling for some years, finally received a third of the attention of the conference, along with the risks of crisis and macroeconomic effects.

Chapter 6 was another invited keynote talk, but at a small meeting of the International Economic Association at a resort in Denmark on the Kattegat, near Copenhagen. My assigned topic clearly called for a reprise on *Manias, Panics . . . ,*[9] rather than on wavelike movements in the overall economy. The meeting had a highly technical bent overall and papers on "Cuspoidal Nets" and "Nonlinear Dynamics," to which I could not warm.

The last item in part 1, a review of Milton Friedman's latest book, *Money Mischief,* written for the *Boston Globe,* came about through my name being given to the book review editor by a reporter friend who knew I was not a dyed-in-the-wool monetarist, but had studied some monetary history.

Part 2, on national finance, has large elements of the international but deals mostly with the United States, in chapters 9, 10, and 11, and with Germany, in chapters 13 through 16. The chapter between these two series, chapter 12, on the economic Golden Age from 1950 to 1973 (plus or minus at both ends) deals with a number of countries but not particularly with the international connections among them. Some question arises as to whether it belongs with national finance, since it is concerned with growth and not finance.

The first two chapters in this part were associated with the Jerome Levy Institute at Bard College in Annandale-on-the-Hudson, New York, and with Hyman Minsky. I first heard of and read Minsky when writing *Manias. . . .* He was closely associated with the founding of the Jerome Levy Institute, and joined it as a research fellow after retiring

---

9. *Manias, Panics and Crashes: A History of Financial Crises,* rev. ed. (New York: Basic Books, 1989).

from the economics department of Washington University in St. Louis. I became a member of the Board of Economic Advisers of the institute for a few years, before finding it too hard to get to its frequent meetings from the Boston suburbs by car, two hundred miles each way. It was a lively group, including Leon Botstein, president of Bard College, James Tobin, Franco Modigliani, and Senator Patrick Moynihan, in addition to Minsky. "The Quality of Debt" was written for an Institute symposium on profits, deficits, and stability. Minsky was particularly interested in various types of debt and their relation to macroeconomic stability. He gave a paper on the subject at a symposium organized by Jean-Pierre Laffargue of CEPREMAP in Paris and by me in Bad Homberg, in the Federal Republic of Germany, in 1979. At that time, Minsky was severely criticized by the late Raymond W. Goldsmith, who contended that financial crises were phenomena of the childhood of capitalism, not its maturity.[10] This view in retrospect looks overly optimistic as one bears in mind the October 1987 stock market crash in New York; Third World debt; savings and loan institutions; boom and bust in shopping malls, office buildings, hotels, and condominia; and to bring it further down to the present-day options, swaps, other derivatives, mutual funds for emerging (country) markets, and the like.

Chapter 10, on intermediation, disintermediation and direct trading, was a contribution to Hyman Minsky's retirement celebration in St. Louis. It sought to enunciate a general tendency in commodity markets, like those in Venice, Amsterdam, and London, over time, where entrepôt centers lose their function as a turntable as information on what is available where and what is wanted where becomes widely diffused and direct trading enables buyers and sellers to mutually economize on transport costs. The same tendency, at a weaker level, is seen in financial markets. It is weaker because the savings from direct trading in money and financial instruments, more or less weightless, are smaller than those in economizing on commodity freight.

Chapter 11, on the lender of last resort, was given in London as a Henry Thornton lecture, named after one of the originators of the concept two generations before Walter Bagehot's formulation in *Lombard Street*.[11] Despite the venue, it dealt mostly with the United States, and

10. Raymond W. Goldsmith, "Comment" (on Hyman P. Minsky, "The Financial-stability Hypothesis: Capitalist Processes and the Behavior of the Economy"), in *Financial Crises: Theory, History and Policy*, ed. C. P. Kindleberger and Jean-Pierre Laffargue (Cambridge: Cambridge University Press, 1982), 41–43.

11. Walter Bagehot, *Lombard Street*, in *The Collected Works of Walter Bagehot*, ed. Norman St. John-Stevas 9 (London: Economist [1873] 1978), 48–233.

with deposit insurance for banks and thrift institutions, especially savings and loan societies. The dilemma for monetary authorities in the choice between saving the system in the short run and weakening it in the long run through moral hazard was mentioned above. The MIT secretary who typed it, Eva Hakala, appended a note as she sent it, saying, "Another depressing paper." Before that she had typed a short book of mine, *Mariners and Markets* (1992),[12] which suggested that the market for seamen in the age of sail was efficient only if sailors, who were crimped (shanghaied), impressed, underfed, exposed to shipwreck in undermaintained vessels, fully insured, flogged, and who were wont to mutiny and desertion could be said to have been "free to choose."

The next two chapters were celebratory. Chapter 12, on the Golden Age from 1950 to 1973 (called by the French *les trentes années glorieuses,* presumably starting earlier and coming down later). As the chapter states, the editor-daughter of the coeditor honoree, Sir Alec Cairncross, asked me to deal with the 1960s instead of the quarter century as a whole, but I used my poetic license to broaden the coverage. The title, "Golden Age," raises a question of half full/half empty, depending on the "counterfactual" one brings to the question: whether the half glass of water was being compared with an empty glass or a full one. It was a golden age for Britain because the rate of growth outstripped any previously recorded in British economic history, but the age was tarnished by comparison with the growth in Japan, Germany, Scandinavia, France, and Italy. The United States also lagged well behind the leaders.

"Rules vs. Men" (chap. 13) is a hoary chestnut in economic policy in many times and places, but in this instance deals primarily with the extended controversy in German economic history over the part played by Chancellor Heinrich Brüning in the early stages of the 1930 depression. The honoree of the Festschrift in which the paper appeared, Professor Knut Borchardt of the University of Munich, played a leading role in the debate, coming down strongly on the side that Brüning lacked alternatives. In his view, he was restricted to deflationary measures by law, rules, international commitments, and by the zeitgeist of the German public, with its strong memories of the 1919–23 inflation. The question is general and raises the issue of Thomas Carlisle's hero in history. One referee for U of M Press thought I should change the title to "Rules vs. People" or "Rules vs. Persons." The term *men* in the title is not gender bound, but generic. The same or similar questions could arise in the policies of Golda Meir, Indira Ghandi, and Margaret Thatcher.

---

12. *Mariners and Markets* (New York: Harvester/Wheatsheaf, 1992).

Chapters 14 and 15 are the volunteers, submitted to refereed journals, not commissioned or invited. Chapter 14 on the *Kipper- und Wipperzeit* of coinage debasement in the early years of the Thirty Years' War (1618–48) deals mostly with mosaic Germany, made up of hundreds of principalities, dukedoms, bishoprics, and the like, organized under the Holy Roman Empire into *Kreise* or circles. I came across the episode first in Max Wirth's *Geschichte des Handelskrisen* (History of Trade Crises),[13] albeit a thin and unsatisfactory account purportedly confined to Lübeck. My curiosity was aroused and in due course I poked and pried. Much of the relevant literature is in journals of provincial history in Germany, emphasizing local conditions. I gained access to a few of the most important of these through the kindly efforts of Professor Fischer of Berlin, the honoree of chapter 1, and his assistants. An anonymous referee who may have had a bias favoring early German economic history liked the paper better than the editor of the journal, who eliminated a number of (to me) interesting asides, presumably in the interest of saving space.

The review article on Gerald Feldman's *The Great Disorder* dealing with the German inflation of 1914 to 1923 arose when I received a copy unannounced from the publisher. This was doubtless on the initiative of the historian-author, for whom I had written a paper on the subject for an earlier symposium. On other occasions, I have been sent a book directly by an author and asked to review it and submit the review for publication. For some reason I find this disagreeable and have chosen not to. In this case, the initiative came solely from me. I called the book to the attention of the *Journal of Economic Literature*, expressed the view that it merited more than the usual 500-word review; in particular, a review article, which I offered to produce. The offer was accepted.

Chapter 16, a normal-sized review of a German book, was written on the request of an editor, but with pleasure. Reading it was a learning experience, as the cliché goes. I have long had a rule to review any book I am asked to, unless there are clear reasons to abstain—such as an enormous like or dislike for the person and his/her other work, or being overwhelmed with work. It is a good rule. I break it rarely.

These papers, mostly written in the half decade from 1989 to 1994, are by-products, as I have said, of a period when I was occupied with a revision of *A Financial History of Western Europe*,[14] the slim *Mariners*

---

13. *Geschichte des Handelskrisen* (History of Trade Crisis), 4th ed. (Vienna 1890; reprint, New York: Burt Franklin, 1968), chap. 1.

14. *A Financial History of Western Europe*, 2d ed. (New York: Oxford University Press, 1993).

and Markets, and getting under way on *World Economic Primacy, 1500–1990,*[15] about to go to press. I have a strong bias, to be sure, but I do not think that the collection constitutes what my old department head, Ralph Freeman, used to call "a dog's breakfast." Running through the papers is a series of themes that strike me as critical to economic and historical analysis: the two-sided Manichean complexity of the world. There are times—perhaps most times—when economic life is simple. Markets work, the overall economy is stable, government is properly restricted to the few tasks listed by Adam Smith: national defense, the maintenance of justice and order, and a few massive public works. Connections between cause and effect are clear; the needs of economic policy do not pose dilemmas. But not always. There are some constants in economic life, perhaps in human nature, that I tried to deal with in a set of lectures of a decade-plus back.[16] The paper on intermediation and direct trading might be added to the list developed on that occasion. But be wary and constantly on the lookout for the exceptions. Some monetarists and free marketers would abolish central banks, government licensing, and regulation, lock the door, and throw the key away. At the very least, keep the key.

---

15. *World Economic Primacy, 1500–1990* (New York: Oxford University Press, forthcoming).

16. *Economic Laws and Economic History,* The 1980 Raffaelo Mattioli Lectures (Cambridge: Cambridge University Press, 1989).

Part 1

CHAPTER 1

The United States and the World Economy in the Twentieth Century

The twentieth was said by Henry Luce, the founder of *Time* magazine, to be the American century. If so, like Adolph Hitler's 1,000-year Reich, it did not last as long as advertised. When it started and when it ended are questions that will be addressed, or at least posed, in what follows. But it is perhaps fair to say that the country was an economic youth as the century dawned, and now may be in some sort of economic decline.

I choose not to try to fit the country into the Rostovian stages of preconditions, takeoff, drive to maturity and age of high mass consumption (Rostow 1960). I have some objection to any and all stage theories, but that particular paradigm lacks a stage of decline. Decline may be implied by high mass consumption, however, if one gives credence to the Cipolla view of the decline of empires—that improvements in the standards of living brought about by a rising economy lead to more and more people demanding to share the benefits, and that incomes increase and extravagances develop as new needs replace those which have begun to be satisfied (Cipolla 1970, from the back cover of the paperback).

One could perhaps fit the country into another paradigm related to the balance of indebtedness: young debtor, mature debtor, young creditor and mature creditor, although the symmetry of the scheme hides the fact that the United States went from the first to the third in the three or four years of the First World War, stayed there for sixty years, and reached the fourth stage only in the middle 1970s. This pattern, too, lacks much attention to the stage of capital consumption, as the mature creditor is presumed to live off foreign income rather than to borrow for consumption and/or consume the capital invested abroad.

There are other patterns one could experiment with, the Gompertz

Reprinted from Carl-Ludwig Holtfrerich, ed., *Interactions in the World Economy: Perspectives from International Economic History* (New York: Harvester-Wheatsheaf, 1989), 287–313.

15

TABLE 1.1. The United States and the World Economy—Twentieth Century

Function	1901–14	1919–29	1930–39	1945–70	1971 to Present	Notes
Goods markets	Strong protection moderated 1913	Antidumping tariff, ignored 1927 tariff truce, resist Stevenson rubber plan	Hawley-Smoot irresponsible Begin reversal RTAA, 1934	ITO, GATT, Dillon, Kennedy etc. rounds, sale out of strategic reserve, Combined Boards, NTBs	Bilateral XR, MFA, soya bean "shocku," AOPEC embargo left to oil companies	Gephardt threat of bilateral retaliation, ambivalence commodity agreements, GSP
Foreign exchange	"Automatic" under gold standard	FRBNY interest in European cooperation	Thomas amendment, change gold price, torpedo WEC, Tripartite Monetary Agreement, silver price	Bretton woods, British loan, Marshall Plan, gold pool, swaps, G-10, SDR	10% devaluation floating, benign neglect, Baker Plan, Louvre to correct 1982–85, appreciation	Gold bugs: Mundell, etc., free fall? Liquidity a nonproblem
Capital flows	Mature debtor repays FDI	Dawes loan, spurt X 1924–28, halted 1928 when NYSE boom	Widespread default, lending stopped to all but Canada	X – M Bank, World Bank, regional DBs, IET, VCRP, MCP	bank lending sovereign states after "crime of 1971," big inflow, Treasury bonds, real estate, equities	Baker insistence on banks continued lending, Black Monday
Coordination monetary, fiscal policy	Gold standard, Aldrich Comm., Fed. Res. Act	Sterilize war gold, 1927 Ogden Mills CB meeting	Feeble attempt to coordinate B of E	IMF, OECD, WP #3, Chequers	Carter program, locomotives, summit meetings ineffective	Inability of U.S. to persuade Japan to limit export-led growth, FRG to relax about inflation
Lender of last resort	Not needed	Isolationism, insist on war debts	Too little too late, sabotage World Economic Conference	Marshall Plan etc., swaps, Paris Club	Mexico 1982, Basel protocol 1975	Unclear where responsibility lies today

Abbreviations:
AOPEC—Arab Organization of Petroleum Exporting Countries; B of E—Bank of England; CB—central banks; DB—development banks; FDI—foreign direct investment; FRBNY—Federal Reserve Bank of New York; FRG—Federal Republic of Germany; GATT—General Agreement on Tariffs and Trade; GSP—Generalized System of Preferences; IET—Interest Equalization Tax; IMF—International Monetary Fund; ITO—International Trade Organization; MCP—Mandatory Control Program; MFA—Multi-Fiber Agreement; NTB—Non-Tariff Barrier; NYSE—New York Stock Exchange; OECD—Organization for Economic Co-operation and Development; SDR—Specialized Drawing Rights; VCRP—Voluntary Credit Restraint Program; WEC—World Economic Conference; WP—Working Party; X—export of capital; X – M—exports minus imports, or trade balance; XR—export restraints.

or S-curve of material transformation as the metallurgist, Cyril Stanley Smith (1975) calls it, or the Kondratieff model of recurring fifty-year cycles, at least prices, and possibly—though I have no faith in them—in such other economic variables as production, income, technical change, or wars that serve as hothouses of economic growth, speeding up capital formation and growth in young countries, decline through capital consumption in ageing countries.

One can of course compare the United States in the world economy with the United Kingdom: when Britain was the world's economic leader it had sterling and the British Navy; the United States in its turn had the dollar and the atom bomb (Hogan 1987: 213). Hawtrey (1952) stated that power is the capacity to produce goods and to move them over distances—a view that focuses on the British navy more than on the battleship: the US analogue presumably lies in the civil air fleet and the air force. Or one could approach the ninety-year (present century) history of the United States in the terms of Paul Kennedy (1987) or of Mancur Olson (1982). Kennedy claims that leading powers take on commitments that grow until they mount beyond the capacity of the country, or its willingness, to discharge them. Olson makes a distinction between countries that remain at peace or undefeated for years on end, in which distributional coalitions form and fight for a growing share, or at least against a declining one, of the national income, blocking the agenda of solutions to problems of production and trade. Thurow (1980) calls it a zero-sum society; Krueger (1974) puts it that a shift occurs from output and marketing to rent seeking. A scheme that focuses more on the world economy and less on the United States is that of Wallerstein (1980) in which the world is organized about a center and consists for the most part of a periphery. On this showing the United States could be said to have started in the periphery, or possibly the semiperiphery as the later versions of the pattern provide (Senghaas 1985), and moved unevenly to take over the position of the center, and in recent years to drift out again.

The dating of decline again presents a problem: one could take the breakup of the London gold pool in 1968, the closing of the gold window in August 1971, floating the dollar in 1973 (at the insistence of the Bundesbank). Benign neglect applied to the dollar exchange rate under President Nixon and later President Reagan while Donald Regan was secretary of the treasury, produced a reaction of reasserted US concern under James Baker, Mr. Regan's successor, in the Plaza (1985) and Louvre (1987) agreements and the Seoul declaration on Third World debt. As I write the country seems to be slipping—in the heat of a forthcoming election campaign—into a catatonic state insofar as it tries to cope with the deficit in the balance of payments, trade and exchange policy, and preparing for upcoming incidents in the continuing Third World debt crisis and a possible free fall in the dollar. A number of proposals of more or less insight are put forward, ranging from a return to the gold standard advocated by Congressman Kemp and a former candidate for governor of New York, Lewis Lehrman, to large-scale negotiations about Third World debt (Senator Bill Bradley, Felix Rohatyn, Peter Kenen, et al.), balanced-budget constitutional amendments, rigorous abstention of government from interfering with markets, regulation of markets, reregulation of banking, etc., but no one seems to be listening.

Goods Markets

The task of a leading country in the world in relation to commodity markets has been interpreted as leaving them alone in ordinary times, but intervening in crisis. Leaving them alone means free trade, that is, imposing no tariffs. The United States is constitutionally unable to tax exports so that this means keeping down tariffs and other restrictions for imports. There are various possible sorts of crises. In periods of glut, the task of a leader is to keep its market open for imports, as Britain did from 1846 to 1860 on to 1915. In periods of acute shortage, it means continuing to supply the good or goods in question to buyers. Crises which affect the resources engaged in an import-competing good, sometimes called market disrupting, pose difficult questions. If the resources involved, especially labor, have opportunities for other employment, even at lower wages, there is a case for doing nothing. If they are isolated and the only alternative is unemployment, some economists would want to impose tariffs on second-best grounds that call for interfering with markets when they don't work. Others would intervene to improve or assist the functions of the labor market. Where the industry is capable of recovery there may be a case for a temporary and disappearing tariff, and so on. Much depends upon whether the authorities are concerned with the welfare of a limited group, of consumers within the nation as a group, or of optimal allocation of world resources. Presumably less-developed countries have limited responsibility for the allocation of resources in the world as a whole, while a leading country looks beyond its borders. As a country declines in the world relative to others its horizons shrink again.

The United States entered the twentieth century with high tariffs enacted in 1890 (McKinley), 1894 (Wilson) and 1897 (Dingley). The British Board of Trade estimated at the turn of the century that its most important export goods paid duties in the United States averaging 70 percent ad valorem. The Payne-Aldrich tariff of 1909, a Republican enactment, changed the details but left the general level more or less the same. A Democratic tariff adjustment in 1913 (Underwood) lowered duties on about half the more important items, left others unchanged, established an official Tariff Commission.

The immediate postwar period was one of considerable chaos in trade. Exchange rates pegged during the war were let go, and many countries adopted new tariffs to counteract "exchange dumping." In the United States this took the form of the Fordney-McCumber tariff of 1922. The United States protested vigorously but vainly against the 1923–4 Stevenson rubber plan to raise prices in the Malay States and Ceylon; ultimately the scheme was undermined by rapidly expanding native production in Indonesia. Along with other countries, the United States participated in the World Economic Conference of 1927 that negotiated a truce in tariff increases, but like other countries, paid little attention to it.

Maintaining high tariffs during the 1920s after it had paid off a lot of its overseas debt during the war, accumulated claims on the rest of the world, and engaging in substantial new lending especially in the period from 1924 to 1928, the United States was attacked as failing to act as a creditor nation should. The reference, of course, was to British free trade from 1860 to 1913 and substantial foreign lending. Modern economic theorists, however, are in general agreement that the criticism was misplaced: tariffs are a microeconomic distortion with but little macroeconomic effect as impact on the balance of payments. A particular tariff may make it hard for a debtor to export to the United States a particular good in which it has a comparative advantage, but the expansionary effect of the restriction in the importing creditor, and contractive effect in the exporting debtor, however objectionable in themselves, will correct most of the effect of the tariff on the balance of payments.

The 1929 depression is usually credited with having given rise to the Hawley-Smoot tariff of 1930. In fact, the origin of the Hawley-Smoot goes back to the presidential campaign of 1928 when President Hoover promised to do something for agriculture, and the Congress reached for what Schumpeter called "the Republican sovereign remedy," the tariff. Logrolling let the matter get quickly out of hand. Increases in duties spread from agricultural products to other raw materials and to manufactured products. Democrats joined Republicans in the exercise, and both were pushed aside by the lobbyists for particular interests. The decline in business may have induced President Hoover to sign the monstrous bill into law in June 1930, over the protests of

1,028 economists inside the country and of forty-five foreign countries. It was a beggar-my-neighbor action of the most parochial sort.

In the first years of the Roosevelt administration that began in March 1933, the US government was even more acutely isolationist in economic terms than it had been under Hoover. The World Economic Conference of June–July 1933 was torpedoed, as will be shown, on unwillingness to stabilize the foreign value of the dollar. The farm program required limiting imports from Canada of products the prices of which had been raised domestically. Strong demands for agricultural protection were voiced within the government by one George Peek in the Department of Agriculture. The secretary of state, however, was Cordell Hull, a former congressman and former chairman of the Ways and Means Committee under Democratic regimes, who came from a district in Eastern Tennessee that exported tobacco, and was adamantly, almost fanatically, a free trader, and especially an opponent of British Empire and Commonwealth preference that discriminated against United States farm products. He kept pushing in the Cabinet for a liberalization of trade, partly also as a political gesture against the autarkic Fascist countries.

In 1934 the President acceded to his program, against that of Peek, and went forward with the Reciprocal Trade Agreement Act. Under this legislation Congress turned the tariff-making function over to the Administration for limited periods of time, and within restrictions, as a means of eliminating logrolling. The first Act provided that tariffs could be reduced by 50 percent (or half the Hawley-Smoot level) against reciprocal concessions made by a bilateral agreement partner. Concessions made to one country were extended to all others with whom the United States had a treaty of Friendship, Commerce and Navigation containing the most-favored-nation clause. The first agreements were relatively innocuous, with Latin American countries, and then, just before the war, new ones with Canada and the United Kingdom, but highly restricted in the commodities and products for which concessions were granted (or obtained). Subsequent renewals, especially after the war, provided for 50 percent reductions not from Hawley-Smoot but from the existing lowered level, for reductions to zero under certain circumstances, few of which were realized in practice, and for multilateral negotiations (actually simultaneous bilateral negotiations in which concessions exchange between countries where one was the principal supplier of the other in a given good were generalized to all other countries in the negotiation).

All this time the Congress and the lobbyists representing the interests of particular commodities and products were yielding ground grudgingly. Each renewal of the legislation imposed new limitations: "peril points" beyond which tariffs in specified commodities could not be reduced, an "escape clause," which provided that a given concession could be withdrawn if it led to a very damaging increase in imports, and the like. In due course the Administration gave further ground by negotiating special agreements with foreign exporting countries to restrict exports to the United States, originally one country-supplier at a time, but when this raised US prices and attracted imports from other foreign countries, at first in successive bilateral agreements and then multilaterally.

The movement of the United States from a protectionist to a relatively free-trade country is explained by economists as the consequence of the rising importance of large-scale industry which exported, as against small-scale industry which was import-competing. Business in the former was organized into such a group as the Committee for Economic Development which was liberal, in the latter in the National Association of Manufacturers, which was protectionist. The position in labor was more complex, as the American Federation of Labor on a craft basis and originally protectionist, merged with the Congress of Industrial Organizations, an industrial union, the biggest constituents of which came from large-scale production and were for low tariffs to stimulate exports. In the early postwar period the AFL-CIO supported the trade agreement acts; as world recovery and growth outside the United States began to lead to imports of such products as automobiles, radio and television sets, and the like, the liberality of the unions weakened. Large-scale industry also lost cohesion on the issue. Some companies undertook foreign direct investment to produce whole products or components abroad and remained in favor of free trade, while others such as steel resisted. Labor's opposition to liberal trade arrangements was expressed in the push for passage of a Burke-Hartke bill, which failed, but would have both restricted imports and put penalties on foreign direct investment.

At the time of writing, one presidential candidate, Representative Richard Gephardt from Missouri, proposed to mingle the trade issue with balance-of-payments again, calling for negotiations with separate countries that have bilateral surpluses in payments with the United States. This appears to be a disguised version of geriatric tariffs, such as have been called for in Britain by the late Lord Kaldor. Whether these will come to pass cannot be foretold, but the discussion indicates that the United States has receded a long distance from its role as a leader in promoting freer world trade.

It must be admitted that there was a strong element of national interest in promoting free trade so long as the United States was a leading producer of the latest manufactured goods. The British equivalent was called "free-trade imperialism" (Gallagher and Robinson 1953; Semmel 1970). When the competition from Japan and Germany became intense, enthusiasm for free trade diminished. The Reagan administration professed an ideological predilection for free markets, but like that of Roosevelt, Truman and others, made concessions to protectionist forces when it judged it expedient. One defense against the protectionist forces in the country was to pressure Japan to reduce its infant industry restrictions faster, a process that became known as "Japan-bashing."

Attention to particular trade items was intense in the First and Second World Wars, when scarce shipping space was allocated in transatlantic carriage, and when the United States organized allied Combined Boards to allocate the supplies of food, raw materials and capital equipment. Pressure was exerted to bring such neutral countries as Argentina within the allocation schemes, and to keep them there during the period of acute scarcity after the war. In due course government allocations were relaxed in favor of free markets. When raw materials became abundant after 1951, some residual anxiety over the availability of supplies built up, and the United States acquired substantial stockpiles of commodities, such as nonferrous metals, that might run short. When scarcities returned with the Korean War, some of these US stockpiles were released to the market, to dampen the rise in prices.

In the 1950s and 1960s as Japanese production rose with a strong export drive, the United States kept its market open for Japanese goods when those in Europe were for the most part closed. In 1973, however, two episodes suggested that the United States was no longer willing to take a leadership role in commodities. An Arab Organization of Petroleum Exporting Countries embargo, a reduction by 25 percent for most countries, but 100 percent for those it deemed hostile—the Netherlands and the United States—hurt the Netherlands with far more reliance on imports than the United States, which has substantial domestic production. Neither the EEC (European Economic Community) nor the US government took action to assist the Netherlands—although they locked the door in November 1974, after the horse had been stolen, by organizing an International Energy Agency. The Netherlands was assisted, however, by the international oil companies which rearranged the distribution of Iranian supplies that lay outside the embargo to spread the hurt more equitably.

In the summer of 1973, moreover, President Nixon cut off the export of soybeans from the United States to hold down the price, which had gone sky-high. Since Japan's diet depended upon imports of soybeans, and US production and consumption were on a far bigger scale, this was an unconscionable act for a world stabilizer to take in the commodity field, and indicated a shift away from attention to world stability to the narrow interest of the United States.

A complete account of US leadership in goods markets would require attention to commodity agreements in which US policy has varied from opposition to tolerance, the latter qualified by the condition that some attention be paid to consumer interests, and to acceptance of some financing of balance-of-payments deficits by the IMF when an exporting country's prices fall. The issue is complicated, and lies outside the present interest in leadership functions.

Foreign Exchange

In my taxonomy of leadership functions in the world economy I duck the question of what the appropriate policy for a foreign-exchange regime should be—though I have views on that subject—to say merely that the regime should be managed. In the nineteenth century to 1914 the regime is characterized as the gold standard, though it is sometimes regarded as a sterling standard, disguised as an objective, immutable, and autonomous institution to which Britain conformed rather than which it directed. In any event, the United States played an entirely subordinate and passive role until the establishment of the Federal Reserve System in 1913 and its operation in the world economy in 1919 and thereafter. Even then it is appropriate to observe that interest in the subject was restricted for the most part to New York, and that the rest of the country, including Washington, was uninterested or antagonistic to involvement in the exchange problems of postwar Europe.

In the 1920s Benjamin Strong, the governor of the Federal Reserve Bank of New York, was an advocate of rapid reconstruction of the system of exchange rates in Europe. He continuously urged the Bank of England to restore the pound to par, consulted with the Bank of France and the Bank of Italy as to what the rates for the franc and lira should be, tried to smooth the ruffled relations between Montagu Norman of the Bank of England and Emile Moreau of the Bank of France. As noted below, he was prepared to accommodate US monetary policy to some degree to the interests of Europe but not, however, to the extent of expanding the money supply by the full range made possible by the gold received by the United States from Europe during and after the war.

The exchange regime laboriously reconstructed after 1925 broke down in 1931 as capital withdrawals, first from Austria and then successively from Germany and Britain, led to restrictions on the one hand, especially the German Standstill Agreement, and then British exchange depreciation on the other. In due course the Japanese yen, which had been restored to gold only late in 1929, was depreciated to relieve the strong deflationary pressure of declining export prices, especially silk. This occurred in December 1931. Continued price declines after sterling depreciation drove the United States off gold in April 1933, and the gold bloc ultimately followed in 1935 and 1936.

There is an open historical debate as to whether the United States and France could have forestalled the spreading collapse in foreign exchanges by a substantial lender-of-last-resort operation for Austria in May 1931. The weakened Britain, a victim of overvaluation from the restoration of the pound to par in 1925, lacked the resources to bolster the Austrian schilling. The United States was reluctant to take strong action. France restricted its modest assistance on Austrian acceptance of political conditions. The United States attempted to assist Germany with a moratorium on war debts and reparations, but France raised legal questions and while they were being discussed, capital withdrawals picked up and drove Germany to inconvertibility. Rescues for Britain were too little, too late, and regarded by the British Labour Party as too political. The appreciation of the dollar and gold currencies (depreciation of sterling and its many linked currencies) in September 1931, accelerated the decline of world gold and dollar prices.

In all this, the United States acted as one among the other states, solicitous of its own interest and disregarding the repair or reconstruction of the system. In April 1933 President Roosevelt accepted the so-called Thomas amendment put forward by inflationists in Congress which would allow him to cut the link of the dollar to gold. There followed abandonment of convertibility. When the delegates to the World Economic Conference of June–July 1933 agreed on an exchange of concessions in which the United Kingdom would stabilize the pound, Germany would relax foreign-exchange control, France give up its trade quotas, and the United States settle war debts, lower tariffs, and stabilize the dollar. Roosevelt backed off as the hint of dollar stability knocked down US commodity and stock market prices.

Some observers have maintained that the United States was altogether wrong to devalue the dollar because the current account of the balance of payments was in surplus, which meant that international transactions were giving a lift to the US economy (Nurkse 1949). This analysis has a narrow base in a foreign-trade-multiplier model, and neglects the effects of exchange rates on prices. In actuality the appreciation of the dollar after the pound sterling, yen, etc., went off gold was so deflationary for US prices and incomes that it produced an export surplus as a residual. The surplus was not an independent autonomous force.

In the autumn of 1933 the United States experimented in raising prices through changes in the gold price. At first higher prices for gold were applied to domestic production. Gradually it was recognized that the lift to prices—in the Greenback period from 1863 to 1879 which supplied the data on which the experiment was based—had come from the exchange rate, not the gold price; the gold price was an effect, not a cause. A change was then made to buying gold at higher prices abroad, with the dollars used to buy, say, sterling, driving down the dollar rate. But the connection between gold prices and commodity prices was generally loose and the United States quickly became disenchanted with the experiment. A year later the government approached the Bank of England to ask whether it would be interested in stabilization, and received a negative reply.

During this period the US Treasury also raised the price it paid for silver at the behest of senators from silver-mining states, dismissing the initial negative impact the action had on the currencies of the two main countries on the silver standard, Mexico and China.

Slowly the US view on exchange-rate management changed. Roosevelt and his secretary of the treasury, Henry Morgenthau, became bored with manipulating the gold price and finally stabilized it without British cooperation in February 1934 at $35 an ounce, up from $20.67. Morgenthau developed fairly romantic notions about the excitement of international finance and participated with the British in providing a cover for French devaluation in September 1936, the so-called Tripartite Monetary Agreement which was limited in its actual effect. The participants agreed to hold each others' currencies only for twenty-four hours before turning them into gold, as contrasted with the six months or more under the swap arrangements that sprang into being in March 1961. The Administration, however, held steady, rather than reducing the price of gold again when the so-called "Golden Avalanche" poured gold into the United States, as private citizens and even central banks sold gold for dollars in a Gresham's Law episode (Graham and Whittlesey 1939).

By the time of the Second World War, the United States took a leading role in preparing the way for a new foreign-exchange regime. The White plan from the US Treasury dominated the Keynes plan from Britain to constitute the core of the Articles of Agreement of the International Monetary Fund worked out at Bretton Woods in 1944. The British loan and the Marshall Plan were put into place to prepare the ground before the IMF could be put into action. When it became impossible to separate trade from capital movements and prohibit the latter without undertaking the impossible task of regulating the credit terms of current transactions, the United States led the way in enlarging the quotas of the IMF. It agreed at Basel in March 1961 on a swap arrangement, under which, in crisis, a country under attack could obtain temporary assistance by swapping its currency for foreign exchange, and in the autumn of that year to extend the Fund's Articles by incorporating the General Arrangements to Borrow, the provision of foreign exchange to this Fund from Group of Ten countries with extensive financial markets.

In the late 1950s foreigners began to accumulate dollar balances in New York and it was thought that the United States balance of payments had changed from positive to negative. The gold-exchange standard was attacked by leading economists, Robert Triffin (1960) and Jacques Rueff (1965) on the ground that the United States was able to extract goods and assets abroad from the rest of the world by persuading it to hold dollars. Triffin, in particular, asserted that when the US corrected its balance the world would be short of liquidity because there was insufficient gold coming into central bank reserves to support the demand for more money. He advocated the creation of a new international (paper) asset and its substitution for dollars and gold in international bank reserves. It was argued, in opposition, that there was an abundance of liquidity in the system, as any country wanting more could borrow dollars long and hold them short, with the United States acting as a bank to the world and supplying liquidity to countries of good credit standing on demand. Just as banks were not in deficit when they lent long and borrowed short, so the United States was not in deficit either (Despres, Kindleberger and Salant 1965).

There was, however, a significant difference in that the United States as bank was expanding its deposits and long-term assets, but its reserves were static or declining, as newly mined gold went into hoarding or industrial use, and the rest of the world borrowed long and bought gold. President de Gaulle of France declared war on the dollar standard in February 1965, and after taking incremental surpluses in gold rather than dollars in 1964, began systematically to convert dollars into gold, $1 billion in 1965 and another $500 million in 1966 before the French balance of payments turned adverse. To buttress the dollar, the United States in 1965 put forward a proposal for the creation of Special Drawing Rights (called SDRs), primarily, I judge, to permit its own reserves to grow, even though any scheme would have to provide reserves for all. The proposal was adopted as part of the IMF, but not pursued after the advent of floating exchanges.

The Vietnam War in the second half of the 1960s produced a real deficit in the current account of the US balance of payments and the run accelerated. In 1968 the United States broke up the gold pool under which it had furnished at least half of the gold bid for at the $35 an ounce price in the London fixing. In August 1971 it closed the gold window, refusing to convert dollars into gold, and additionally imposed a 10 percent tax on all imports in an effort to get the other countries of the world to agree to a depreciation of the dollar. If it had raised the gold price other countries might have followed to achieve the same set of exchange rates at a higher gold price. The 10 percent depreciation was achieved in December 1971 at the Smithsonian agreement, named after a museum in Washington, DC where the conference was held, that raised the gold price to $42. The dollar remained under pressure in the next years until finally the notion of a dollar tied to the price of gold or of any other currency was abandoned altogether.

There followed a period of what has been called "benign neglect" of the exchange rate by the United States. Other countries might intervene in their own currencies by buying and selling dollars already owned or acquired through swaps, but the United States took no steps to control the rate of the dollar until tight money under the Federal Reserve's attempt to raise interest rates to bring down the rate of inflation led to five years of appreciation ending in February 1985, followed by two years of depreciation. In September 1985 Secretary of the Treasury James Baker negotiated the Plaza Agreement with Britain, France, Japan and West Germany to stabilize foreign-exchange rates. When this wobbled a further negotiation produced the Louvre agreement in 1987. The emphasis was clearly on correcting the fluctuating dollar that was embarrassing the United States rather than providing a stable world system.

Capital Flows

To achieve economic stability the world needs a steady flow of capital from rich countries with excess savings to those embarked on the development process with capital needs in excess of national saving. Some economists recommend countercyclical lending, to provide exchange to developing countries when depression or recession in industrialized areas cuts down on purchases of less developed countries' exports. It is awkward, however, to have a spurt of foreign lending suddenly cut off by the diversion of savings to home use. As it happens the rhythm of capital flows is not readily subject to policy control. There tends to be a regular pattern in the course of development, borrowing while rapidly developing, paying back as a country achieves new industries and expands exports, then accumulating foreign investments. Ultimately a country lives off the income of accumulated investment and may even consume its foreign capital.

At the start of the twentieth century the United States was in the process of moving from the stage of young debtor to mature debtor. The country was also beginning to undertake direct foreign investment abroad in those industries in which it had innovated—agricultural machinery, office machinery and the like—typically labor-saving devices, and in oil, an industry in which it had pioneered. The outbreak of the First World War speeded the process of change inordinately, allowing the United States to pass rapidly to the stage of young creditor in a few years. Much of the accumulation of claims on the rest of the world took the form of intergovernmental debts, provided to European allies during the war and in its immediate aftermath. J. P. Morgan & Co. took the lead after the war in private lending for stabilization purposes, but after the successful oversubscription of the New York tranche of the Dawes loan in 1924, the rush to lend abroad became general—especially to Germany, Latin America, Australia, New Zealand and Canada.

When the New York stock market started an ascent in the spring of 1928, however, sale of foreign bonds in New York became difficult. Foreign borrowers shifted from long-term issues to short-run bank loans, based not on trade credits but on accommodation. Some US houses such as Lee, Higginson of Boston kept trying to float funds for preferred clients, for instance Germany and Ivar Krueger, and went bankrupt in the process. With the spread of depression worldwide, default on outstanding debt became general in Latin America and Germany. New lending continued during the 1930s only for Canada and Israel, the latter selling bonds to supporters in the United States on drives in which the economic motive was diluted by political and religious ties.

It seemed clear after the Second World War that private lending would take a long time to recover from the defaults of the 1930s. Accordingly the United States made generous settlements on Lend-Lease and various relief loans—in place of the business attitude toward war debts after the First World War. At Bretton Woods US proposals provided for an International Bank of Reconstruction and Development (the World Bank) to lend government monies to borrowers in need of capital, and also to mobilize private savings for the purpose by selling to the public its bonds bearing governmental guarantees. The first issues were sold in the United States for dollars, the currency then most in demand. Gradually, as national capital markets recovered the Euro-bond market grew to strength and goods became available from other sources, monies were raised outside the United States in the Euro-currency market, Germany, Switzerland and Japan, and after 1973 in the oil-producing Arab states. While the World Bank was getting organized in 1945 the United States enlarged the capital of the Export-Import Bank from $1 billion to $4 billion, took the lion's share of the assistance furnished by UNRRA and in 1946 undertook a $3.75 billion loan to the United Kingdom to assist sterling's postwar recovery as a key currency. When these measures proved inadequate to the task of reconstruction the United States in 1948 enacted a European Recovery Program—the so-called Marshall Plan—with assistance made available partly on a loan basis, but for the most part in grants.

The recovery generated by this governmental assistance finally began to attract private capital abroad from the United States, initially as direct foreign investment and ultimately in debt form, both as new bond issues and as bank loans. In the 1960s the capital outflow began to exceed the US current account surplus in the balance of payments by a substantial margin. First President Eisenhower, then Kennedy and Johnson, became concerned about the balance of payments and tried to inhibit the outflow. A tax levied on interest received from bonds, the so-called IET (Interest Equalization Tax), was set at a prohibitive level. Subsequent legislation, known as the Gore amendment, applied the tax to bank loans to which the lending had shifted. When the wedge between returns available in the United States and those in Europe widened, the flow shifted once again to direct investment. In 1964 President Johnson called for a Voluntary Credit Restraint Program that permitted direct investment but tried to limit the amount of capital brought from the United States. In 1968 the program was made mandatory.

None of these measures proved effective. The IET applied to bonds had a major loophole in that it did not apply to foreign bonds bought from other residents in the United States, and the procedures for establishing the residence of the sellers were poorly enforced. In direct investment, allowing new investments made with foreign profits which would otherwise have been repatriated had the same impact on the balance of payments as allowing a capital outflow. Moreover, loans raised abroad by Americans had to be repaid, so that direct investment undertaken with foreign loans was equivalent, with a time lag, to the export of capital or direct investment.

In the early 1970s the monetary authorities in the United States made a mistake with substantial consequences for the world economy. Largely to assist in the reelection of President Nixon in the autumn of 1972, the Federal Reserve System loosened credit in 1970 and 1971 to stimulate business (Greider 1987). The action was taken at a time when the Bundesbank in Germany was trying to control inflationary tendencies by tightening interest rates. The result was that an enormous outflow of short-term capital went abroad to the Euro-currency market that had been gradually building up since about 1960. There it was borrowed by German residents, including multinational corporations, to pay off internal debt, and when sold to the Bundesbank for deutsche marks was redeposited by the Bank in the Euro-currency market. The "deficit" on the balance of payments of the United States under the (unacceptable) liquidity definition, rose from an average of $2–$4 billion a year to $20 billion in 1971 and $30 billion in 1972. Interest rates fell in the Euro-dollar markets, and Euro-banks started to look for loan outlets. Well before the Yom Kippur war of November 1973, the large price increase in oil, and the accumulation by OPEC (Organization of Petroleum Exporting Countries) of massive dollar balances which were deposited in New York and the Euro-currency market and recycled by major banks to Third World oil importing countries, the burst of sovereign lending by syndicates of banks had begun. The sudden and unanticipated fall in interest rates stimulated foreign lending much as had happened in the 1820s and 1880s in Britain when government debt conversion to lower levels had taken place.

The burst of lending to Third World debtors, notably Mexico, Brazil and Argentina, continued with a spurt for oil-producing countries like Mexico in 1979 when the second OPEC price increase occurred. This increase was short-lived, however, as new production came into play in the North Sea, the North Slope in Alaska and elsewhere. When Mexico found it impossible to maintain debt service at lower oil prices without help, the Third World debt crisis ensued in August 1982. Various stop-gap measures to adjust the position were worked out. The United States made a bridging loan to Mexico, and an emergency purchase of $1 billion worth of petroleum to be delivered to the US Strategic Reserve while the commercial banks and the International Monetary Fund negotiated a debt rescheduling. This and subsequent reschedulings undertook to provide for new loans so as to avoid the disastrous pattern for world stability of 1873, 1890 and 1928 when rapidly rising lending was suddenly stopped. The commercial banks in general, and especially the regional banks in the United States which had been drawn into the lending syndicates belatedly, were reluctant to lend more. Handling of the debt problem proceeded country by country, year by year, on a thoroughly ad hoc basis.

Not only did the United States stop lending to Third World countries after 1982, but it began to attract the savings of the rest of the world, not for investment so much as for consumption, private consumption as personal savings continued to decline in the country, and public consumption as the US government deficit mounted in the 1980s, along with the deficit on the balance of payments on current account. Much of the effect can be traced to tight monetary policy after 1979 when an attempt was made to reduce the rate of inflation which had risen over 10 percent a year, while loose fiscal policy with substantial tax reductions in 1981 and a rising rate of military spending continued. The tax reductions failed to raise personal savings: the government and household spending attracted imports and crowded out exports. Countries like Japan, Germany and Taiwan piled up savings and dollar balances that they invested in government bonds, takeovers of US companies, real estate and ordinary equities. While figures of balances of indebtedness are notoriously uncertain because of problems of valuation, it is generally believed that the United States went from a creditor position vis-à-vis the rest of the world of some several hundred billions in 1980 to a net debtor position of half a trillion dollars by 1987.

Coordination of Macroeconomic Policy

Under the gold standard, in effect at the opening of this century, monetary policy was understood to be coordinated automatically: countries receiving gold expanded their money supplies; those losing it (apart from newly mined specie) contracted. In addition, in the pre-Keynesian era, governmental budgets were expected to be balanced in peacetime, if not overbalanced to pay down government debt.

US interest in monetary policy in the years before the First World War arose primarily from financial crises experienced in 1893 and 1907. A National Monetary Commission was appointed in 1910, under the chairmanship of Nelson Aldrich, and produced a series of studies of central and commercial banking in the United States and in other countries. The concern was primarily with the inelasticity of the money supply in crisis and, despite the fact that the 1907 panic had been communicated through London and Paris to Italy, its focus was local.

Following the First World War the country got drawn in to questions of policy at the international level. The United States had accumulated a large stock of gold during the war through exports to the Allied powers, and it was anticipated that this would lead to increased money supplies and higher prices. Sterilization of much of the gold frustrated this hope. In Britain, which was struggling to restore the pound to par in the first half of the 1920s, it was sometimes proposed that she should send $100 million in gold as a payment on war-debt account to cause inflation in the United States. The suggestion was vetoed by Montagu Norman of the Bank of England on the ground that the Federal Reserve System would probably sterilize that too.

The imbalance between the pound, restored to par and overvalued in 1925, and the French franc, stabilized de facto in 1926 and undervalued, led in 1927 to an ad hoc attempt to coordinate monetary policy internationally. Benjamin Strong, Montagu Norman, Hjalmar Schacht of the Reichsbank and Charles Rist, the deputy governor of the Bank of France, met on Long Island in July 1927 at the estate of the secretary of the US Treasury, Ogden Mills, to discuss what steps might be taken to ease the British difficulties. It was agreed that the Federal Reserve Bank of New York would lower its discount rate to discourage the inflow of capital from London, and adjust its gold price so that the Bank of France would purchase gold to match its balance-of-payments surplus from New York rather than from London. The exercise in international cooperation is regarded by some as a mistake insofar as it contributed to the rise of the stock market in New York, and a detour from an appropriate policy based on US requirements (Friedman and Schwartz 1963: 289 ff).

Coordination of macroeconomic policy became a nonissue during the depression, the war, and the immediate years after the Second World War when each country was fully preoccupied with its own problems. With the establishment of the Bank for International Settlements in Basle in 1930 as part of the Young plan dealing with German reparation, there were monthly meetings of central bankers that permitted an exchange of views, but the United States was not represented formally as the Federal Reserve System was not a stockholder of the Bank in spite of its having an American president from time to time and an observer attending the meeting, usually in the person of the US Treasury attaché in Paris. It was not until after the war, of course, that transatlantic air travel developed to the point where it was feasible to bring members of the Washington establishment to Europe for meetings on a regular basis.

In the course of the Marshall Plan, economic policies came under discussion in the OEEC, at which the United States had a representative of the US Economic Cooperation Agency in the person of its Special Representative. When the OEEC was converted, after the termination of aid under the Marshall Plan, to the OECD, with the United States as a regular member along with Canada and later Australia and New Zealand, a series of working parties was established of which No. 3 dealt with macroeconomic questions. This functioned for a number of years with regular meetings attended by representatives of the US Treasury, the Council of Economic Advisors and the Federal Reserve system. Its work was gradually allowed to lapse, as it was recognized that various countries had different objectives as in achieving low unemployment, low inflation, balance-of-payments equilibrium and the like. In 1966 Secretary of the Treasury Henry Fowler urged at a meeting of finance ministers at Chequers in England that the Europeans lower their interest rates. This was largely an ad hoc appeal to assist the US balance of payments. Under the Carter administration from 1976 to 1980 the United States appealed for the major powers, especially Germany and Japan, to join it in expansionary fiscal policy as "locomotives" to pull the rest of the world and each other into greater prosperity. The response was at most halfhearted, and US efforts to expand income and employment largely alone worsened the country's balance of payments. Under Presidents Carter and Reagan there began a series of Summit Meetings among seven leading countries—the United States, Germany, Japan, France, Italy, Canada and the United Kingdom—that met for a few days a year, with elaborate agendas prepared by staff, covering a wide variety of political and economic subjects but reaching few agreements, and constituting, for the most part, ceremonial meetings for photographic opportunities.

On this showing, coordination of macroeconomic policies—monetary and fiscal—has been both sporadic and ineffectual. There is, moreover, the disastrous experience of 1970 and 1971 when the Federal Reserve System and the Bundesbank pulled strongly in different directions, the United States to lower and the Bundesbank to tighten interest rates. Such lapses into cross-purposes have happily been rare.

The Lender of Last Resort

I have written so profusely and redundantly on this issue at various earlier times (Kindleberger 1978) that I can afford to be brief here. In the prewar period the United States was preoccupied with its own affairs and took little if any interest in how it might assist the troubles of others, if only to prevent their spread. The war loans of 1918 and 1919 can be interpreted as rescue or salvage operations, though not in the narrow sense of relieving finance markets in acute distress. Insistence on collecting war debts and denying any connection between reparation and war debts can be interpreted as the opposite of last-resort lending; refusing to relieve economic trauma because of the potential cost in giving up a good asset for a poor one. (The analogy that comes to mind is that of the Intra-European Payments Scheme of 1949 under the Marshall Plan, where possibilities of a given country cancelling its claim against its liabilities were divided into two classes: those on the same country, which proceeded automatically, and those where a claim on A was cancelled against a liability to B which was turned over to A. In this latter case the cancellation was undertaken only if the creditor agreed to accept the claim on the debtor. Few cancellations of this order took place.)

It is generally recognized that the United States (and France) were niggardly and dilatory in serving as lenders of last resort to Austria,

Germany and Britain in 1931, permitting international disintermediation to ramify. In addition, the French attached political conditions to their limited assistance, not to Britain but to Austria and Germany, and followed up the depreciation of sterling by accelerating the liquidity crisis, converting dollars into gold, as did Belgium, the Netherlands and Switzerland. As indicated earlier, the Tripartite Monetary Agreement provided little assistance among the several partners—holding foreign exchange by agreement only twenty-four hours. It did, however, turn the direction of pressure from liquidation to support.

During and after the Second World War Lend-Lease, the Bretton Woods institutions, the Export-Import Bank capital infusion, British loan and Marshall Plan transferred resources for more or less long periods rather than serving as last-resort lending. That came into being spontaneously at Basle in March 1961 with swaps, the provision of instant foreign exchange to help in this case Britain, later Canada, Italy, Britain again, the United States. The swaps were expected to be reversed at the end of a fixed time period, usually six months, and if this could not be done with the besieged country's resources because the reversal of capital flow had not been complete, it was expected that any unreconstituted portion would be otherwise funded, usually by a drawing on the International Monetary Fund. The Fund was of little avail as a lender of last resort on its own because of the time-consuming nature of its decision making when rescue operations were often needed in hours and days rather than weeks and months.

A residual ambiguity as to which country could undertake responsibility for meeting the liabilities of its banks arose in 1974 when the German authorities delayed meeting obligations of the bankrupt Herstatt Bank of Cologne to foreign banks with which it had exchange contracts. The so-called Basle protocol of 1975 provided that each national authority should be responsible for the obligations of its national institutions worldwide. In 1982, however, the Bank of Italy declined to meet the liabilities of the Banco Ambrosiano's Luxembourg subsidiary (as contrasted with branch) when that bank failed. The 1984 failure of the Continental Illinois Bank found the US Federal Deposit Insurance Corporation making good Japanese-held certificates of deposit in excess of the prescribed $100,000 limit in order to restore confidence in the international money market.

In 1988 there is some uncertainty as to where matters stand with respect to the lender-of-last-resort function. The Plaza and Louvre accords negotiated by Baker call on the leading five financial powers to stabilize each other's currencies but make no provision, as under the swap arrangements, for any country whose currency is supported by the others to compensate a foreign central bank that experiences losses on its foreign-exchange holdings from depreciation or devaluation of the currency in question. The central banks of West Germany and Japan, in particular, hold large amounts of dollars bought at rates well above present levels. Swaps would doubtless be set in motion if other currencies than the yen, deutsche mark or dollar were to be dumped on the market by speculators. The Bank of Japan and the Bundesbank have large holdings of dollars with which they can support their currencies. But if the dollar were to come under attack and threaten to go into a free fall it is not clear at what point, in terms of exchange rate or amounts of support, other countries would rally around. As the US role as world stabilizer is undermined, there is no clear country interested to take its place. We approach again the position in the early 1930s when the former stabilizer has weakened in relative strength and zeal to uphold the role and other possible candidates for the post hold back.

Some economists and political scientists put faith in bilateral or trilateral arrangements to stabilize the world economy in the foregoing respects. A distinguished German banker and legislator, Ludwig Bamberger, commenting on the need for a central bank, made a remark that bears on the point: "shared responsibility is no responsibility" (Zucker 1975: 78).

REFERENCES

Cipolla, Carlo M. (ed.) (1970), *The Economic Decline of Empires,* London: Methuen.
Despres, Emile, Charles P. Kindleberger, and Walter S. Salant (1965), "The dollar and world liquidity: a minority view," *The Economist,* vol. 218, no. 6389, London (5 February).
Friedman, Milton, and Anna Jacobson Schwartz (1963), *A Monetary History of the United States,* Princeton: Princeton University Press.
Gallagher, John, and Roland Robinson (1953), "The imperialism of free trade, 1815–1914," *Economic History Review,* 2nd ser., vol. 6, pp. 1–15.
Graham, Frank D., and Charles P. Whittlesey (1939), *Golden Avalanche,* Princeton: Princeton University Press.
Greider, William (1987), *The Secrets of the Temple: How the Federal Reserve Runs the Country,* New York: Simon & Schuster.
Hawtrey, Ralph G. (1952), *Economic Aspects of Sovereignty,* London: Longmans, Green.
Hogan, Michael L. (1987), *The Marshall Plan: America, Britain and the Reconstruction of Western Europe, 1947–1952,* New York: Cambridge University Press.

Kennedy, Paul (1987), *The Rise and Fall of Great Powers: Economic Change and Military Conflict from 1500 to 2000,* New York: Random House.

Kindleberger, Charles P. (1978), *Manias, Panics and Crashes: A History of Financial Crises,* New York: Basic Books.

Kindleberger, Charles P. (1986), *The World in Depression, 1929–1939,* 2nd edition, Berkeley: University of California Press.

Krueger, Anne O. (1974), "The political economy of the rent-seeking society," *American Economic Review,* vol. 64, no. 3 (June), pp. 291–303.

Nurske, Ragnar (1949), "Conditions of international monetary equilibrium," in American Economic Association, *Reading in the International Trade,* Philadelphia: Blakiston.

Olson, Mancur (1982), *The Rise and Decline of Nations: Economic Growth, Stagnation and Social Rigidities,* New Haven, CT: Yale University Press.

Rostow, Walt W. (1960), *The Stages of Growth: A Non-Communist Manifesto,* Cambridge: Cambridge University Press.

Rueff, Jacques (1965) in J. Rueff and Fred Hirsch, "The rule and role of gold, an argument," *Essays in International Finance,* no. 47, Princeton: Princeton University Press.

Semmel, Bernard (1970), *The Rise of Free Trade Imperialism: Classical Political Economy, the Empire of Free Trade, and Imperialism, 1750–1850,* Cambridge: Cambridge University Press.

Senghaas, Dieter (1985), *The European Experience: A Historical Critique of Development Theory,* Dover, NH: Berg Publishers.

Smith, Cyril Stanley (1975), "Metallurgy as human experience. The 1974 distinguished lectureship in materials and society," *Metallurgical Transactions,* vol. 6Aa, no. 4, pp. 604–14.

Thurow, Lester (1980), *The Zero-Sum Society,* New York: Basic Books.

Triffin, Robert (1960), *Gold and the Dollar Crisis,* New Haven, CT: Yale University Press.

Wallerstein, Immanuel (1980), *The Modern World System II: Mercantilism and the Consolidation of the European-World Economy, 1600–1750,* New York: Academic Press.

Zucker, Stanley (1975), *Ludwig Bamberger: German Liberal Politician and Social Critic, 1823–1899,* Pittsburgh: University of Pittsburgh Press.

CHAPTER 2

Europe in the World Economy

I have taken on an impossible assignment. How can one feel in any way confident in describing the role of Europe in the world economy in the months and years to come, if one is unclear about the economic prospects facing Europe, Japan, the Middle East, the so-called Third World and the United States, in the light, especially as I write, of: the deadline facing Iraq in Kuwait in less than a week; the threatened collapse of the Soviet economy, especially in the production and distribution of consumer goods and food; frustration in Eastern Europe; a new government in Britain; deepening recession in the United States, apparently spreading to Japan and parts of Europe; continuing problems in Third World debt, raw material prices, and so on. If various elements of the picture are obscure, it takes a prophet or the son of a prophet to see the whole picture as they come together. The task is made particularly difficult as I write on the last day of the Uruguay-round negotiations without knowing whether Europe, the United States, Japan and the grain-exporting countries will reach agreement or let the negotiations fail.

My diffidence in forecasting is not universally shared. Two highly respected political scientists in the United States, Henry Nau and Joseph Nye, brush away signs of American weakness that others think may lead to a reduction of the US role in the world economy. The first calls American decline a myth with the subtitle *Leading the World Economy into the 1990s.* Nye's book is called *Bound to Lead,* though it is concerned as much with political as with economic leadership. A third entry in the debate, by Myron Ross, relies on Kondratieff long-wave theory to predict a *Coming Economic Boom, 1992–2020.* For the moment I reserve my positions on these views, to turn first to the general problems facing the major national and regional economies in the provision of

Reprinted from "Building the New Europe I: Single Market and Monetary Unification in the EEC Countries," *Rivista di Politica Economica* 81, 3d ser., no. 5 (May 1991): 619–30 and from Mario Baldassarri and Robert Mundell, eds., *Building the New Europe* (Basingstoke: Macmillan, 1993).

public goods, and then discussing how the world economy has been and may in future be organized and world public goods produced.

Adam Smith thought in terms of only three public goods (which he called the duties of the sovereign): national defense, the administration of justice, and the few works so large that they could not be undertaken by the private market. Modern economists have added to this list. Public goods, I may remind you, form that class that cannot be exhausted short of some very high degree of congestion, and from which no one can be excluded so that they are available to all, whether they pay for them or not. They are produced by government with the power to tax, since if they were produced by the market, inability to exclude consumers would lead individuals to ride free without payment for the cost of production. For international public goods, where there is no government with power to tax, there is a grave risk that the goods may not be produced at all. The difference between private and public goods is akin to that between a market and a budget. Values are exchange in a market. In a budget funds are expended on some basis, perhaps need, perhaps to favor political interests, and raised by taxation on some basis, perhaps by borrowing, or by the inflation tax.

Within an economy with a government, the public goods beyond defense, justice and infrastructure may include competitive markets, stable money, standards, and perhaps some means of softening the harsher results of competitive markets by providing certain services at a reasonable standard, as in health, education, perhaps housing, and social security. At times of crisis the list may be extended. My list of international public goods includes, on trend, open markets, stable exchange rates, access to supplies in acute shortage and to markets in glut, and a lender of last resort in financial crisis. In the absence of international government, other means have to be provided if these public goods, including the most important of all, peace, are to be produced at all.

Before I come back to public goods, I offer a brief *tour d'horizon* of the economic problems facing Europe, Japan and the United States, and then move to the role of Europe in the world economy. Everything I say is provisional, subject to change without notice. If no economist to my knowledge predicted the implosions of the stock market in Octobers 1987 and 1989, or the collapse of the socialist economies in Eastern Europe in 1989, you will understand my insistence on not rushing in where angels fear to tread.

First Europe. The Continent is embarked on two great journeys, one to assimilate Eastern Europe into the European economy as a whole, the other to complete the forging of a single economic community, begun in this city in 1957. I am concerned that the two journeys are substitutes rather than complements. The current and capital costs of absorbing Eastern Europe into the market system of the West will be substantial. The crisis problem of feeding the Soviet Union has been assisted by the adventitious existence of stocks of food assembled years ago in Berlin in defense against another Soviet blockade. Provision of stocks against possible disaster is one sort of public good, exemplified by the grain offices of Italian city-states and the US petroleum reserves. Sometimes, as in US stockpiles of grain and cotton built up in the 1930s to support farmers, but invaluable during the war, serendipity comes to the rescue. But subsidies for eastern Germany, for moving out Soviet troops, for equalizing the social security systems, and the like will be expensive currently. And the capital demands for deferred maintenance and obsolescence in the East, for correcting cumulative pollution, for accommodating the migrants to the West, will be on top of the current expenditure.

Capital requirements in Europe are virtually certain to raise world interest rates, cut off the flow from Europe and perhaps Japan to the United States. Optimists are not troubled that this will intensify recession or depression in the United States because the cut-off of capital can be offset in the foreign-exchange market by further depreciation of the dollar. Much further depreciation of the dollar, however, poses an inflationary danger as the rise of foreign trade prices spreads through the cost of living and wages. The choice between further depreciation and inflation, or higher interest rates and deflation, is not an agreeable one.

The other mobile factor of production, labor, poses a question, and perhaps a problem. The *Treaty of Rome* provided for free movement of labor across national boundaries, although apart from South Italians among the original six, little movement took place. Migration to the West from Eastern Europe, however, is now substantial; indeed, that from the People's Republic to the Federal Republic through Hungary and Austria in 1989 precipitated the Socialist collapse. With the razing of the wall, it was anticipated that this would dry up. It appears not to be doing so. East Germans, moreover, are being joined by citizens of other Eastern countries, both those of ancient German origin and those with no ethnic claim on the West. Austria faces a harrowing problem of whether to send refugees back to such a country as Romania or to let them stay.

There is a danger that this migration may go so far as to deprive Eastern Europe of the minimum of professional, semiprofessional and skilled cadres needed for a modern economy. A riot in Leipzig in November 1990 could not be contained because of the absence of adequate numbers of police. Rapid economic recovery in Eastern Europe that gives the populace sufficient hope in the intermediate run of matching Western productivity and standards of living may be difficult or impossible to achieve. Bear in mind that this movement of population is different in its effects than that that produced the wall in 1961. In the 1950s, the refugees and expellees moving to the Federal Republic, and the guest workers, proved stimulating to economic growth, holding wages down and profits up, with the profits reinvested in further productive capital, along the lines of the Lewis model of growth with unlimited supplies of labor. These migrants were originally single men for whom infrastructure in the form of housing, schools and hospitals need not be provided beyond simple barracks. The migration of whole families produces a different result. The earlier movement from the South stimulated the sending economies, as well as the receiving, as disguised unemployment was cleared away, and rising wages encouraged both savings and labor-saving investment. Today the risk is that the wholesale movement of workers East to West may hurt growth in both areas.

If we turn from these immediate issues, building the complete common market by 1992 on which the experts here have been discoursing promises to be difficult enough. Harmonization of tax systems, social security, regulations in pure food and drugs, safety standards and the like is a tedious, specialized and time-consuming task. Building the European Monetary System with a common currency, European central bank, and consistent fiscal policies seems moving along nicely after twenty years of setbacks and new starts, but questions remain that will take economic expertise and especially political will to solve. How rapidly will Europe move how far: to a confederation? Federation? United States? Union? How much sovereignty, that is, are the constituent countries ready to surrender to the Continent as a whole? Different visions of the future are held by the leading protagonists, Germany, France, Italy, Britain, with some uncertainty remaining in the last instance after the change in conservative leadership. Mrs. Thatcher's resistance to grants of sovereignty seemed to me to have provided a cover behind which President Mitterand and Chancellor Kohl could assert more devotion to the European ideal than perhaps they felt at heart. The new twist in Ostpolitik, and the problems of Eastern European recovery, reconstruction and integration into the East seem likely in my uninformed judgment to extend the achievement of current goals of Western integration beyond 1992.

There are problems enough in the economic field, to be sure, but an American may be pardoned if he mentions the differing responses of the Community's members to the military crisis in the Middle East. Creating a European political Community may be even more difficult than building the economic one.

On Japan, I am, again, far from expert. Like Germany, Japan has had a superb record of economic growth since the end of the second world war. More than Germany, it has made economic hay under the American defense umbrella, Americans are impressed by Japanese innovative prowess, saving habits, export drive, and faithful support of American economic leadership in the past, at the same time that many insist that Japanese support for free markets is limited in particular respects, such as competition for rice farmers, ease of entry of foreign direct investment, readiness to streamline wholesale and retail distribution. In a number of financial circles, moreover, there is worry that security and real estate prices remain still dangerously high, despite the substantial 1990 declines from 1989 levels.

In the last few years, Japan has become more economically assertive, making the point, for example, that with its new high status in international finance, it should have enhanced voting power in the International Monetary Fund and World Bank. (Parenthetically, the same could also be said about the United Nations Security Council where both Germany and Japan will one day obtain permanent membership in recognition of the realities.) The rise of the yen has continued for five years with substantial paper losses for the Bank of Japan and Japanese insurance companies that have been financing a large proportion of the United States cumulative budget deficit. Japanese investment in the US has increasingly moved from debt into real assets like direct investment and real estate, in the latter case not always with exquisite timing. I have nonetheless been surprised that Japanese lenders to US bodies have not insisted on denominating the loans in yen, rather than dollars, to shift the exchange risk to the borrowers.

A word or two about my own country before getting to the world economy. Wide differences of opinion exist not only over whether the United States is in secular decline, but also over the short-term prospects of recession or depression. Long-term decline, of course, may be merely relative to faster growing countries or areas elsewhere. Despite Nau, Nye, Ross and others, I view the United States as an aging economy, its interests shifting from trade and industry to finance, from capital accumulation to consumption, from individual enterprise to what Mancur Olson calls "distributional coalitions" or vested interests, that seek to protect what the French used to call in the prewar days of Malthusianism, *positions acquises*. I detect a decline of team-play, not only in sport but in business and professions, as takeovers break up existing management structures,

firms in law, accounting, advertising reshuffle partners and even liquidate. Even academic departments appear to be succumbing to the star
system that so dominates sport and entertainment.

Moreover, the short-run outlook looks dangerous with its fragile
financial structure of high levels of debt owed by government, industry,
real estate, Third World countries and consumers. Insurance companies
and banks are awash with defaulted real estate loans and depreciated
junk bonds. While low by 1930 standards, bankruptcies are rising. The
possibility that government has to take over a huge load of debt as
lender of last resort poses a threat of inflation. If on the other hand
banks and insurance companies work their way out of the problem by a
return to conservative lending and investing, the prospects for rapid and
extensive recovery become less than bright. I hasten to warn you, however, that I have been bearish on the immediate economic outlook in the
United States for some years, and have only recently begun to find a
swing of opinion in my direction. Roger Babson predicted a crash of the
stock market in 1928. He found it did not pay to be right prematurely.

There are then short-run problems of absorbing the shock of the
collapse of Eastern Europe, financial tensions in Japan and the United
States. Assuming these difficulties can be overcome, we have a longer-
run question of how the world economy is to be organized, and the place
in it of the New Europe, how, that is, international public goods will be
produced in the absence of world government.

The primary international public good, as noted, is peace. Its provision poses problems well beyond my capacity to expound. I restrict
myself to economic public goods, starting with five I have discussed
many times before: open markets, stable exchange rates, coordinated or
at least not inconsistent macroeconomic policies, international capital,
and a lender of last resort. To these can perhaps be added some of the
intractable issues already mentioned: economic breakdown as in Eastern Europe, hunger because of breakdown, drought, pestilence, disease, earthquake; the settlement of massive numbers of refugees or
would-be refugees; and economic development in general. In all these
first responsibility rests with the countries concerned. Once their capaci-
ties are overwhelmed, however, the threat of human, economic or political disaster becomes a challenge to the world.

Assume that national governments are moderately successful in
providing domestic public goods. International public goods may not be
furnished at all if countries free ride, each looking after its national
interest whatever the cost to other countries. This is international anarchy under which the strong and aggressive exploit the weak and the
passive, a condition of the world not without historical precedent. If, on

the other hand, international public goods are to be provided, a number of ways lie open. One country may be a hegemon, as political scientists like to term it, what I prefer to call a leader to dilute the implication of force; second, instead of one leader, duopoly of power, or an oligopoly or cartel, what is thought of today as trilateralism, with Europe, Japan and the United States sharing the world's burdens; third, regional blocs; fourth, "regimes," another concept of political science, described by Stephen Krasner as "principles, norms, rules and decision-making procedures around which actor expectations converge in a given issue area"; fifth, a system of functional international organizations. Apart from anarchy, these are of course not mutually exclusive. I may also add that any system decays over time. Entropy is endemic, if you can abide a short sentence of Greek roots.

Anarchy, the absence of international economic order, is abhorred in the same way that nature abhors a vacuum. I have lately been studying monetary anarchy in the seventeenth century in the Holy Roman Empire, and been struck by how the many territorial units detested the inflation that followed the gradual breakdown of rules for minting coin under the imperial ordinance of 1559. The breakdown was initially gradual, picked up speed and culminated in hyperinflation in 1618 to 1622. Even as the Thirty Years' War broke out, various circles covering usually one or more principality, duchy, bishopric, city, etc. reached out to agree with its neighbors to restore monetary order. There are economists who think an absence of authority is desirable because of normal government malversation or blundering. By historical revealed preference, some provision of the public good of stability is sought in anarchy. It may evolve in Darwinian fashion; it is probably desirable to plan it.

In due course, as the world continues to get smaller, world government will evolve. After World War II there were idealists or utopians who wanted to write constitutions to install one immediately. For as far ahead as one can now see, the notion is premature. The road probably lies through international organizations such as—to name a few in alphabetical order in English—BIS, ECOSOC, FAO, GATT, IBRD, ICAO, IFA, IMF, IPU, UNESCO, WHO and dozens more. Experience going back to the League of Nations, if not earlier, reveals that few of such organizations adequately fulfill their purposes unless they are pushed by powerful nations. Most too are paralleled by similar regional organizations, or by additional organizations in the less-developed world, or both. GATT, for example, has a counterpart in UNCTAD among LDCs, and in the North American Free Trade Area, now in embryo. In finance, in addition to the World Bank there are regional funds for Latin America, Asia and Africa, plus the European Social Fund, European Investment Bank and the

European Overseas Bank for investment in former colonies. Nor do most of them have the powers that inhere in national ones. The IMF is far from a world central bank in its inability to create money. No opinion that has come to my attention has suggested that the hunger problems of the Soviet Union should be turned over to the rather moribund Food and Agriculture Organization.

Regimes are one step down in terms of organization than these formal bodies, just as they are a long step down from world government. In a well-known book, *After Hegemony,* Robert Keohane notes that regimes are sometimes habits formed in a period of hegemony. On the whole, the world economy has performed fairly well on trend and in crisis since the perceived (by some) decline in the hegemonic power of the United States. Rampant protectionism has been held in check even if there has been some backsliding. Oil crises in 1973 and 1979 have been overcome—the returns are not in for 1990–1991—with the help of the international oil companies in the first instance. Third World debt presents an ongoing crisis in some views, or is being muddled through on another. The Uruguay round underlines the limits of dependence on old habits, however, whether it squeaks through or fails. Without injections of national energy in the international interest rather than the national or parochial, regimes run down.

Regionalism has been put forward as a solution for the organization of the world economy for many decades, and especially since World War II. It calls for fairly tight regional arrangements, such as are under construction in Europe, and less rigorously in North America, for the most part only talked about in the rest of the world—with little structure among the separate blocs. There is a good deal to be said in favor of regional cooperation, close cooperation in relevant instances, but I think it a mistake to raise an expedient into a principle. Many individual countries trade more outside the geographic confines of a region than within them—Australia, for example, though both Australia and New Zealand may be cited for the affirmative in the debate as they have increased their trade and cultural ties with Asia since they were orphaned by Britain's joining the Common Market. While Brazil has close trade ties with the United States because of coffee, Argentine connections run to Europe. The prospect for close regional cooperation in the Middle East looks dim. A recipe for close African integration is one for turmoil. It is unclear whether Mexican adherence to a North American trade arrangement would help or hurt Mexican growth. Evolutionary regionalism is desirable; forced regionalism is not.

We come to trilateralism, the notion that Europe, Japan and the United States should lay out the lines along which the world economy organizes caucus in international bodies to decide what needs doing, and rig the voting arrangements, mostly weighted, to ensure that the agenda is followed. One variation of this might be the G-5, G-7, or the G-8 with the inclusion of the Soviet Union, raising the question of vetoes as in the Security Council. Another question is whether the European vote would be cast by the Community as a whole (the EEC) or by Germany. After the successes of Ostpolitik, the German role in the Common Market seems dominant in much the same way that Prussia dominated the path leading to the unification of the Reich, and Piedmont that of Italy. If regional units have to arrive at decisions before tackling world problems, the process becomes time-consuming and extremely awkward in crises when decisions may be required in weeks, days or even hours. The Federal Republic has acted like a leader of Europe in relation to the problems of the Eastern bloc, taking on major costs in the integration of the two Germanies and the payment to hasten the removal of Soviet troops.

The trilateral solution can work for the lender-of-last-resort function since the swap arrangements are conducted by central banks, some of which are independent of governments (in the short run). For the other international public goods, trade, exchange rates, capital flows and macroeconomic coordination, the troika solution assumes either that the three participants are prepared to serve the international rather than the national interest, in cases where they conflict, or that the national interests of the three coincide. Both assumptions seem unlikely to be fulfilled.

This takes me back to the hegemonic or leadership solution. As I noted at the outset, scholars such as Nau and Nye think that the United States is "bound to lead" in future, "leading the world economy into the 1990s" as it did from 1945 to some uncertain date in the 1970s. US leadership in the military field was demonstrated when after the rape of Kuwait, President Bush moved to shield Saudi Arabia from Iraqi aggression. US policies, moreover, obtained international support from the United Nations. In the economic arena, however, the record is one of weakness and following along. American contributions in aid of Eastern European relief and reconstructions have been derisory, and organized by other countries. The country has passed the hat to get substantial contributions to pay for the costs of its deployment. Assistance to the USSR has taken the form of grain exports which serves a parochial interest. United States preoccupation with Third World growth of the 1950s and '60s has given way to attempts to collect debts and hold down restrictions on some leading US exports, such as computers in Brazil. From its position as economic leader of the world in the third quarter of this century, the United States has slipped back into the pack, while Germany (Europe?) and Japan have moved up.

Some of you may know that I ascribed the length, depth and width of the world depression of the 1930s to the fact that Britain was no longer capable of acting as world economic leader and the United States then was unwilling to assume the role. There is a danger—how serious, I am at a loss to measure—that with its problems of debt, productivity, savings and the rest, the United States is becoming like Britain in the interwar period, with no replacement in sight. Germany and Japan have been faithful followers of the United States lead after World War II, and while they are becoming more assertive, neither seems poised to claim a dominant and expansive world role. That the position bears a resemblance to the 1930s is seconded by a passage from José Ortega y Gasset's *The Revolt of the Masses* which I recently reread. To bring it up to date, I substitute the United States where he writes Europe, and Germany and Japan for his New York and Moscow. The book appeared in 1930, more than sixty years ago: "United States commandments have lost their force, though there is no sign of any other on the horizon. The United States—we are told—is ceasing to rule, and no one sees who is going to take her place. . . . It would not matter if the United States ceased to command, provided there was someone to take her place. But there is not the faintest sign of one. Germany and Japan represent nothing new . . . one does not know what they really are . . . United States loss of command would not worry me if there were in existence another group of countries capable of taking its place in power and in the direction of the planet." Ortega thought that provincial England, Germany and France were in decay, but that a United States of Europe could overcome the suffocation caused by the narrow boundaries of the separate countries. This notion, wildly premature in 1930, has a new lease on life two generations later.

I have no great optimism that Europe will recapture its "command" of the world as Ortega put it, or take its rightful share of the responsibility for the international public goods of peace and economic stability and growth in the immediate future. It is fully occupied at the moment with more parochial concerns, completing the common market and integrating Eastern Europe into the West. For the years immediately ahead, it would appear we have to rely on all the methods of producing public goods, trilateralism, regional-bloc building, international organizations, and perhaps especially regimes. It embarrasses me to confess that I do not fully share the American predilection for drawing up and attempting to implement written constitutions. The most interesting economic institutions of the postwar period, in my judgment—the Euro-currency market and the swap network—were not the result of complex negotiations as at Bretton Woods, but evolved. I am a wobbly—not firm—believer in proceeding as the way lies open, muddling through, unwritten constitutions. But it is important to have a fairly clear idea of the direction one wants to go. In the longer run, the world economy wants an institutional equivalent of world government to produce international public goods. I fervently hope that the experience of the next years in building the new Europe—to which this conference is contributing, will provide a pattern that can be followed with necessary variations in moving to the needed larger scale.

CHAPTER 3

Economic Growth and Decline: A Look at the World Economy of the 1990s

I am delighted once again to be in Tokyo, and to speculate with this distinguished audience about what the future holds for the world economy, and especially for my country, yours, and our great partner in the world, undergoing great changes at a rapid rate, Europe. I should warn you, however, that my studies these last decades have concerned the past, rather than any attempt to foretell the future. While I believe that some economic laws have great generality, I am also impressed by the new social science theory of chaos, that is, of random mutations, as in Darwinian evolution, that lead off in unanticipated directions. I shall speak as if I had more confidence in what I am saying than I really do, and should warn you that it would be unwise to bet the store on any hint or implication you may gain from these remarks.

In the course of looking at the last half millennium, I, along with many others, have been struck by the changes in world economic leadership—dominance, hegemony—whatever word you prefer. In the sixteenth century the Mediterranean countries were the top of the economic heap, notably the Italian city-states and Spain. Then came a shift to the Low Countries, initially Bruges, then Antwerp, but in the early seventeenth century Holland, with its economic capital at Amsterdam. In due course, leadership crossed the North Sea to England, with London as the great entrepôt center, and the Midlands, focused on Manchester, Birmingham, and Sheffield, producing the industrial revolution that revisionists want to transmute into an evolution. Britain was clearly in ascendence in the nineteenth century, gradually moving from trade to industry and then to finance. After the Second World War in the twentieth century, it was the United States that finally accepted a responsible role in helping to manage the world economy, until toward the end of the century, where we are now, its leadership is seen to be faltering.

Based on a keynote lecture at the International Economic Symposium of NHK Enterprises, Tokyo, March 28, 1990.

My task this afternoon is to peer into the future and suggest what may happen next.

First, however, let me rehearse succinctly the various theories that have been put forward to explain this succession of rises and declines. There is, as you may imagine, no lack of such theories, dealing for the most part with decline. They deal with:

war;

increases in consumption at rates faster than the growth in output;

ossification of interest groups that dig in and fight over the distribution of income, or on how to share new burdens that may be imposed on the economy;

rapid spurts followed by slower declines in rates of productivity increase, and failure to match innovations in product and process abroad;

a withering of the entrepreneurial spirit, including shifts from trade and industry to finance and the rentier status;

success in one or two lines of endeavor—the Spanish or Dutch disease—that leads to demands for higher wages in other activities that lack the same increases in output.

While I can devote only a few sentences to each of these, I would point out by way of introduction that (1) they are not mutually exclusive; (2) a decline may well be relative to faster growth elsewhere, rather than absolute; and (3) each of the reasons listed, and doubtless others, fits into a general pattern of economic adolescence, maturation, and arteriosclerosis, or aging. Just as Shakespeare noted the seven stages of man, so may there be an inexorable rise and decline of civilizations and countries, as Toynbee and others have noted. The S- or Gompertz curve is in this view more general than geometric growth at steady rates. It is this last possibility of economic aging that makes it difficult to be highly optimistic about using policy measures to halt or reverse the declines in savings, productivity gains, the digging in of distributional coalitions, and so on.

First, war. There are a lot of theories here. A popular book in the United States a short while ago was Paul Kennedy's *Rise and Decline of Great Powers,* which blamed senescence on military expenditure, emphasizing the weakening of Spain as a result of the religious wars in the Spanish Netherlands and Germany (the Eighty Years' War from 1572 to 1652, and the Thirty Years' War from 1618 to 1648). This theory is related to such striking modern-day contrasts between United States defense expenditures of 6.7 percent of its GNP, West Germany's 3.1 and Japan's 1 percent. But war can stimulate as well as depress. While Spain, the Nether-lands, and Britain declined as a result of wars, U.S. industrial power was stimulated by World Wars I and II. And war has another dimension, related to Mancur Olson's theory of increasing rigidity of "distributional coalitions." Winning a war may be harmful to growth if it strengthens existing vested interests and pressure groups that resist taxes or encour-ages war-weary populations to spend accumulated monetary reserves in order to make up for lost consumption, while defeat, if it destroys such interests, may clear the way for sensible policies. Survival of most interest groups in Germany after World War I, for example, made it impossible to adopt effective monetary reform and led to the hyperinflation from 1921 to 1923, whereas the failure of the Junkers, industrial cartels, farm inter-ests, labor unions, and civil servants to survive the Nazis and defeat in World War II as powerful political groups produced acceptance of the brilliant monetary reform of 1948. Some credit for the magnificent growth of Japan after 1950 may be owing to the similar wartime and immediate postwar destruction of vested interests.

The decline of the Italian city-states in the seventeenth century is held by the economic historian, Carlo Cipolla, to have been a function of rising consumption and debt, at a time when the growth of output was slowing down. Such a theory well fits the falling and low rate of saving in the United States, compared with the high rates in Japan and West Germany. Saving in my country seems to have been unaffected in its downward course by the 1981 tax reduction designed to favor higher incomes and increased saving. Saving rates, of course, are consequences of many other factors than levels of income and past and present rates of growth: for example, the cost of land and housing in Japan, the system of wage and salary payments with annual bonuses, the absence or avail-ability of consumer credit. But fast-growing countries tend to save more than slow.

Inability of a country's entrepreneurs to resist or match competi-tion from new and thrusting foreign producers finds many examples, including the British victory over Venice in the manufacture of woolens and soap; Germany and the United States pushing past Britain in the 1880s and 1890s in electrical engineering, chemicals, and automobiles; and Japan overtaking and surpassing the United States in automobiles and electronics. At an early stage in all these countries some technol-ogy was begged, borrowed, or stolen from the leading rival, but in due course the rising country developed entrepreneurs who undertook new products and found markets at home and abroad, sometimes using inventions conceived in mature economies that had lost some of their capacity to innovate. There is a question here, too, whether productivity can be stimulated by policies, such as governmental support of research and development and tax policies to promote risk taking and the like, or whether research, the patent numbers, and the desire to innovate are dependent rather than independent variables, driven in an S-shaped profile by growth, as well as in some degree contributing to it exogenously.

Closely related to falling productivity is the waning of the entrepreneurial spirit after a country has been growing for an extended period. New lines of output require new men, and the previous generation of industries and industrialists tends to take it easy. This is sometimes expressed as "three generations from shirtsleeves to shirtsleeves," implying that the third generation loses its wealth and has to start over again. The more usual experience is for the third generation to withdraw from trade and industry into aristocratic agriculture, stately homes, sometimes public service, the professions, and often finance and investments. Having made a fortune, the successful merchant in Venice moved to terra firma, cultivating big estates on the mainland. In Holland, trade gave way to finance. The professions and public life, as well as the City of London, have attracted the British.

The "Dutch disease" is a concept developed from the discovery of North Sea gasfields that raised wages throughout Holland and squeezed those industries that had not benefited from the lucky find. The concept is an old one, however, and applied especially to the riches earned by the Spanish discoveries of silver in Peru and Mexico. Its current American equivalent may perhaps be the enormous salaries earned by outstanding professional athletes, Hollywood stars, top company executives and lawyers, and especially by financial manipulators. In a world where many are getting rich quickly, it is difficult to settle down to humdrum contentment with modest returns that accumulate slowly. Team play seems to have been affected adversely, not only where Most-Valuable-Player competition and hotdogging (enthusiastic celebration of a good play by the player) pervade the field of sport, but in law, advertising, accounting firms, and financial houses, which break up currently because younger associates and partners want theirs now, rather than, as in the past, waiting until they have attained seniority. Many are called but few are chosen, for example, in professional football, and especially basketball, but the returns of the few that are chosen are so huge that they turn the steps of the many into what constitutes for the vast majority a dead end. The rise of state lotteries is another indication of wealth for a few that undermines the incentive to work.

Most economists appear to believe that rates of saving, productivity increase, innovation, and the like can be affected by policy manipulation, especially by changes in taxation and by the skillful application of "industrial policy." There is, of course, much that correct policy could do, such as correcting the U.S. deficits in the federal budget and the balance of payments by raising taxes to balance the budget while lowering interest rates through monetary policy to stimulate investment and offset the negative impact of the tax increase on consumption. But this assumes that devising proper policies is a technical question for economists, rather than a politico-sociological one. The fiscal problem in the United States has been set back by President Bush's adamant stand against raising the levels of income tax that were lowered in 1981. That position was not taken quixotically, however, but as a response to public attitudes. Even if the Bush administration were resolved to correct the deficits, it is by no means clear that the Congress could enact such a measure in the teeth of the pressure groups resisting their share of the burden. As for industrial policy, strongly advocated in many quarters, it is easy to be skeptical about the ability of government to pick winners in new industries, which for the most part seem to evolve in Darwinian fashion from chaotic beginnings. One may also question whether government is able to close down the losers, as for example, in the case of the M-1 tank and the F-16 fighter plane, where the Pentagon wants to get away from obsolete or poorly functioning weapons, but is unable to resist the pressure to maintain them from legislators representing the districts affected by the potential loss of employment. It may be remarked, however, that Britain slimmed down cotton textile production, and the Common Market undertook to rationalize steel production on the Continent in the Davignon Plan with some modest success.

Chaos theory leaves open the possibility that new S- or growth curves may grow out of the old as they slow down. There may be a fountain of economic youth awaiting an economic Ponce de Leon, the Spanish explorer who searched for such a fountain in Florida in the sixteenth century. To rely on it, however, is risky. I start peering into the future, then, with a somewhat pessimistic attitude.

The future I am supposed to deal with stretches out ten years to the end of the present century in 2000 AD. I confess I would rather talk about this year and next, looking at the problems that are looming up. Let me start with a look at the fascinating series of problems posed by the November-December 1989 revolution in Eastern Europe, move to the domestic problems of the United States, proceed to the bilateral problems facing the United States and Japan on the one hand, and the United States and Europe on the other, concluding by an examination of world economic organization as a whole, and its stability.

The most exciting problem facing the world economy in the several years ahead is what will happen to the Socialist bloc, the so-called Second World, as compared with the First World of the developed countries, broadly congruent with the membership of the Organization for Economic Cooperation and Development (the OECD), and the Third World of countries that have been successively called backward, underdeveloped, and developing. I write necessarily somewhat in advance of today and run the risk that anything I say will have been rendered obsolete during the first months of 1990. The economies of some countries of the Eastern bloc have practically broken down (for example, the Polish) and need relief, rehabilitation, and reconstruction, just as Europe and Japan needed them in 1945 and the first few years that followed the end of World War II. Others had been making progress toward democracy, as opposed to authoritarian control by the Communist Party, and from a command to a market economy, before the wave of change of last November and December. The progress has been and will be uneven. Foreign debts of the past weigh heavily over many of these countries and such debt, like consumption loans of the poor generally, are difficult, even approaching impossibility, to service on the original terms. One billion dollars of aid for Poland from fourteen countries seems small, but may loom large in terms of competing demands, especially when one contemplates the preoccupation of the Federal Republic of Germany with the Democratic Republic and of France with Rumania. Perhaps most important of all is the fact that the Bush administration has painted itself into a corner on taxes. If there is a peace dividend from the prospective end of the cold war, a legion of other claimants stand in line for a share: the budget deficit, the war on drugs, the educational deficit, the environment, the undermaintained infrastructure, health care, housing for the homeless, some, perhaps a substantial amount, of reversal of the redistribution of income against the poor and in favor of the rich . . . the list seems endless.

It is impossible to forecast the impact of the 1989 revolution on the world economy, even with a full panoply of economic models provided by rational expectations. I believe that the revolution will slow down the European schedule for completion of the Common Market and creating a single European currency and a central bank, laid down for the end of 1992, projects that the unification enthusiasts dragooned the politicians into adopting with a timetable, but to which the major powers—West Germany, France, and Britain, the last openly, the others in their hearts, are not yet ready to yield the necessary sovereignty. *Ostpolitik* appears to me a substitute for the Common Market, not a complement. President Mitterand of France has boxed the compass over German unification, once ignoring the issue, then appearing to condone reunion, and finally emerging with his real position that it is advisable to go slow. He must think that two Germanies of 61 and 16 million, respectively are preferable to a single Germany of 77 million, lying along the border of a France of 56 million.

The dissolution of the Second World is liable to be hard on the Third. Barber Conable, president of the World Bank, hastened in December 1989 to Africa to reassure his borrowers there that more for Eastern Europe did not mean less for Africa, nor presumably for Latin America or the Middle East. That must mean that the Bank, and presumably the International Monetary Fund, have to grow, with the diffidence of the United States in this regard posing an obstacle. Japan may take over provision of most new capital for the Bretton Woods institutions, but that raises an issue I postpone to the end.

The strategic goals of moving Eastern Europe to democracy and market economies, more or less integrated into the world economy, pose hundred of questions, but it is difficult to focus on these until the tactical problems of avoiding breakdown, chaos, and massive emigration to Western Europe, Israel for the Jews of Russia and Rumania wanting to leave, and anywhere else they can be taken in have been taken in hand.

For the United States, I choose to look at the business outlook, the debt problem more generally, and the balance of payments together with the dollar. The outlook for business, in my unsophisticated judgment, is far less attractive than the stock market with its new highs seems to hold. Real estate and banks with large portfolios of real estate loans are in trouble, so that the prospects for construction in housing, hotels, office buildings, and shopping malls are less than brilliant. Automobile sales are widely off, despite rebates and other stimulants. Unemployment is rising, not only in automobiles, but also in high-tech industries like computers and in Wall Street. Real estate troubles me most. A book written in 1933 by one Homer Hoyt described the cycle in real estate associated with the stock market (*One Hundred Years of Land Values in Chicago*). On the rise, they advance together. When a crash comes in the stock market, speculators in real estate who have shared the stock market's euphoria on the way up, congratulate themselves; they have real assets, not depressed pieces of paper, they are financed by term loans, not day-to-day debt that is instantly callable. But liquidation in the stock market such as followed the October 19, 1987, crash, takes place in a few months, or perhaps a year plus, whereas that in real estate is extended in time. Demand falls off sharply as new buyers wait for prices to come down. Interest and tax burdens on the speculators continue. Instead of months or a year and a fraction, liquidation in real estate stretches out for three, four, sometimes as long as eight years. I mentioned this in an economic conference last fall and was told that econometric studies show no correlation between stock market and real estate prices. So much the worse for econometrics. In the months since October the press has been filled with more and more bad news about nonperforming and problem real estate loans. At first this seems to have been confined to the Southwest of the United States, where the boom had been accentuated by the high prices of oil in 1979 and 1980, followed by collapse. Since then, however, the troubles have spread to New England in condominia, Florida, New Jersey single-family houses, Chicago hotels, New York office buildings, and so on and so forth. Some bank stocks have lost 90 percent of their value. The thrifts—savings banks and savings and loan societies—have a problem on their hands that grows larger daily. One knows how to prevent a strung-out liquidation from turning into a panic: throw money at it or, in more scholarly terms, produce a lender of last resort that ensures that unsophisticated holders of claims on threatened institutions do not lose. Since central banks can create money with a stroke of the pen, there is no technical limit to the capacity of a country to bail out its domestic institutions. There may be, however, political limits. The taxpayer may not want to bail out bankers and depositors who have been carefree in their chase for profits. In addition, if the institutions ensuring bank deposits have to take over a large amount of real estate from insolvent institutions, its liquidation is likely to take time on the one hand, and to slow down recovery in construction, on the other.

Real estate debt, to be sure, is not the only debt problem in my country. There are the burdens of Third World debt with which the world has been contending since the revelation of the morass in August 1982; consumer debt, continually reaching new highs; junk bonds from leveraged buyouts and mergers; not to mention the piling up of government debt as the federal deficit continues from year to year. The late Raymond Goldsmith developed a theory that the financial-intermediation ratio (the ratio of total debt to national income) starts out in the early stages of a country's development at some level such as 0.25 and rises with development to 1.75 or so when the financial structure of a country is fully developed. In the 1980s, the U.S. ratio has passed 3.0. Banks with bad loans and mortgages started to work it out at book values by lending the sluggish debtors new money to pay overdue interest. Lately, however, they have been forced to write bad and problem loans off. This has led the U.S. regulators, and indeed national authorities in the leading financial countries, to require banks to raise more capital, a difficult task when bank stocks are depressed. The same choice between work-out or write-off now confronts the government regulators who have to deal with the assets of the taken-over banks.

One disturbing facet of the American debt problem is that much of it as been accumulated in foreign hands, along with a rather mixed bag of American plants, equipment, real estate, and companies. In the past many economists claimed that a domestic debt is not a burden because we owe it to ourselves, whereas foreign debt requires us to reduce our level of living to sustain debt service. Since then, economists have become more subtle in comparing domestic and foreign debt. Nonetheless, there is a substantial kernel of truth in the view that foreign debt is a greater burden than domestic. Perhaps the greatest issue is the use to which the debt is put. If it is consumed, including military expenditure, there is no asset with capacity to produce the debt service. By the same token, if foreign investment in the United States buys up existing assets, with the monies received not reinvested but consumed, the flow of profits to foreign owners reduces the income available at home. One can, to be sure, postpone the cuts in consumption by borrowing the interest and dividends paid abroad from foreigners, as the Third World has been doing along with the United States, or allowing the foreigners to use their profits to acquire new productive assets. Sooner or later a day of reckoning arrives, to borrow the title of a book by Benjamin Friedman. There is a strong possibility that it will arrive in the 1990s.

The balance of payments of the United States will of course be affected by debt service paid to foreigners in the future. I am not a great believer in the concept of the balance of international indebtedness, toting up the claims of the world on a country, and of the country on the world and taking heart from a positive balance, fear from a negative. There is no unambiguous way to measure either assets or liabilities, including in the latter foreign ownership of assets in a country. Should one use cost? book (cost minus depreciation plus appreciation)? the capitalized value of the stream of income? market? or replacement? Despite the fuzzy character of the balance of claims, a continuous loss of assets and piling up of liabilities does pose problems, and the balance of interest and dividends received compared with those paid to foreigners has importance for the future standard of living, even though the effect may be staved off for a time by borrowing what is owed abroad, and foreigners investing here what they earn here.

One particular form in which the day of reckoning might arrive is if foreigners after a time regard the outlook for the dollar as dubious and choose not to continue lending in dollars, and even to withdraw some of their dollar debts as they matured. This might send the dollar into a free fall if foreign central banks stood aloof. I have been surprised in recent years that foreign investors in the United States have not tried to denominate their loans to United States borrowers in their own currencies, though perhaps not in a synthetic currency such as the ECU or the SDR, which have their own problems both of understanding and of higher transactions costs. A shift of foreign investment from debt to real assets is part of this uneasiness. Central banks undertaking swaps have an implicit exchange rate guarantee for the six months before the swap is reversed, but I have been expecting the development of foreign currency lending, or something more akin to the Roosa bonds of two decades back.

A free fall of the dollar and a possible shift to U.S. borrowing in foreign currency or with foreign currency guarantees may well have been prevented by the relative high interest rates in the United States. The New York financial press writes continuously as if the Federal Reserve System were conducting monetary policy with the fear of inflation in mind. There are two links of monetary policy to inflation, one through the quantity theory that especially applies in a closed economy, the other through exchange depreciation, which usually drives up the prices of foreign trade goods. The Fed may have both in mind.

It takes two to tango, of course, and the mirror image of the United States' current account deficit is the surpluses of other countries, including, notably, Japan, Taiwan, West Germany, and perhaps Switzerland. If the United States consumes too much, they may be said to consume too little, if the United States saves too little, they save too much; if the United States exports too little and imports too much, they the reverse, and so on. The United States has tried to address the deficit in the balance of payments through depreciation of the dollar. The reduction of the dollar from 360 to the yen to 140–50 seems to have had as little effect as the 1981 tax reductions had on the savings ratio. The country has worked on the bilateral imbalance in other ways, none satisfactory: through appeals to Japan to import more, especially rice, beef, and citrus fruit, reduce its exports through direct controls, or allow export prices in dollars to rise when the dollar depreciates. I deplore Japan bashing, but regard it as something that goes with the territory. In the seventeenth century, Britain went in heavily for Dutch bashing, introducing into the language a series of ironic expressions that have survived: a Dutch treat, in which each party pays his or her own way; a Dutch uncle, who is a strict disciplinarian rather than avuncular in the usual benign sense; Dutch courage, which comes from being drunk, and many more. As a footnote on the quirks of history, observe that when the British bashed the Dutch they were on the way up, while today too many U.S. persons go in for Japan bashing when the United States is in the process of being overtaken. The rising assertiveness of Japanese industry, if not yet of politicians, may indicate a prospective reversal in the direction of bashing.

This afternoon's panel will discuss the international position of Japan in greater detail, but let me briefly sketch out two scenarios in U.S.-Japanese relations, one pessimistic, the other optimistic. Reality, to be sure, will lie perhaps somewhere between, or even lead off in an entirely different direction.

First, the pessimistic. Japan will continue to save at a declining but still high rate to build houses on land that is kept high in price by subsidies to rice growers, and United States savings will not respond to the new Bush initiative in the form of tax-free savings accounts that will primarily divert existing savings from other outlets. Japanese industry will continue to compete effectively in lines where the United States has had a comparative advantage—computers, copiers, chips, aircraft—and to shift out of obsolete industries by moving production to other parts of the Pacific Rim. Exports will continue to rise as fast or faster than imports. Savings will be used to buy up U.S. real assets, to a greater extent than debt, and investments in the Third World will be in kind or debt, intermediated through international organizations or by way of Chicago and New York. At some stages Japanese companies and even official institutions may slow down and even stop buying U.S. Treasury obligations. I do not necessarily predict financial crisis, though I am interested in the species. The most likely outcome is bickering, fussing, unending negotiation, and a continuous increase in the economic power of Japan and a decline in that of the United States. Japan will resist taking on its own defense and that of the Far East and the United States will cut its defense spending worldwide, increasing the likelihood of regional brushfire wars. If push comes to shove, it will be unclear who is in charge, in either a regional conflict that threatens to spill over or a financial crisis with a potential for spreading.

The optimistic scenario may not strike Americans as particularly cheerful, as it calls for a transition of economic leadership from Washington, or at least its continued dilution. Adjustments in the economic sphere occur on both sides, as Japanese consumption rises and savings fall, United States consumption is contained, and savings rise. The budget is overbalanced and the deficit in the balance of payments on current accounts is eliminated, even if there is no debt repayment or buyback of assets. (As an aside it may be mentioned that if households and industry do not save enough, total saving can perhaps be raised through government surpluses, just as in Norway after the war when the public refused to save, but capital formation was required. It would be awkward, however, if the government ran surpluses to crowd investment in and found it resulting in current-account surpluses and debt repayment abroad.)

Japanese contributions to the World Bank and IMF will be raised, along with Japanese voting power in those institutions and even a loss of the United States' veto. Japan and Germany will be given permanent seats in the U.N. Security Council, and their military forces will relieve the United States of its sole responsibility for maintaining the uneasy peace in the Middle East. Japan will widen its bilateral aid for economic development of the Third World beyond Asia, and even contribute importantly to the critical need for aid for the Second World.

On narrower economic lines I should like to see Japanese security prices stop rising, because, despite my profound ignorance of it, that market makes me nervous. I suspect that the hidden reserves of Japanese banks and companies are well understood by Japanese investors, if not by passive foreign observers, just as the hidden losses of American banks are understood in markets in my country.

What this scenario calls for is a smooth transition to greater sharing of economic responsibility in the world between our two countries, a greater readiness on the part of the United States to abandon the chauvinist and puerile claim to be "Number 1," and a greater acceptance by Japan of world responsibility.

I leave too little time for First World Europe. I have already suggested that the revolution in Eastern Europe will slow down the process of creating a true Common Market. I do not think it will stop it altogether. The groundswell against nationalism in favor of a confederation or federation, perhaps the former with its emphasis on the retention of national sovereignty slipping into the latter where such sovereignty is compromised, is too strong to be frustrated for long. The remaining countries of the European Free Trade Area (EFTA)—Iceland, Norway, Sweden, Finland, Austria, and Switzerland—will join the Common Market, if not immediately the Community. In due course East Germany will be unified with the Federal Republic, and Poland and Czechoslovakia, both of which wanted to join the Marshall Plan in 1947, plus Hungary, will enlarge the European economic area still more. The question remains how parochial Europe will be and especially whether it will work to reduce the slight influence there of Japan and the major role that has been played by the United States.

There is a possible historical analogy; for 150 years from 1783, Britain served as a protector of the United States of America—with a brief interruption in 1812. Two world wars reversed the position; instead of the United States depending upon the United Kingdom, the latter relied on its "special relationship" with the United States. Military dependence for Europe was expressed through the North Atlantic Treaty Organization (NATO), to which France may be said to have belonged de facto, if insisting on its independence de jure. Economic dependence of Europe on the United States gradually declined after the Marshall Plan, most recently slowly as the OECD—originally a European organization, later broadened to include Japan, Canada, the United States, Australia, and New Zealand—lost the greater part of its operational functions but carried on as a quasi-academic institution. With the likely end of the cold war—a conclusion that some may regard as debatable—NATO has lost most of its raison d'être. U.S. armed forces will increasingly be brought home from Europe and from the Far East. An American presence in Europe is still required in the war against terrorism that extends well beyond Europe's borders, but not, I think, for peace keeping more generally. But the end of history, as Francis Fukuyama regards the end of the cold war, does not mean the end of economic history, even though the direct role of the United States in Europe is bound to shrink.

How then will the world economy be organized? Postulate with me the decline of American hegemony, leadership, prime responsibility for world economic stability—whatever you choose to call it. As of the moment, I see no rival country challenging for the position, as Britain challenged Holland and Germany, Britain in the years from 1875 to 1914, and as Japan challenged the putative leadership of the United States in 1941. The Federal Republic of Germany and Japan have been faithful followers of the U.S. lead in the three decades after 1945, and if in the following decade and a half they have become more assertive, I see no strong urge in either to issue challenges to take over the position that the United States appears to be vacating. That leaves several possibilities:

leadership of a cabal, consisting of the United States, Japan, and the Common Market, or perhaps of Germany in the guise of the Common Market;

reliance on worldwide and regional institutions built up since World War II—the ITO, IMF, IBRD, the regional U.N. economic commissions, and the regional development banks;

a more sharply divided regional arrangement of Euro-Africa, the Americas, and the Far East, in financial terms, organized into ECU, dollar, and yen blocs; and

muddling through in a limping or hybrid system, until some country with a powerful economy once again accepts responsibility for world economic stability and is accepted by most of the world in that role, without two or more countries contending for the prestige and what some insist have been for the United States the gains.

I happen to find none of these alternative possibilities—I hesitate to call them options—overwhelmingly attractive.

In writing a history of the Great Depression of the 1930s, I remarked that there were certain functions that needed to be discharged for the world economy to be stable, three in ordinary times or on trend, two in crisis. On trend, the functions were maintaining a flow of capital to needy countries, providing some sort of order in foreign-exchange rates, at least among the key currencies, and arranging for a modicum of coordination of macroeconomic policies among the leading countries. In crisis, more is needed: open markets for distressed goods in depression, a source of extra supply when goods are tight, as in the oil crises of 1973 and 1979, and a lender of last resort in financial crisis. Lacking a leading country able and willing more or less to discharge these functions, the crises of 1873, 1890, and 1929 were followed by prolonged depressions. Let me call these functions, for short: steady capital lending, a foreign-exchange regime, macroeconomic coordination, open markets, and last-resort lending.

Today's system as U.S. leadership shrinks has a mixed scorecard. On steady lending, there is the Third World debt crisis, with the Baker Plan, followed by the Brady Plan, widely debated, praised, and scorned, and the prospect for new capital and assistance for Eastern Europe, in which no country at the moment points the way. I am unclear about which country orchestrated the $1 billion package for Poland as I write, but the amount is derisory and the countries of Western Europe seemed to be pulled in different ways. The system does better with the foreign exchanges, though hardly brilliantly, and some coordination of macroeconomic policy is provided in the preparations for summit meetings of the G-5 or G-7. Open markets do not do well. Last-resort lending, which used to be led by the United States, has been transformed into last-resort borrowing by the United States through open markets and the G-10 swap network.

I see little likelihood of a trilateral leadership that would pull together for long. The interests of Japan, a united Germany, and the United States differ at the national level, and each country has a changing interest in and commitment to the international public interest. If responsibility for this international interest were thus shared, it is likely in my judgment that it would dissolve in wrangling over the comparative size of the various burdens.

Regional solutions have been proposed steadily since World War II, and progress is being made both in Europe and in the free-trade area between Canada and the United States. In Europe, especially, exchange rates are converging in the European Monetary System and macroeconomic policies have become better coordinated. It is hard to see similar progress in either the yen or the dollar area. A more fundamental objection, however, is that for many countries economic relationships across area boundaries are more important than those within them, and that some countries are unwilling to submit to the wishes of the area leader. After having struggled free of Belgium, France, Portugal, and the United Kingdom, the African countries, for example, are prepared to receive aid and trade from Europe, but not direction. Latin America seems to be suspicious of any attempt to renew the Alliance for Progress. Regional economic organization on a voluntary basis is desirable within a strong global framework—say, ultimate fixed exchange rates among the dollar, yen, and ECU (or deutsche mark), but fixed rates within blocs with gyrating rates between them do not constitute a stable system.

I am a muddler-through. It is not a heroic position, but big planners do not succeed unless there is strong leadership, called in some quarters "arm twisting," to drive the plans through interests when they do not fully converge. At the moment there is no leader, no country willing to assume the heavy burdens of leadership, no country recognized by the others as fully responsible, no hegemon, if you will, to concoct and enforce such plans. Each country should tackle its own problems to the greatest possible extent, the United States its deficits, declining savings, crumbling infrastructure, spreading pollution; Japan its level of living, especially in housing; Europe unification, both in the Common Market and with the East. International bodies should be encouraged to push harder and more insistently to solve international problems. That calls for the gradual reorganization of the responsibility for decision making in these institutions in line with contributions to them. I should like to see the OECD reverse its decline and strengthen such units as Working Party Number 3 that was established to address the coordination of macroeconomic policy. The changes that are possible, however, are marginal, not structural. In time, another system of organization will emerge, perhaps with a new hegemon. In a world that recognizes chaos theory, I choose not to predict which country, federation, or continent that will be.

It is a matter of some moment that the two most far-reaching organizations of the postwar period—the Euro-currency market and the swap network among the G-10 central banks—grew like Topsy rather than springing full blown from the brow of an economist. An eclectic approach along broad theoretical lines, such as I have outlined, is safer and more likely to succeed than would be adoption of a heroic nostrum, such as flexible exchange rates, the gold standard, annually balanced budgets, M_2 growing at a fixed rate, free banking, or whatever your favorite cure-all happens to be. It is, to be sure, a recipe for tension and nervous making. I firmly believe, however, that "Proceed as the way lies open" is, in economics, a better motto than "Damn the torpedoes; full speed ahead."

Thank you very much for your considerate attention.

CHAPTER 4

International Finance in Perspective:
The Second Half of the Century Compared
with the Interwar Years

The changes in international finance over the twentieth century can be described in various ways: as a movement from the gold and dollar standards to flexible exchange rates; as a move from the dominance of trade in international dealings to that of capital movements; as a loss of importance of national boundaries and governmental intervention with a rise in the proportion of international to national dealings; as a change from stable personal relationships between the personnel of nonfinancial and financial corporations to highly competitive and variable ones based on price; as a move to increased national liquidity with an awareness of the opportunities for earning higher returns, commensurate with risk, in other countries; or as the development of new financial instruments, covering many more time spans. Perhaps the change can be summed up as one from a few assets with limited liquidity to many more instruments with far more liquidity, and from a narrow horizon to one spanning the world. In the course of these changes, finance has become more volatile in some dimensions, more stable in others. I explain this further with brief potted histories of the interwar and post–World War II years.

The interwar years divide naturally around 1925, 1929, 1933, and 1936. The year 1925 marked the end of the tortured recovery from World War I, a period of unpayable reparations and war debts, foreign exchange depreciation, heavy speculative capital inflows to Germany and Eastern Europe in the hope that their currencies would recover to prewar pars, the chaos of hyperinflation in Germany, and finally, the successive stabilization of the replacement Reichsmark, the pound sterling (at prewar parity), the depreciated French franc, and the Italian

Originally published in French as "Finance international en perspective: La seconde moitié du siècle comparée à l'entre-deux guerres," *Revue d'Economie Financière* 14 (Fall 1990): 11–24.

lira. The Dawes Plan of 1924 that created the Reichsmark was a watershed in another dimension, in long-term capital movements. During and immediately after the war there had been intergovernmental loans, giving rise to war debts, and a few loans to governments by private institutions, notably among the latter the J. P. Morgan stabilization loan of $100 million to France that enabled the government briefly to squeeze the speculators going short of the franc. The Dawes Plan contained provision for a Rm 800 million loan for Germany, divided among a number of capital markets. The American tranche of $110 million, more than half the total, was oversubscribed ten times and gave rise to a burst of foreign lending by American financial houses new to the business, all over the world. In Latin America the manic surge of lending was called "the dance of the millions." Widespread defaults in the 1930s underlined that the quality of U.S. loans had deteriorated sharply after 1924. Among the largest borrowers were the German government and German municipalities, which stopped service on the debt in 1931 with the Standstill Agreement.

The flurry of foreign loans was cut off in the spring of 1928 by the start of a boom on the New York Stock Exchange, diverting attention from abroad to home, and from bonds to shares. A brief resumption of underwriting of foreign bonds took place in the second quarter of 1930 after the stock market collapse of October 1929, but could not be sustained. When long-term lending was halted, some borrowers such as Germany shifted to short-term loans from London and New York banks. Australia, New Zealand, Argentina, and Uruguay could not do so because of a different pattern in their borrowing from London. Instead of originally issuing bonds abroad and drawing down the proceeds over time, they would typically borrow through overdrafts, paid off when they became large with the proceeds of long-term loans. When the long-term bond market dried up, they were already indebted and hence forced to depreciate their currencies.

The stock market collapse in New York in October 1929 was precipitated by the revelation of a Hatry swindle in London in September, which tightened interest rates there, pulled London funds in brokers' loans in New York home, raised interest rates there, and started a liquidation of securities that gathered speed. World commodity prices had been declining gently since their postwar peak in 1925, but the stock market crash pushed them into a sharp dive. In this era, with a few exceptions such as sugar, commodities imported by the United States were shipped on consignment to New York, to be sold on arrival. The buyers were commodity brokers, as a rule, who depended for credit on the New York banks. After the crash, however, these banks were seized up with trying to sort out brokers' loans undermargined by the fall in stock prices. With credit unavailable, commodities were dumped on the market and fell sharply in price, import commodities falling much more sharply than export. With the price decline, the value of imports fell, and as a consequence the value of exports of foreign countries. An important difference between the stock market crashes of 1929 and 1987 is that the latter was not communicated to commodity prices or to foreign trade.

A second important sequel of the stock market crash was a "flight to quality" in investments. Interest rates recovered quickly after the crash, returning to preboom levels as early as January 1930. This movement, however, was limited to high-grade corporate and government bonds. Bonds of less than investment grade continued to fall in price. The first banking crisis in November and December 1930 was the result of the falls in commodity prices and in second- and third-grade securities, including corporate and municipal bonds and mortgages. The first flight to quality was evident in foreign bonds in March 1930, the second in domestic securities in September.

The course of the depression in the early 1930s is well known. As commodity and security prices fell, banks, in Europe as in the United States, came under pressure and capital sought safety. The Young Plan of June 1930 to help transfer German reparations barely managed to get placed. By May 1931, the Austrian Creditanstalt, a major bank, was forced to close after failing to get international help, starting an unraveling of short-term credits. This led to the German Standstill Agreement of July 1931, the abandonment of the gold standard by Britain in September, and by Japan at the end of the year. Apart from Argentina, Latin American countries defaulted on their foreign bonds, in some cases, as in Colombia, after sizeable depreciation had raised the domestic currency cost of debt service. The Hawley-Smoot tariff in the United States in June 1930 had produced a wave of retaliatory protection and accelerated the declining spiral of world trade. Spread of collapse from stocks to commodities to real estate in the United States induced a wave of bank failures there that finally pushed the United States off gold in April 1933. In due course, and despite measures to limit outflows of capital and to hold up commodity prices, the gold bloc of France, Belgium, the Netherlands, and Switzerland abandoned the gold standard in September 1936 (Belgium in 1935) under cover of a Tripartite Monetary Agreement among France, the United Kingdom, and the United States.

The years from 1936 to the outbreak of war in 1939 saw further disintegration of the world economy in both trade and finance. A number of countries tried to support exports of capital equipment with government credit. In Britain an Export Credit Guarantee Department, in the United States an Export-Import Bank, and in France a comparable organization with the acronym COFACE were set up. They continued to operate after World War II because of the gap in private trade finance between short-term credit and long-term bonds. After the war, too, the Federal Republic of Germany established a similar unit, the *Kreditanstalt für Wiederaufbau* (credit agency for reconstruction).

Efforts at maintaining or expanding international credit were limited, however. Some special relationships held up within regional and currency blocs, Canada borrowing at long term in the United States, and the British recovery based on a housing boom spilling over to Scandinavia through expanded imports. German clearing agreements kept some trade going with southeastern Europe and Latin America. With the outbreak of war in September 1939, all efforts to revive international trade and finance came to an end.

Wartime planning in the United States produced a resolve to build a more liberal world economy when peace arrived, especially in trade and in the management of exchange rates. Less attention was given to the revival of international capital movements, and the Bretton Woods Agreement of 1944 tolerated and indeed sanctioned capital controls. So hopeless was it thought to be to reestablish private lending that a world bank was established to provide quasi-governmental lending where it was needed. To assist the recovery of the world's economies from war, United Nations organizations were established for relief and rehabilitation (UNRRA), reconstruction and economic development (the IBRD or World Bank), and monetary stabilization (the IMF was founded to stabilize exchange rates and fund short-term balance-of-payment disequilibria). This program took time to get started, so that other assistance was necessary: military relief; increased capital for the U.S. Export-Import Bank; a British loan on the key-currency principle that world currencies should be stabilized in decreasing order of importance; and, in due course, post-UNRRA relief, Interim Aid, and the Marshall Plan. The World Bank and the IMF did not participate in European or Japanese recovery, apart from one or two emergency advances in slight derogation of the articles of agreement.

One financial feature of the Marshall Plan was the European Payments Union, established, after two false starts, as a means of restoring at least limited convertibility among the leading countries of Western Europe, convertibility, that is, into one another's currencies if not into dollars. Unlike the Bretton Woods articles, which were virtually dictated by a determined U.S. Treasury assistant secretary, Harry D. White, when the world's attention in wartime was elsewhere, EPU rules were negotiated in hard bargaining among the recipients of Marshall Plan aid, especially between Belgium, a perennial trade surplus country, and deficit Britain, which hoped to restore its world financial leadership. After its foundation in June 1950, the Union encountered a series of crises that it overcame one by one until, with general convertibility in 1958, it was wound up, it is fair to say, though it was officially succeeded by a European Monetary Agreement of limited content. The subject of a 1989 book by two of its officials, Jacob J. Kaplan, an American, and Günter Schleiminger, a German, the exercise was an outstanding achievement in continuous bargaining, helped by a U.S. investment in dollars that could be circulated among the participants.

The World Bank set up at Bretton Woods gradually grew in size, with capital replenishment, and in prestige, but confined its operations for the most part to advising and lending to less-developed countries. Other official regional funds for the same purposes were established: an Inter-American Development Bank, an Asian Development Bank, one for Africa, and, in connection with the European Common Market created by the 1957 Rome Agreement, a European Investment Bank, and a European Social Fund to make grants available to peripheral parts of Europe adversely affected by the centripetal forces of the market. In 1990, plans were approved to create a European Bank for Reconstruction and Development to operate in Eastern Europe after the economic revolution there.

Bit by bit in the 1950s, private international lending that had been expected to remain moribund recovered. A number of countries and governmental organizations, led by Scandinavians, issued bonds in New York, a large portion of which were bought by European investors. Specialized securities were sold to the Jewish community in the United States, first for Palestine and then for the state of Israel. These had a substantial eleemosynary component. Canadian borrowing from the United States resumed on the basis of strong regional and sentimental ties between the two countries, so strong indeed that some U.S. insurance companies that routinely bought Canadian bonds had policies against "foreign" investments. London prepared to lend the sterling area in principle, but initially assigned it a priority far back in the queue, so that Australia and New Zealand turned to New York.

The origins of U.S. direct investment went back to the middle of the nineteenth century. It picked up in the 1890s and especially flourished in the 1920s. Economic theory has established that the motive for this was not cheap capital in the United States so much as an advantage in a branch of industry or in particular companies on which "rents" could be better protected by foreign production, as opposed to exporting or licensing the technology. To some extent companies established "tariff factories" abroad behind tariff walls that made exports unprofitable, but direct investment occurred mostly on innovative products to forestall imitation and to get ahead of potential competition. A new surge of investment by companies "going international" took place after European economic recovery in the 1950s, especially as the costs of management declined with easier international communication by telephone and jet aircraft. In the 1970s and especially the 1980s, a reverse movement took place as European and Japanese companies invested in the United States. In addition, a number of U.S. companies, under pressure from service on debt contracted in taking over other companies or in resisting being taken over, sold foreign or domestic subsidiaries to foreigners. The two movements brought foreign capital to the United States and reduced the domination of the ranks of multinational corporations by American companies.

While private capital movements were building in size through securities and direct investment, the U.S. debit on foreign aid and long-term capital account gradually came to exceed the current-account surplus on trade and services, including interest and dividends. In the late 1950s economic analysts developed a concept of "liquidity balance" in which increases in short-term liabilities to foreigners were counted the same as losses in gold on the ground that foreigners might one day choose to convert them to gold. Robert Triffin warned against a world shortage of liquidity that would occur when the United States corrected its liquidity deficit and dollars were no longer added to world reserves. World gold production was limited, and much of it was flowing not into central-bank reserves, but into private use and hoards. These ideas gained acceptance in official Washington circles, and beginning with President Eisenhower in the fall of 1960, U.S. policy was directed to correcting the deficit, largely by restraining the long-term capital outflow. An Interest Equalization Tax was applied in 1963 to raise the cost on lending abroad through bonds, and shortly extended to foreign bank loans. In 1964 President Johnson called for a Voluntary Credit Restraint Program on direct investment abroad, and in 1968 for a Mandatory Control Program. None of these efforts produced significant results, as there were too many conduits through which U.S. capital could flow to higher interest rate and profit areas abroad. Corporations with foreign earnings could retain them overseas with the same effect as if they had invested "new money." Regulations under Democratic administrations became increasingly complex without increasing in effectiveness, and when the Republican president Richard Nixon took office, the program was eliminated.

Other proposals to deal with the problem of world liquidity included raising the price of gold. Triffin proposed the creation of a new international paper asset to replace both gold and dollars in central-bank reserves. A minority view held that the liquidity definition of an overall balance-of-payments deficit was misleading: when the world needed reserves, it borrowed from the United States and held the balances. Some borrowing was for capital formation, some primarily to increase liquidity. Concern about what would happen when the United States corrected its "deficit" was misplaced, because like any other bank, the United States furnished liquidity to the world by lending long and borrowing short. There was no shortage of world liquidity, nor any prospect of one.

None of these ideas appealed to the French, either to such officials as President deGaulle, who believed that the United States was acquiring good assets with worthless dollars, or to Jacques Rueff, a leading economist. In 1965, when deGaulle returned to office, the Bank of France undertook a program of regular sizable conversions of dollars to gold as a means of enforcing discipline on the United States. The effort had to be halted in 1968 when the events of May and June led not only to the resignation of deGaulle but to an outflow of capital from France that had to be met in gold or dollars. It is noteworthy that in the following years the French authorities bought gold when France had a surplus but borrowed dollars through French nationalized agencies when there was a deficit to meet, in so doing building up a substantial indebtedness in dollars and a stock of gold. This represents a speculative policy that has been successful thus far as the price of gold has risen more in the 1970s and 1980s than the dollar, in terms of francs. Over the longer run, however, it may prove difficult for any country to dispose of large amounts of gold without depressing the price substantially, already at $360 an ounce well below its peak of $850. The price of the dollar has been highly volatile, it is true, but owning gold and owing dollars puts France in a highly leveraged position in two markets.

In 1965, the Johnson administration in the United States undertook to push the Triffin proposal of a new paper reserve asset for central banks, the Special Drawing Right (SDR), but as a supplement for gold and dollars rather than a replacement. The nature of the asset or credit was widely debated. One ambiguity in the United States position was that the SDR should be the equivalent of gold in value, no better than the dollar, and both at a time when the value of the dollar was less than gold. It was not universally clear that the SDR was to provide pure liquidity, that is, to constitute an asset to be held rather than spent, or whether it would be used, as less-developed countries sought, to increase their capacity to import. The less-developed countries differed from the financially advanced countries, concerned with liquidity to be held to meet a possible financial crisis. The advanced countries, organized into the Group of Ten at the World Bank, were interested in liquidity for availability in a financial crisis; the less-developed countries wanted funds for spending. For political reasons, it was impossible to create assets and distribute them only to the G-10 (or primarily to the United States, which had the major liquidity problem) and omit the rest. After a couple of distributions, and with the adoption of floating exchange rates that were thought to solve the world balance-of-payments problem in another way, the SDR was allowed to languish.

The French borrowing referred to above took place not in New York, but in the Eurobond market. This grew out of so-called Eurocurrency market for short-term funds that came about in an accidental and unforeseen way. It is of some interest to economists to compare institutions that evolve in Darwinian ways, such as the Eurocurrency market, and those that are thoroughly planned, like the World Bank and IMF. The Bank and Fund, to be sure, after their initial idleness in standby during the Marshall Plan, evolved both in size and in function through a series of changes in practice.

The Eurocurrency market grew out of a discrepancy between the rate of interest allowed on time deposits in the United States for domestic depositors and that for foreigners. There was a profit to be made by shifting dollar deposits from New York to London to banks that kept them in dollars redeposited in New York. One of the earlier outside holders of dollars in London was the Soviet Union, which needed dollars for trade but wanted them out of U.S. jurisdiction. The British authorities tolerated the existence of nonsterling funds held at British and foreign banks in London without feeling a necessity to provide surveillance. As it developed, the Eurodollar market was a wholesale one, with minimum deposits of $25,000 and borrowings of $1 million or more. In due course similar markets in currencies other than the dollar (and sterling) came into being, both for deposits and for bond issues. In the credit crunches in the United States in 1966 and especially 1969, U.S. banks would borrow in the Eurodollar market to add to a bank's reserves in the United States. At this stage dollar deposits in Europe were matched, dollar for dollar, by funds in New York, earning slightly higher returns than local deposits, so that the borrowing in London by one American bank resulted merely in a transfer of money from another American bank, and total U.S. bank reserves were not affected.

In 1970, however, a significant change came about that increased world liquidity. Under the chairmanship of the Federal Reserve Board of Arthur F. Burns, an attempt was made to assist in the reelection of

President Nixon by lowering interest rates to stimulate the American economy. The action was taken at a time when the Bundesbank was tightening interest rates in an effort to restrain German inflation. Funds flowed from New York to the intermediary position of London. There, first American multinational corporations, and then German firms, refinanced their German loans by borrowing dollars in London. The monies were sold to the Bundesbank for deutsche marks to repay German banks, and the Bundesbank redeposited the funds in the Eurodollar market, giving that market the basis to expand its operations further. Interest rates fell in London, liquidity rose, and the world-leading Eurodollar banks set about finding new outlets for lending. As on earlier occasions, including the 1924 surprise success of the Dawes Loan, their eyes lit on Latin America. A wave of lending to those countries gave a start to the Third-World debt problems of the 1980s more than a year before the Arab oil-price rise of November 1973. When this occurred the path had been explored and the large OPEC oil profits were deposited in the Eurodollar market, pending their ultimate dispersal, and re-loaned. Oil-importing countries borrowed from world banks to buy oil in what became known as the recycling of OPEC dollars; oil-producing and exporting countries such as Venezuela, Mexico, and Peru borrowed in order to expand output and take advantage of the new high price. The world became awash with dollars.

The vast number of dollars created in the processes just described led the United States to stop converting dollars into gold for central banks. Support of the London private gold market had been abandoned earlier in 1968. In the summer of 1971, with the recognition of a sharp decline in the current account of the U.S. balance of payments, the United States moved to devalue the dollar, which was accomplished at the Smithsonian Institution in Washington, D.C. in December. The flow of funds out of the United States and into the Federal Republic was hardly affected, however, and in the spring of 1973, the Bundesbank stopped holding the Deutschemark down in relation to the dollar, thus ushering in a regime of flexible exchange rates.

It had long been thought by economists that flexible exchange rates would inhibit the flow of capital internationally, except for speculative funds, because of exchange risk. Either the borrower or the lender would have to take an exchange risk, and in a few cases both. In a risk-averse world this would deter the borrower or lender because of the chance of having to pay more or receive less than the original amount when the loan ended. This judgment proved wrong. Foreigners continued to borrow dollars and Americans continued to buy foreign currencies for investment, not only to go short of dollars, or long of foreign monies, but also because the risk of foreign-exchange rate change was deemed less significant than differences in rates of return. Major money markets remained highly liquid, capital flows substantial; balances of payments and exchange rates were driven by the capital account, more or less disregarding the fundamentals of price levels and changes in national incomes that shape the current account.

The next major turn in international finance came at the end of the 1970s and the beginning of the 1980s, when the Iraq-Iran war led to a second sharp rise in oil prices—from $10–12 a barrel to $30, with occasional higher peaks. This stimulated a boom in oil-producing areas, especially Mexico; the U.S. Southwest, including Texas, Oklahoma, and Louisiana; and western Canada. The resultant threat of inflation led the Federal Reserve System, under Paul Volcker as chairman of the board, to attempt restraint by tightening money supplies, producing a sharp recession in 1981. Mexico proved unable to service its debt, revealing in August 1982 that lending to Third World countries had been excessive. Negotiations in the resulting crisis were conducted sporadically to the end of the decade with one major debtor and another. Banks loaned interest owed as it accrued to the debt, granted temporary delays in payment, and swapped debt for equity in limited amount. Governments forgave a great deal of the debt of the poor nations, proposed moratoriums and new lending by banks. A host of debt-adjustment proposals were put forward by government officials, research institutions, and private individuals. Realism can be said to have broken into the problem in May 1987, when Citicorp, one of the leading lending banks, wrote off $3 billion in foreign loans against income and surplus. In due course, the Third World debt problem moved off center stage, giving way in the United States to the savings and loan crisis, discussed below.

The enormous volume of liquid funds continuing to flow among the major currencies produced movements in foreign-exchange rates that overshot generally conceived equilibrium levels. The dollar rose continuously from 1982 to February 1985, as high interest rates and a stock market boom attracted foreign capital, this despite large current-account deficits. The finance ministers of the leading financial countries met in New York in September 1985 at the Plaza Hotel to agree on the need for steps in the direction of stabilizing the currencies. The Reagan administration had relied through benign neglect on markets to achieve desirable results. In 1987, however, it came to the realization that a careening exchange rate was disturbing to business, however profitable it was for banks trading in foreign exchange.

The movement to stabilize exchange rates advanced more rapidly in Europe than in the world as a whole, as the European Economic Community (EEC), after several false starts constructed the European Monetary System (EMS) on the way to monetary integration, that is, a single European currency, or at least fixed rates, and a single central bank, or at least a federal structure encompassing national central banks. In the eyes of many, the projected European Currency Unit (ECU), the acronym also standing for the name of an ancient French coin, looked like the deutsche mark with a new name, just as in German monetary unification in the 1870s the Prussian thaler became the national currency, taking over the name of the Hamburg unit, the mark. In the early stages of developing the EMS, there were frequent but small depreciations among the constituent currencies, as one country and another inflated at rates faster than the average and developed balance-of-payments deficits. Gradually the depreciations became smaller and less frequent as coordination of monetary and fiscal policy improved. Progress proved sufficiently rapid, in fact, that Britain under Prime Minister Thatcher tried to slow down the process, and even West Germany and France appeared to hesitate. At the end of 1989 and the beginning of 1990, the revolution in Eastern Europe and the prospect of unification of the West and East German currencies drew attention away from European monetary advances and put them on hold.

The rise of Eurocurrency and bond markets, increases in oil prices, and booms in the New York stock market, real estate, office buildings, shopping malls, condominiums, and luxury housing produced a near frenzy of financial activity in the United States that spread worldwide. American banks established branches abroad to accompany American multinationals and to lend and borrow in less regulated climates. A combination of cultural differences and regulation, however, made it difficult to break into Japanese financial markets. Foreign banks and investment houses moved to the United States especially to operate, with their large savings and the Japanese export surplus, in the market for U.S. Treasury securities, with the demand for funds swelled by governmental deficits. Banks at home and abroad developed new products, all kinds of futures, options, swaps, repos, and "securitization" of instruments such as mortgages, automobile paper, installment credits, and, in the United Kingdom, export credits, packaged and then sold off in pieces to investors. Mutual funds grew both in shares and in money market instruments. As international diversification spread in the United States, special mutual funds were established to invest in foreign shares, sometimes in a variety of countries, sometimes in a single one. A practice developed of floating bonds of less than investment grade—so-called junk bonds—to finance takeovers of one company by another in leveraged buyouts and mergers or acquisitions. Junk bonds provided a striking illustration of a generalization in a report by experts of ten central banks, published by the Bank for International Settlements, that innovations in financial markets tended to be underpriced at the start and therefore overused.

One financial innovation in the United States—stock-index futures— came in for criticism in connection with program trading—the triggering of buying and selling programs by small differences in prices for spot shares and futures, detected by computers. In particular, program trading was blamed for increasing the volatility of stock prices and for the sharp declines in New York of October 19, 1987, and October 13, 1989, declines that spread worldwide through psychological infection. Stock-index futures made it easier to speculate in the stock market because the margin required to buy futures was only 5 percent, whereas that in the regular spot market was 50 percent. With well-financed arbitrage, the two markets are in effect one, despite the technical difference of the number of shares traded in the index, and the introduction of the futures index enlarged the possible volume of speculation.

One of the foremost shifts in financial practice was the move by large nonfinancial companies to deal directly with large institutional investors, such as life insurance companies and pension funds. Small businesses continued to rely on banks for loans and financial advice, but large companies, with their own financial experts in the corporate treasury department, began to increasingly deal directly, bypassing the banks. These large companies might issue commercial paper or place longer-term debt directly with the purchaser. Similarly in shares large blocks were traded off the floor of the New York Stock Exchange to save commissions, helping to break down the rigid commission structure. Disintermediation leading to direct trading is analagous to the substitution of direct trade for organized markets in commodities, and the waning role of entrepôt centers as information about sources and outlets for commodities has been diffused.

Disintermediation has occurred elsewhere in financial systems, especially among the thrift institutions in the United States, where interest-rate ceilings had been imposed by government regulation. The sharp increase in interest rates in 1979–81 led savers to withdraw funds from savings banks and savings and loan associations and place them with unregulated money funds for higher returns. The banks losing deposits had to turn to the capital market and sell certificates of deposit, paying market rates. The movement over the postwar years has been described as one from asset management by banks to liability management. The acute phase of disintermediation in 1981 led Congress to deregulate the thrift institutions, with harmful results. In combination with deposit insurance, deregulation led to a wave of speculative lending and buying of high-risk and high-return junk bonds, with considerable malfeasance, which may cost the insuring agencies hundreds of billions of dollars.

Deregulation in the United States under the competition of foreign banks, because of disintermediation and for ideological reasons under the Reagan and Bush Republican administrations, spread abroad. Constricted Japanese financial markets opened to a degree under the pressure of strong growth, high savings, a restructuring of industry, and foreign pressure. Financial houses migrated to Europe, especially London, and brought competition to London banks, acceptance houses, discount houses, brokers, and merchant banks, leading to financial deregulation, climaxing in October 1986 in what was called a big bang, but proved less apocalyptic. Responses of financial houses to the widening of horizons proved excessive and a number of banks, brokers, and investment houses that charged into new markets have, after some years of disappointing profits, pulled back.

At the beginning of the 1990s it is possible to detect a sense that deregulation, innovation, and rapid change in financial markets may slow down to allow the changes of the 1970s and 1980s to be digested. The financial problems of Eastern Europe divert capital and attention from the main markets of Europe and the United States. In addition, despite high stock markets, uneasy feelings are widespread that security markets in the United States and Japan are too high in the light of unresolved crises in Third World lending and real estate and financial institutions, including savings and loan associations and possibly insurance companies. Employment in financial institutions is down, and the mood is one of consolidation rather than advance.

Over the longer run, there is little doubt that world financial integration will proceed. Supersonic aircraft, satellite communication, and computerization will bring financial markets into still closer touch. Richard Cooper's 1986 forecast that the world will have fixed exchange rates by 2015 may put the date too late. The dollar and U.S. treasury bonds that are now traded around the world around the clock will be joined by the Ecu and yen, and by the bonds and shares of leading countries.

I have one reservation. The world economy needs a number of public goods: peace, open markets for goods, stable exchange rates, coordinated macroeconomic policies, a steady flow of capital to developing countries, and, in the event of crisis, a lender of last resort. Because it does not pay private individuals or groups to bear the cost of public goods when they cannot be excluded from their enjoyment, they must be provided by government. In the absence of international government, other means must be found. Simple cooperation has a habit of breaking down in difficulty. It may be that trouble is avoided, but the historical record is not reassuring. For a quarter century after 1945, the United States managed to provide the needed stability, but its will and capacity to continue to do so may be in decline. Nationalism is on the rise, and not only in Eastern Europe. A forecast of continued progress in international finance, after regrouping in the years just ahead, must rest on an assumption of crises limited in number and intensity, solutions for them by worldwide cooperation, and a new assertion of responsibility by Europe.

CHAPTER 5

International (and Interregional) Aspects of Financial Crises

My usual role in a conference of this sort is the opening paper entitled "Blank-Blank-Blank Financial Crises, the Rise of Financial Centers, Capital Flight—whatever—A Historical Perspective." It is pleasant to be relegated to the role of cleanup, although I recognize that the last paper of a conference in the afternoon tends to find the audience diminished as some conferees head for the airport to get home for dinner.

Instead of history, I choose to start with some theory. Connections between national (and regional) economies run through many channels. Most theorists think of their specialty as the most important of these connections and sometimes as the only significant one. The list includes money (initially gold and silver, later short-term capital); other capital movements, including those through securities (bonds, shares, and, most recently, securitized mortgages), direct investment and real estate; trade mostly in goods rather than services and associated largely with income changes of the Keynesian variety; foreign-exchange rates; prices; and psychology. A Milton Friedman looks mainly at money flows, especially of high-powered money, in 1921 and 1929 gold, asserting that the case for the United States initiating the depressions starting in those years was that the gold flows were to this country. In his 1989 Robbins lectures, Peter Temin pointed to income changes brought about by the deflationary policies of Hoover, Baldwin, Laval, and Bruning, who were clinging to the gold standard; in his earlier volume, *Did Monetary Forces Cause the Great Depression?* (New York: Norton, 1976), he points to shifts in consumer spending on automobiles and housing, somehow brought about. Those who blame the Hawley-Smoot tariff for the depression of the 1930s focus on trade and the blow to it of tariff increases and retaliation. Few join me in thinking that the start of a recession can come from cutting off a flow of capital that then forces the recipients to

Reprinted from Martin Feldstein, ed., *The Risk of Economic Crisis* (Chicago: University of Chicago Press, 1991), 128–32. Copyright © 1991 by the National Bureau of Economic Research. All rights reserved.

cut investment and imports. One current fear, however, is that West Germany, Japan, and, to a lesser extent Taiwan and Switzerland, may stop supporting the U.S. bond, stock, and real estate markets, putting pressure on investment here.

Another of my pet views about 1929 is that the decline in share prices communicated itself rapidly to commodities, especially raw-material imports, normally then shipped to New York on consignment and bought on arrival by brokers on bank credit. When New York banks seized up because of the troubles in brokers' loans, this credit was cut off, making commodity prices plunge. The decline in New York prices spread worldwide through arbitrage and instantaneous markdowns, without the necessity for slow-moving trade changes, though the volume of U.S. imports fell. The debt-deflation model of Irving Fisher is still relevant, despite the propensity of some theorists to say that it smacks of money illusion, which their analysis does not allow. My answer is that producers facing falling prices know they have lost income, as do their banks, whereas consumers are slow to recognize their increase in real income and unlikely to found new banks.

One important channel of communicating price changes is through changes in exchange rates. There are some, such as McCloskey and Zecher, who think that the exchange rate is always at the purchasing-power-parity level, and hence neutral. This seems to me to misread the history of 1931 when a downward ratchet operated in a buyer's market, with depreciation leaving domestic prices unchanged and appreciation depressing them. In a seller's market, the ratchet may work the other way, as in the 1970s. In the uneasy balance between buyer's and seller's markets, an exchange-rate change lowers prices partway in the appreciating country and raises them partway in the depreciating one—a matter of considerable assistance to the world economy in the 1980s.

The psychological connection among markets is brilliantly revealed at the end of each quarter in the chart of contemporary *New York Times,* which traces out the profiles of share prices in a dozen countries for the previous three months. They run along broadly similar lines, despite the fact that only a handful of securities are traded in several markets. Similarly, the implosion of 19 October 1987 was echoed in equity markets worldwide.

Now I would like to make a methodological point that I have been belaboring for a number of years. Most theorists seize one of these connections among international markets—money, goods and the income changes behind them, securities, prices inclusive of exchange-rate changes, and psychology—and run with it, whereas in my judgment, the situation changes from time to time and calls for a change in model. In 1929, the stock market crash spread to commodities and, through them, to the banking system. A flight to quality in 1930 hit hard at institutions with low-grade securities and today hovers over the low-grade bond market. Deflation in stocks may also spread to real estate, in 1987 also hurt by the decline in oil prices, especially in the southwestern United States. The patterns among markets may differ. If deflation spreads from stocks to commodities, the effect is almost instantaneous. The impact on real estate is slower. Homer Hoyt's neglected classic, *One Hundred Years of Land Values in Chicago* (University of Chicago Press), written in 1933 and recapitulating five cycles in Chicago real estate prices, underscores the differences on the upside, speculation in stocks spreads easily and quickly to real estate. On the downside, when stock prices collapse, real estate speculators congratulate themselves that they have claims on tangible assets and term debts, as opposed to day-to-day brokers loans. Over time, this consolation proves limited. Demand for real estate turns down sharply as buyers wait for prices to decline, but interest and tax payments stay up. Supplies of houses and other buildings continue to emerge from the long pipeline. Whereas a crash in securities is over in months, attrition in real estate, according to Hoyt, may take three, four, sometimes as many as eight years. A similar prolonged attrition takes place in sovereign debt where default has been avoided thus far, since the crisis began in 1982, because earlier defaults interrupted capital flows to developing countries for periods as long as thirty years.

The international propagation of booms and crashes occurs readily in markets for money, bonds, stocks, commodities, and direct investment. It has not operated in the past through real estate, although increasing integration of the U.S. real estate market into the world may produce a similar synchronization in the future as securitization of mortgages and foreign investment in hotels, office buildings, apartments, and the like occur. The 1925 Florida land crash and the 1974 Arab-induced bubble in London real estate were both localized, though psychological contagion today may link the extended real estate market in Japan to other national markets, including the one in the United States. Or it may work the other way. I know of one operator who is reacting to the troubles in Boston real estate by assembling a fund in London to pick up bargains.

We know from the days of Henry Thornton and Walter Bagehot that national financial crises may be halted by a lender of last resort who props up markets by making money available to hard-pressed debtors with illiquid assets. (There are other devices, such as the guarantee of liabilities of institutions threatened with failure, but I restrict the analysis to last-resort lending.) International "lending" at last resort is less well understood but has occurred historically in a variety of forms: exchanges of gold for silver, discounting of foreign bills of exchange, promises not to draw on foreign deposits, forward purchases of oil for cash, bridging loans, and swaps under the Basle Agreement of March 1961. These are invoked when financial crisis in one country threatens to spread abroad. Last-resort lending is short-term therapy. What happens next?

In Bagehot's formulation, last-resort lending should be undertaken only on good collateral. In English financial history, this proviso has been honored in the breach as well as in the observance, and for all kinds of reasons. The Bank of England acquired titles to a copper works, a coal mine, a West Indian plantation, and, in 1836, the assets of three American "W" banks that it was able to liquidate only in 1848. In its various "salvage" operations, the Bank of Italy acquired the problem loans of various Italian banks to prevent them failing in 1907, 1922, 1926, and 1930–33, finally consolidating them into the Istituto Ricostruzione Industriale (IRI) in 1933 to hold more or less in perpetuity. The Reconstruction Finance Corporation in the United States at the end of 1932 saved a number of banks, though it failed to forestall the collapse of the banking system in March 1933. Its assets were safely liquidated in the wartime expansion after 1940. Swaps used to halt foreign-exchange crises that are not undone by a return flow of capital after a stipulated period, such as six months, are funded into long-term obligations of the IMF or between central banks or governments.

The initial lender with bad loans faces an agonizing choice between write-off or workout. In Third World debt, American banks first sought to work out their nonperforming loans, but ended up writing off substantial portions of them. It is seldom recognized that the lender of last resort has the same problem. Unreversed swaps may get funded, but central banks that hold foreign exchange that declines in price keep it on the books at cost until sold, rather than "mark to market," which is the conservative banking rule. This is tolerable since central banks with power to create money cannot fail. If they lose money from buying high and selling low, it reduces the profit they normally pay to government, shifting the loss to the nation at large. The contrast between the successful workout of the RFC and the unsuccessful one of the IRI has been mentioned. The Resolution Trust Corporation set up under the 1989 legislation in the United States to rescue the thrift institutions in trouble is expected to liquidate a substantial portion of the bad debts taken over and to write off other amounts estimated as high as $190 billion. The liquidation process—the working out—is likely to prevent the recovery of the real estate market in this country, or depress it further, except in the event of a vigorous, unexpected continuation of the 1982–89 boom.

As therapy for financial crises, last-resort lending has the difficulties of moral hazard on the one hand and liquidation of the acquired assets on the other. There is a third possibility: that the function will get caught up in politics and thereby be prevented from effecting the necessary and salubrious work of rescue. In 1931, France refused to come to the aid of Austria, after the first feeble step, on foreign policy grounds. The legislation to assist the thrifts in the United States almost became entangled in political questions that divided the parties after the highly partisan political campaign of 1988: how much to put on the 1990 budget; whether to raise any of the loss repayment by taxation, a step the president refused to consider; and whether the taxpayer should bail out the bank officials guilty of bad judgment and in some cases malfeasance and fraud. The great benefit of central banks as lenders of last resort is that they are mostly not immediately subject to political debate and decision. Crises must be handled with dispatch, which is why a voting body such as the IMF is more successful in cleaning up arrears than in mounting the barricades in moments of crises.

In the series of financial crises since 1979, this country and the world have been fortunate in that the lender-of-last-resort process has escaped being caught up in political disputes. At the domestic level, some of these escapes have been narrow. Internationally, while the U.S. role as leader of the world economy has slipped, there is no challenger that refuses to cooperate in crisis, management or offers competing solutions that might stalemate decision. If a new economic world leader is called for in the interest of stability and the United States tries to hold on to its position as number one, the transition may give rise to difficulty as occurred in the 1930s when Britain proved unable to provide stability and the United States was unwilling to.

CHAPTER 6

Business Cycles, Manias, and Panics in Industrial Societies

Let me clear the decks by first limiting my discussion to the cycles of about ten years, disregarding the Braudel cycle of 150 years (with peaks in 1350, 1650, 1817 and 1973–4 (Braudel, 1984, p. 78), the Kondratieff (1935) of fifty years, and the Kuznets cycle of twenty years (Kuznets, 1958), not to mention the Brinley Thomas international cycles linked across the Atlantic by migration, again of twenty years (Thomas, 1954). I have in mind much more the nineteenth- and twentieth-century cycles with breaks in 1816, 1825, 1836, 1847, 1866, 1873, 1890, 1907, 1914, 1921, 1929, 1937, perhaps 1949, and then again perhaps 1974–75 and 1981–82. I will have great difficulty in explaining the cyclical character of the movements, but am unwilling to accept that there is anything in nature, apart from human nature, that makes for the regularity, such as it is.

My interest, moreover, is in the international character of these events. Many observers write about cycles in a given country as if they were purely local, and some insist that the origin of a given international cycle is purely local (Friedman, 1970, p. 78, on 1929; Clapham, 1910, II, p. 267 on 1866; four economic historians on the 1893 Australian financial crisis which they denied was connected with the Baring crisis in London in 1890 (Butlin, 1961, p. 280; Hall, 1963, p. 148; Boehm, 1971, chaps. 9, 10; Pressnell, 1982, p. 160). There have been many accounts of the 1873 crises in Germany and Australia on the one hand, and in the USA on the other, but few connect the two.

The other salient issue is the extent to which given cycles, or all cycles are primarily financial, primarily real insofar as they involve a structural disequilibrium or misallocation of resources, or some combination of the two.

Reprinted from Niels Thygesen, Kumaraswamy Velupillai, and Stefan Zambelli, eds., *Business Cycles: Theories, Evidence and Analysis,* Proceedings of a conference held by the International Economic Association, Copenhagen, Denmark (London: Macmillan, in association with the International Economic Association, 1991), 41–55.

On the international front, I assert that the connections between the course of economic events in one country and one or more others are many and varied. Friedman and Schwartz (1963) base the judgment that the USA was responsible for the depressions of 1921 and 1929 on the fact that at both turning points the flow of gold was toward the USA. Money flows, including gold flows, form one connection, working through monetary changes and changes in short-term interest rates. Long-term capital movements—especially when they are suddenly cut off—form another. In 1866 tight money in France and Britain cut off lending to Italy and pushed that country into recession and incontrovertibility of the lira. In 1873 the German and Austrian boom interrupted the capital flow to the USA cutting down railroad investment there. The Baring crisis of 1890 led to a halt in British lending not only to Argentina but also to Brazil, Chile, South Africa, Australia and the USA. The brilliant rise in the New York stock market from March 1928 interrupted lending through foreign bonds to Germany and Latin America and pushed those countries into relapse. Tight money in the USA starting in 1979 halted long-term lending to the Third World, although policy measures were taken after 1982 to ease it down, rather than cut it abruptly. In these cases, especially 1928–9, the downturn in the borrower deprived of capital may well feed back to the lender in the third sort of connection—i.e., through reduced imports—by way of a fall in national income and the foreign-trade multiplier.

A fourth connection runs through arbitrage that reduces the prices of internationally traded commodities and internationally traded securities in two or more markets, and has an effect on the incomes of producers and the wealth of asset holders. Some observers deny that price changes within an economy can lead to depression, as they deny the existence of money illusion. In their analysis, consumers gain from price declines, offsetting the losses of producers. But this is a static view that overlooks the dynamics of the matter. Producers know rapidly that they must cut back spending when the prices of their outputs fall, while consumers are slower to recognize and respond to a gain in real income. Moreover, the bankruptcy of producers may cause banks to fail, whereas the gains of consumers are not only slow to be recognized but are unlikely to lead to new banks.

The fifth and final connection is purely psychological, though it is connected with arbitrage in securities traded in common. In 1929 when the New York stock market crashed, all stock markets over the world marked down their prices, even though the number of stocks traded on more than one exchange was limited. The same phenomenon was observed in 1987 on Black Monday, 19 October.

I see no way to measure the relative weight of each of these five connections—gold, money and interest rates as one; long-term capital flows and their cutoff; income changes that lead to changes in foreign trade; commodity and security arbitrage, and psychological connections that lead to marking prices up or down in two markets not directly joined. No doubt, the weights will differ from case to case, and I am skeptical that an average of the weights over a significant number of cycles would be helpful in enabling economists to forecast what may happen in the next international cycle, just as I doubt that there is a typical business cycle such as Wesley C. Mitchell tried to measure at the National Bureau of Economic Research in the 1920s and 1930s. That effort produced superb by-products such as the studies in income and wealth, but the direct output can be said to have been exiguous. In my judgment any analogy between predictable cyclical paths of stars and galaxies and the economy is flawed. Economics less resembles celestial mechanics than evolutionary biology in which mutations can be confidently predicted to occur and later explained, but forecasting their nature and timing is hazardous.

In my lexicon, there are two general models of business cycle with strong but variable links between them. One is real, sometimes called structural, sometimes resulting from overinvestment because of too low a rate of interest (Hayek), or a market rate below the natural rate (Wicksell). The other derives from the title of this paper and is financial in origin. It is sometimes called the Fisher-Minsky model. I start describing the latter.

The Fisher-Minsky model starts with some autonomous event, shock or "displacement," which alters investment priorities. It can be real: the start of a war; the end of a war; a good harvest; a bad harvest; the coming to fruition of a major and wide-ranging innovation such as the railroad; a discovery; and also of wide-ranging impact—some salient political event such as the independence of the Spanish colonies in Latin America around 1822. It may also be almost entirely financial: a refunding of maturing high-interest government debt, as in 1822 and 1888; a change in financial legislation, as the adoption of limited liability; banking deregulation; a financial innovation, the unexpected success of a large security issue (the Baring loan of 1817, the Thiers *rentes* of 1871 and 1872, the Dawes loan of 1924, or the many times oversubscribed Guinness public issue of 1886, the success of which was like "the crack of a starting pistol" for the issuance of other brewery shares not only in England but in Canada and the USA (Cottrell, 1980, pp. 168–70).

The altered investment opportunities lead to a shift in investor interest and new investment which may—I do not say must—lead to overshooting. Rational expectations holds that new information leads a market economy to establish a new set of prices according to some widely recognized economic model, presumably a new set of equilibrium prices. This no doubt does happen. It is my contention, however, that it occasionally does not. Rational expectations assumes that the participants in the market all have equal sophistication, information, and purposes, or at least that the market is dominated, so that prices are established by a dominant group that is intelligent, sophisticated and well financed. History shows, however, that participants in a market often have very different interests, degrees of experience, purposes, information and the like. To take one example, early railroad investment in England that led to the railway mania of the 1840s was undertaken by the gentry along the right of way, hoping to enhance the value of their land, especially when it contained deposits of coal and other minerals; by manufacturers served by a given line gaining access to inputs and transport for outputs; by pure investors seeking income from dividends and interest; by sophisticated speculators who bought the securities with the intention of selling them for capital gain; and by unsophisticated speculators, sometimes referred to as "servant girls and greengrocers," who observed the early capital gains of the professional speculators and entered the game late (Reed, 1975). In addition to these, when the mania collapsed in 1847, half-built lines made a determined effort to sell securities to their suppliers of construction materials and rolling stock, speculating in a different way by buying so-called vendor's issues. Without more research than has been given to the problem it is not self-evident that any one group was sufficiently dominant for its notion of an equilibrium price to prevail in the market.

Assume that the market for railway shares, brewery shares, Latin American bonds, whatever asset is subject to revised valuations, does develop euphoria and positive feedback, as rising prices entice more numerous and less-sophisticated speculators to enter the market and bid prices up still further. At some point expectations of continuously rising prices will moderate, and more sophisticated investors may judge that the market has gone too high. They begin to sell. Investors along the right of way (of a railroad), manufacturers hoping to gain from the finished line, and pure investors, typically unleveraged, buy securities to hold. The last two groups, however, seek action. They hope to buy low and sell dear. Their purchases are leveraged by borrowed funds or installment purchases. So long as new investors continue to enter, the early ones can sell and pull out. But uncertainty may come to prevail. This is a period that I call "distress," by analogy with a term in corporate finance that obtains when a company can contemplate the possibility that it may be unable to meet its obligations. No certainty is involved, merely recognition of a possibility. Distress may subside and leave a given market in equilibrium with market-clearing prices, balancing new demands and supply from former holders. Or the expectations of higher prices that led to rapid advances may give way to expectations of a large decline, on the ground that the rise has been overdone. In these circumstances a crash and perhaps a panic may ensue. The rush out of money into the asset or assets gives way to a rush out of assets into money. Prices fall.

The bare bones of this model must be fleshed out in a number of directions, especially covering the propaganda of euphoria and overshooting from one market to another, and one country to another; the possibility of curbing an excited market with monetary policy or even by moral suasion, and the possibility that a market crash of some sort may lead to business depression.

A plausible case can be made that overshooting and collapse in a single market are of no general macroeconomic interest. The Florida land boom that crashed in 1925, for example, burned unwary investors, but had only localized effects. For a mania to have serious potential, it must spread. In the 1820s, for example, the independence of Spanish colonies that started a boom in Latin American bonds and mining shares coincided with the 1822 refunding of British debt from the Napoleonic wars, which stimulated a boom in domestic shares, especially in insurance, as investors sought to maintain their incomes in the face of lower interest rates by buying higher-paying and riskier securities. In the 1830s the boom was in cotton, public lands in the USA, and British industries exporting to the USA; in 1847 in railroad shares (the mania), and in grain which soared in price because of the short crop and the potato blight in 1846. In the boom leading to crisis in 1866, there was a rise in cotton and in shipping to countries that might overcome the cotton famine produced by the Civil War in the USA, plus an Italian boom brought on by public works, especially railroads, in the newly unified country. The German boom that spilled over to Austria was partly financial in origin, based on receipt of the Franco-Prussian indemnity with more than 500 million francs paid in gold and silver, partly construction from the so-called *Gründungsfieber*—exultation over the establishment of the German Reich, and partly a railroad boom in the USA, financed in part by German and Austrian investors. These examples could be multiplied.

Of particular interest for contemporary observers is the link between the 1981 oil-price collapse and the financial crises of Mexico, Venezuela, etc. on the one hand, and the southwest banking community on the other. Also in the southwest, but elsewhere in the USA as well, is the connection between financial crises in security markets and those in real estate. The two cycles have different patterns. A stock market crash as in 1921 or 1987 has effects which are completed—unless the deflation spreads relentlessly as in 1929—in a few months or at most one or two years. In real estate, the profile of difficulty is different (Hoyt, 1933, chap. vii). At the time that the stock market collapses, real estate speculators congratulate themselves. They own real assets instead of pieces of paper. Their debts consist in term loans, not demand obligations. But demand for real estate falls sharply. As real estate prices level off and start downward people stop buying, waiting for the bottom, but taxes and interest keep up. Attrition among the real estate speculators is slow, but if there has been a boom in office buildings, shopping malls, luxury houses, condominia and the like to parallel that in shares, the shakeout of open positions may go on for four, five even eight years, with strong negative effects on the industry and on banks lending to it.

Something of the propagation from one country to another has been indicated for Britain-Latin America (1826), Britain-USA (1836), Germany-Austria and the USA (1873). The collapse in London in 1847 can be traced throughout the world by a record of the number of bankruptcies (though the volume of assets involved would be better). In 1857 the collapse started in the Ohio Life and Trust Company in New York, spread to London, Scandinavia and Hamburg. One of the more interesting possibilities is for a convulsive deflation to be transmitted from A to D through B and C without B and C being much affected. In 1866 Paris did not suffer greatly but communicated the tightness of money from London and Berlin to Milan and Genoa by cutting off French lending. In 1907, a stock market panic in New York sent a shock wave through London and Paris to Italy again, without significant consequences for the mediating markets. Some of these connections, both up and down, are monetary or involve capital flows; some psychological. The foreign trade multiplier seems less involved for financial boom and bust as they work slowly when most of the propagation is close to instantaneous. The table of spreading failures starting in London in August 1847 and arriving in the USA in October to December 1848 (Kindleberger, 1978, p. 127) may well have been caused by declining British imports.

In explaining the euphoric phase of a boom, Minsky places great stress on the growth of debt of dubious quality (Minsky, 1982). His taxonomy of debt is not universally applauded (e.g. Goldsmith, 1982), and it is, moreover, difficult to establish a characterization of debt by quality. Monetarists such as Friedman and Schwartz (1963), however, believe that the expansionary phase of the cycle could be curbed by holding the money supply constant or growing at some predetermined rate. This view presupposes, first, that the velocity of money is constant, and second, that there are no innovations that relate to means of payments. Neither assumption seems warranted historically. Short-term variations in money turnover are frequent. Of greater importance, however, has been the fact that the definition of money is constantly undergoing change, as new means of payment and new forms of credit are devised. Coin, banknotes, deposits, bills of exchange, brokers' loans, other forms of selling in installments, savings deposits as well as demand deposits, certificates of deposit, NOW accounts, credit cards, options, repos, etc., can extend the amounts available for payments to buy assets, and so on, successively, under conditions of agitated speculation. Along with an outrush of money into some form of assets in euphoria, there will be extensions of credit in new forms and new directions, based on a given amount of "money," however defined. Monetary control of manic investment booms is a theoretical construct that is belied by historical experience.

On the downside, as debt is paid off, the money supply shrinks rapidly. To prevent a market crash from leading to depression, and the price collapse in the agitated area from spreading to other assets, especially goods and services, there should be a lender of last resort, as rationalized by Bagehot in *Lombard Street* (Bagehot, 1873). Such measures take many forms: suspending the Bank Act of 1844 that limited the amount of banknotes the Bank of England could issue, open-market operations in the USA, relaxation of rigid rules of central bank discount, guarantees of bank liabilities as in the Baring crisis, the actions of the Federal Deposit Insurance Corporation (FDIC) or the Federal Savings and Loan Insurance Corporation (FSLIC) in guaranteeing deposits up to a limit which has been increasingly raised, governmental loans of the Reconstruction Finance Corporation (RFC) or Istituto per la Ricostruzione Italiana (IRI) type. All have political implications and sometimes require political action—for example, to expand the resources of the FDIC or FSLIC after its appropriated funds and borrowing authority have been exhausted. This may be particularly anxiety provoking in a situation when the executive and legislative branches of the US government are in different hands, when the contending parties have just emerged from a bitter electoral campaign and when there is a substantial budget deficit that the executive wants eliminated but for which it is unwilling to raise taxes.

It is my contention that financial crises lead to depression only when there is no lender of last resort to halt the spreading collapse of credit and money. Using the meteorological metaphors that are frequently encountered in the popular literature, one may say that a financial crisis halted by a lender of last resort is like a summer storm, short, sharp, useful in clearing the air of the oppressive atmosphere of the period of distress, but without serious consequence. Where there is no lender of last resort to check the spread of deflation from one asset to another, and from assets to banks that have made loans to asset holders, financial crisis may lead to prolonged depression. This, in my view, is what happened in 1873 and 1929. In 1890 the London financial market was righted by the guarantee of liabilities of Baring Brothers; the deflation continued in the world overseas—Latin America, Australia, South Africa, and the USA, until the expanding gold production of the Rand served, after a fashion—and belatedly—as a lender of last resort, or more accurately as an ultimate provider of more liquidity. Especially have I maintained that international markets might have been able to recover if the spreading collapse in 1931 from Austria in May, to Germany in July, Britain in September, Japan in December, the USA in 1933, and the gold bloc in September 1936 had been arrested in timely fashion by a significant lender-of-last-resort action by the USA and France to prop up Austria as the first casualty of the causal chain (Kindleberger, 1986, 2d ed., chap. xiv). Failure to take such action internationally can be ascribed to the lack of international government on the one hand, to the politicization of the process by France, over foreign policy, and to the isolationism of the USA. It should be noted, however, that this view is contested by Moggridge, who holds that the 1929 crash was far more structural than purely financial, and needed some more thoroughgoing therapy, perhaps some such measure as the Marshall Plan after the Second World War (Moggridge, 1982). At the same time, a number of respectable economists felt then, and feel now, that the Marshall Plan was not needed and the recovery of Europe from the Second World War could have been accomplished by such elementary measures as halting the inflation and depreciating the exchange rate (in still more elementary terms, balancing the budget and setting the exchange rate at the purchasing-power parity [for this brand of opinion, see Kindleberger, 1982, chap. 14]). It is evident that the distinction between financial business cycles and structural ones, and the links running between the two, are a matter of some debate and confusion.

Within the financial causes of business cycles, there is a distinction between those who think in monetary terms, believing that the quantity of money determines the course of national income, and that mistakes in monetary policy are responsible for excessive expansions and contractions which would be nonexistent or perhaps only greatly moderated, if monetary policy were perfect, and those who follow a Keynesian mode of thought, ascribing the cycle to changes in investment, consumer, or government spending, autonomously determined. In his recent Robbins lectures, Peter Temin, for example, ascribes the 1929 depression to deflationary policies of the British, French, German, and US governments, and the recovery to a change in "regimes," with their altered expectations, that led to enlarged investment (Temin, 1989; see also Temin, 1976). Opposed to this class of views is a more structural view that emphasizes the misallocation of investment. The classic example is the Empire State Building, finished in 1930, and not fully occupied until 1940 during the first year of the European war, a "stranded investment" in the terminology of Hayek, that may have had monetary origins in too low an interest rate that caused investment to be too roundabout and capital-intensive, but produced a structure of investment unsuited to final demand.

In one of his semantic essays, Fritz Machlup excoriated the use of the term "structural," calling it a weaselword, from which all the meaning had been sucked out, as a weasel sucks the meat out of an egg (Machlup, 1958, reprinted 1964). I took exception to this characterization, especially as he quoted something I had written about "structural disequilibrium," in which I had defined precisely what I had meant. In the second reprint of the paper, he added a footnote saying he had not meant to impugn my use of the term. By structural disequilibrium I meant a failure of markets to adjust to changes in underlying conditions of demand and supply, including those produced by nature, war, or discoveries. In a different context relating to calculations of purchasing-power parity, I specifically included such changes as a loss of foreign assets (sold off during war), or the necessity—because of a peace treaty—to pay reparations, or because of aid during a war, to pay war debts. The need to service old debts could be subsumed under the term. In all this, it is assumed that other things are equal, or that they change, if they happened to consist of macroeconomic variables such as national income, the money supply, and the budget, in some appropriate amount. Typically structural disequilibria result from failure of resources to adjust as required by some change in demand, supply, institutional condition or arrangement, and are to be distinguished from a purely macroeconomic expansion or contraction. The distinction is of course overdrawn, since not all income elasticities are identical and any expansion or contraction requires some rearrangement of resource allocation. But at a heuristic level one can distinguish such cycles or disequilibria that can be handled with merely monetary and/or fiscal policy (excluding from the former, exchange-rate adjustment that directly alters relative prices of foreign-trade and nontraded goods) and with the appropriate microeconomic adjustment left to the market to achieve the appropriate allocation of resources, from those cycles or disequilibria occasioned by changes in demand, supply or institutional arrangements that require more deep-seated therapy.

As already indicated, judgment will differ from case to case. Viner, Machlup, Graham and Lutz believed that the disequilibrium after the destruction caused by the Second World War could be handled by macroeconomic policy. Moggridge and I did not. I thought that the disequilibrium after the First World War, including some destruction but more fundamentally the institutional trauma involved in war debts and reparations, plus the recovery of European production in lines that had expanded greatly outside Europe during the war, could have been corrected by the market, provided that the spreading collapse that started in Austria could be rapidly halted. Moggridge (1982) did not.

A business cycle that starts as a simple expansion and then goes too far, or as a simple contraction and spreads too widely and deeply because of the absence of a lender of last resort, can convert a Fisher-Minsky model of debt expansion and deflation into a structural cycle. On the upside, investment in a set of industries or assets may go so far as to strand Hayek-type investments that have to be worked off slowly over time if they are not taken over by government to rescue their owners from bankruptcy, and the banks that financed their owners rescued from failure in their turn. On the downside, especially in the international cycle that proceeds from a boom in lending that goes too far and is then cut off, the accumulation of interest and principal repayments to the overseas creditors may mount so high as to be beyond the capacity of macroeconomic policy, in this case even including exchange depreciation, to service the debt and at the same time discharge normal obligations to domestic resources. This is the issue today in Third World debt, where bankers and until recently the World Bank and the US Treasury have been insisting that sensible macroeconomic policies in the Third World would enable them to pay up, while the countries themselves seek wider measures, such as limits on debt service or partial forgiveness and write-offs, suggesting that the boom in Third World lending after 1970 went so far as to constitute a structural disequilibrium.

Simple cyclical and structural disequilibrium do not exhaust the possibilities. In the second and third editions of *International Economics* (1958 and 1963) I suggested there might be secular disequilibria as well, in which balance-of-payments disequilibrium could be ascribed to long-run income forces related to growth and decline rather than to cycles. There are pervasive structural changes not necessarily connected with either cycles or secular change. These include the discovery of the route to the Far East around the Cape of Good Hope, of the New World by Columbus, the sharp decline in ocean freights from the introduction of the ironclad vessel, steam, diesel, refrigerated ships, etc., in the second half of the nineteenth century. Secular disequilibria are connected with economic growth and decline. Some economists dismiss such analysis as Spenglerian nonsense, but the facts that Britain was overtaken by Germany and the USA at the end of the last century, and that the USA is being overtaken by Germany and Japan currently, raise the question. If one believes unreservedly in the equilibrating capacity of the market, all that is needed to correct the US balance of payments currently is to fiddle with tax and other incentives in the USA and Japan, to raise savings in the USA, lower them in Japan, and increase research and development in the USA to bring it up to or beyond the Japanese level along with adjusting the exchange rate further. If the trouble lies deeper in the growth process, however, American profligate spending, Japanese hoarding and the steady decline of productivity increases in the USA are unlikely to be readily reversed in the short run. The monetary and fiscal policy measures needed for the cycle, and the price measures such as depreciation of the exchange rate to assist the reallocation of resources from nontraded to traded goods will not go all the way to restore balance.

This paper is addressed to international business cycles on the one hand and manias, panics and crashes on the other. It is not therefore incumbent upon me to discuss anticyclical policy with its problems of recognition, decision and action lags, the choices in fiscal policy whether to act in the spending or tax field, and the possibility of gridlock in action from vested interests, called by Mancur Olson (1982) "distributional coalitions," with opposing programs. (In this last connection, the difficulty in raising taxes in the USA today offers a powerful illustration). Instead, I pose two questions: first, why have these financial crises occurred on an average of one every ten years up to 1949? and why did the early rhythm that had prevailed for close to 400 years then break? The first question is the harder, so that I take the second one first.

It seems evident that even without purposeful design, government finances serve as a built-in stabilizer of the economy. To the extent that government taxation varies with the cycle, rising in boom and falling in recession or depression, and to the extent that expenditure for such matters as unemployment assistance or relief of the poor behaves countercyclically, there is an inherent tendency, without policy decision, for governments to run surpluses, or at least relative surpluses, in boom and deficits in depression. Before the Second World War, government budgets formed a relatively small portion of gross national product, except in wartime, so that the dampening of national-income changes initiated in the private economy under capitalism was small. With the growth of expenditure and taxation after the Second World War, however, from the order of 10 percent of gross national product (GNP) or less around 1900 to more than 20 percent after the Second World War, the different behavior of government from private expenditure patterns, altered the macroeconomic scene.

The first question—why booms followed by busts repeated themselves at intervals of about a decade—is harder to answer. One would have thought that economic actors would learn. Sometimes they do— as in US government policy after the First and Second World Wars— insistence on collecting war debts and the sanctity of commercial loans after the First World War and relief, rehabilitation, grants and reconstruction loans on generous terms and the Marshall Plan after the Second World War. On the other hand, the French general staff failed to learn after the First World War and built a Maginot line that was circumvented through the undefended French border along the Low Countries.

Two possible theories can be adduced on an *ad hoc* basis, without, so far as I can see, any adequate means to test which of the two is superior. First, there is the hypothesis that as the nature of the displacement and the objects of speculation change from time to time the participants in the manic phase are persuaded on each occasion that this is different—i.e., that the freedom of the Spanish colonies in the 1820s, the demand for cotton in the 1830s that drove expansion west from Georgia and led to booms both in public land and in purchases of British goods in the USA, the railway boom of the 1840s, and so on were so unlike that the old pattern was by no means certain to be reproduced. The second possible hypothesis is that the astute speculators may learn, and repeat their successful maneuvers of the past decade, but the amateur, inexperienced and late-coming crowd that gets caught up in the excitement of a rising market is a new group each time. Some individuals may learn and move from the large class of outsiders that gets fleeced in the crash into the charmed circle of insiders that consciously or unconsciously does the fleecing, perhaps, but their places are taken by newcomers as uninitiated as they were the first time. A third possible theory is that the players recognize the nature of the game and its dangers, but enjoy the action thoroughly and sustain their hopes of winning even though in a contemplative mood they would realize that the chances of emerging successful are not high. Lotteries are played continuously on this basis, both by the unintelligent who focus upon the winnable amounts rather than the chances of losing—in cognitive dissonance— and by intelligent players who hope to get in and out fast—like the originators of chain letters, but are sufficiently sophisticated to realize that they may not. I see no way to determine which of these theories explains the repetition of the pattern for 400 years. Especially is this the case when there is no agreement in the economics profession, first, on why the 1929 depression was so extended and, second, why the Stock Market crash of 1929 was followed by prolonged and deep depression, when those of 1921 (in the USA at least) and 1987 were not.

Let me conclude with a series of short blunt declarative sentences:

1. The persistent pattern of financial crises at ten-year intervals is impossible to explain in terms of the theory of rational expectations.
2. Financial crisis may turn into depressions if there is no lender of last resort.
3. Business cycles may have primarily financial, primarily structural (resulting from changes in demand, supply or institutional relationships) or mixed origins.
4. It is hard to explain why economic actors in capitalist societies have not learned from experience so as to avoid financial crises.
5. The larger role of government in national income expenditure since the Second World War has both dampened financial crises and extended their periodicity.
6. Financial crises are generally international in character, with the connections between a crisis in one country and others running through money and capital flows, including changes in interest rates, asset and commodity arbitrage, the foreign-trade multiplier, and purely psychological infection.
7. One particular pattern frequently encountered is that of a flow of foreign lending burgeoning in manic or quasi-manic form and then being suddenly cut off, leaving the borrowing country with a recession or depression that may feed back to the original lender.

REFERENCES

Bagehot, Walter (1873) *Lombard Street: A Description of the Money Market,* (London: John Murray, 1917) reprint edition.
Boehm, E. A. (1971) *Prosperity and Depression in Australia, 1887–1897* (Oxford: Clarendon Press).
Butlin, S. J. (1961) *Australia and New Zealand Bank, the Bank of Australasia*

and the Union Bank of Australia, Limited (Croyden, Australia: Longmans, Green).

Braudel, Fernand (1984) *Civilization and Capitalism, 15th–18th Century,* vol. 3, *The Perspective of the World* (New York, Harper & Row).

Clapham, Sir John (1910) "The Last Years of the Navigation Acts," *English Historical Review* (two parts, July and October), reprinted in E. M. Carus-Wilson (ed.) *Essays in Economic History,* vol. 3 (London: Arnold, 1962).

Cottrell, P. L. (1980) *Industrial Finance, 1830–1914: The Finance and Organization of English Manufacturing Industry* (London: Methuen).

Fisher, Irving (1913) *The Purchasing Power of Money: Its Determination and Relation to Credit, Interest and Crises* (New York: Macmillan).

Friedman, Milton (1970) "Column" in *Newsweek,* 25 May 1970.

Friedman, Milton, and Schwartz, Anna J. (1963) *A Monetary History of the United States, 1867–1960* (Princeton: Princeton University Press).

Goldsmith, Raymond W. (1982) "Comment" on Hyman P. Minsky, "The Financial-Instability Hypothesis: Capitalist Processes and the Behavior of the Economy," in C. P. Kindleberger and J.-P. Laffargue (eds.) *Financial Crises: Theory, History and Policy* (Cambridge: Cambridge University Press, and Paris: Editions de la Maison des Sciences de l'Homme) pp. 41–43.

Hall, A. R. (1963) *The London Capital Market and Australia, 1870–1914* (Canberra: Australian National University, Science Monograph) no. 21.

Hayek, Friederich (1931) *Prices and Production* (London: Routledge & Kegan Paul).

Hoyt, Homer (1933) *One Hundred Years of Land Values in Chicago: The Relationship of the Growth of Chicago to the Rise in Its Land Values, 1830–1933* (Chicago: University of Chicago Press).

Kindleberger, Charles P. (1973, 1986) *The World in Depression, 1929–1939* (Berkeley: University of California Press).

Kindleberger, Charles P. (1978) *Manias, Panics and Crashes: A History of Financial Crises* (New York: Basic Books).

Kindleberger, Charles P. (1987) *Marshall Plan Days* (Boston: Allen & Unwin).

Kindleberger, C. P., and J.-P. Laffargue (eds.) (1982) *Financial Crises: Theory, History and Policy* (Cambridge: Cambridge University Press, and Paris: Editions de la Maison des Sciences de l'Homme).

Kondratieff, N. D. (1935) "The Long Waves in Economic Life," in *Review of Economic Statistics,* vol. 17, no. 6 (November).

Kuznets, Simon (1958) "Long Swings in the Growth of Population and in Related Economic Variables," *Proceedings of the American Philosophical Society,* vol. 102, no. 1.

Machlup, Fritz (1958, 1964) "Structure and Structural Change: Weaselwords and Jargon," *Zeitschrift für Nationalokonomie,* no. 3, pp. 280–98, reprinted in his *International Payments, Debts and Gold* (New York: Charles Scribner's Sons).

Minsky, Hyman P. (1982) "The Financial-Instability Hypothesis: Capitalist Processes and the Behavior of the Economy," in Kindleberger and Laffargue (eds.) *Financial Crises*, pp. 13–39.

Moggridge, D. E. (1982) "Policy in the Crises of 1920 and 1929," in Kindleberger and Laffargue (eds.) *Financial Crises*, pp. 171–87.

Olson, Mancur (1982) *The Rise and Decline of Nations: Economic Growth, Stagflation and Social Rigidities* (New Haven: Yale University Press).

Pressnell, L. S. (1982) "The Sterling System and Financial Crises before 1914," in Kindleberger and Laffargue (eds.) *Financial Crises*, pp. 148–64.

Reed, M. C. (1975) *Investment in Railways in Britain: A Study in the Development of the Capital Market* (Oxford: Oxford University Press).

Temin, Peter (1976) *Did Monetary Forces Cause the Great Depression?* (New York: Norton).

Temin, Peter (1989) *Lessons from the Great Depression* (Cambridge, Mass.: MIT Press).

Thomas, Brinley (1954) *Migration and Economic Growth* (Cambridge: Cambridge University Press).

Wicksell, Knut (1935) *Lectures on Political Economy*, vol. 2, *Money* (New York: Macmillan).

CHAPTER 7

The Evolving Organization of the World Economy

The summer of 1991 is an awkward time to think, much less write, about the future organization of the world economy. The outlines of President Bush's New World Order are unclear. The Soviet Union has broken up and if there is no union among the republics that remain, the nature of the confederation among them remains to be settled. Reunited Germany faces a fiscal problem of substantial proportions and murky consequences to complete in orderly fashion the integrating of the Peoples' Republic. Yugoslavia may well be breaking up. The outlook for the Middle East economy remains dim, although there is a ray of hope for some resolution of the Arab-Israeli confrontation in the future conference. Voices in the United States are becoming insistent that we are not facing up to the problems of low savings, declining productivity, substantial deficits in the federal budget and the national balance of payments, a weakening infrastructure, and high and mounting health costs, to say nothing of the social problems of drugs, homelessness, abortion, teenage pregnancy, and the like. We appear to some to be slipping back into the feeling of malaise for which President Carter was so roundly mocked in the 1970s. The question is sometimes asked whether the United States, despite its success in Desert Storm, has lost its world leadership, or even lost its way. At the same time, there are strong opinions to the contrary, not only in the Republican administration, but in academic circles, to cite only *The Myth of America's Decline* by Henry Nau, *Bound to Lead* by Joseph Nye, and *America's Economic Resurgence* by Richard Rosecrance.

I am enough of an angel fearing to tread in short-run problems not to offer my views on the prospects for Eastern Europe, the rate of recovery from the U.S. recession if we avoid a double dip, the likelihood that the European Economic Community will meet its goals for 1992, or the Dow-Jones industrial average for December 31 of that year, if I had such views. Nor will I try to push a hard line on monetarism versus

---

Based on a paper presented at a private seminar in New York City, October 11, 1991.

Keynesianism, privatization, free versus managed trade, deregulation or regulation. I have become a Manichean, a word I first learned in the last year or two, meaning that like Dr. Jekyll and Mr. Hyde, the world is partly good and partly evil, and that in policy questions other circumstances call for other remedies. On trend, markets should be left alone; in crisis, some intervention may be salutary. Rather, I propose to take a long-run view of the organization of the world economy, using a certain amount of economic history and some unrigorous economic theory. Like Richard Cooper, who on the fortieth anniversary of the Bretton Woods agreements said that we would have reached a system of world fixed exchange rates in 2015, I think I know more about desirable ultimate goals and outcomes than I do about the path or paths the world will follow in getting to them. Admittedly, a stumble or an unexpected success in the short run, like a mutation in biology, may change directions for the long-run pull.

Let me start by referring to a couple of polar views of world economic organization, one of hegemony versus pluralism, and the other borrowing from Nau, the "structuralist" as opposed to the choice-oriented perspective. Hegemony is a word so widely adopted by political scientists that it is difficult to evade, although I prefer to think of a hierarchical system of world economic organization, where one country is a leader, or accepts an unusual share of responsibility, rather like the father of a family before militant feminism and children and animal rights, or the captain of a ship, or in a weaker simile, the conductor of an orchestra. Pluralism in international relations means one country, one vote, equality of sovereignties. Between these polar extremes, of course, there are many compromises, such as one country first among equals, vetos for a few "great powers," weighted voting, regional blocs, and the like. Structuralists, in Nau's analysis, believe there is an inevitability about changing roles of leading countries in the world economy, starting perhaps at first quiescent, then challenging an existing leader, with some country ultimately taking over leadership, and finally subsiding into quiescence again. The human individual, I am told, goes from neonate to adolescence, maturity, and senescence, or, in Shakespeare's model, through seven stages of man. Countries are hardly "born," and do not die (though they may break up), but in a structuralist view, as defined by Nau, they may slip from leadership to followership in an aging process difficult to evade or control. In his more cheerful choice-oriented perspective there are national will and power of decision making, not perhaps free will because of constraints, but the possibility, with the appropriate political resolve, for a country to retain its world dominant role. It is hard to offer theoretical arguments against this possibility, and the historical record is not a reliable predictor of the future. Nonetheless, revealed historical preference, to borrow a term from consumer economics, suggests that no nation (or city-state) has continuously remained a dominant economic and political power. The cycle or S-curve of slow start, rapid rise, and then slowdown has sped up since the time of Persia, Egypt, Sparta, Athens, Rome, and Constantinople, who ruled for centuries, but the process of rise, followed by decline and in some cases fall has been often repeated. Before I come to Venice, Florence and Genoa, Spain, Flanders, Holland, Britain, and the United States, with bows to other less successful challengers such as France, Germany, and Japan, a word on the relations between military and economic power.

Desert Storm showed the might of the United States in a military way so outstanding, despite the puny army and air force of Iraq that were overcome, that many of the optimists, as opposed to those structuralists who believe in the likelihood of at least relative decline, threw their hats in the air and asserted that the United States was number one again or still. It is true that military and economic primacy generally go together— generally, but not universally. Spain, the central country of Paul Kennedy's *The Rise and Fall of Great Powers,* began to experience financial crises in the second half of the sixteenth century, well before its decline in military capacity in the seventeenth. Germany and Japan today are economic giants and military midgets. In Venice, Genoa, Amsterdam, Britain, and the United States, however, military and economic power have gone together. Military power typically emphasizes either sea or land, or now air forces. Economic strength may start out by stealing, then adapting and finally creating new technology, but it also involves high rates of saving, new types of financial institutions, creative destruction, or the abandonment of output lines in which other countries are catching up. There are many elusive aspects to economic development. A recent manuscript I saw discussed Florence in the high Renaissance in terms of creativity, and a research project with worldwide coverage being undertaken from Luxembourg focuses on economic vitality, both concepts hard to define, but not completely without meaning.

In a review article on the books seeking to refute the thesis that the United States is in some sort of decline ("Fin-de-siècle America," *New York Review of Books,* June 28, 1990), Paul Kennedy argues that while history does not produce forecasts, it raises questions that are risky to ignore. The Italian city-states declined in the sixteenth century, Holland in the eighteenth, Britain in the nineteenth—more or less declined, that is, in each case. The elements contributing to decline draw different emphasis from different authors, Kennedy stressing military adventure for Spain; Carlo Cipolla consumption; Mancur Olson the growth and gradual ossification of what he calls "distributional coalitions," but what are usually known as vested interests; William Baumol, with a team of collaborators, the decline of rates of innovation and productivity growth. These forces, of course, are not mutually exclusive, and the decline is usually not absolute but relative to other countries at more creative or vital stages of their S-curve. In a study of Venetian and Dutch elites in the seventeenth century, Peter Burke notes that both shifted from sea to land, from work to play, from thrift to conspicuous consumption, from entrepreneur to rentier, from bourgeois to aristocrat (*Venice and Amsterdam*, 1974, 104).

With the list of leading or hegemonic economies—early Italian cities, perhaps Antwerp, certainly Amsterdam, London, and New York—one should mention failed challenges from Spain, France, Germany, Japan, and the Soviet Union. The leader may then beat back some challenges. Sooner or later up to now, however, a leader at a given time has been displaced by another. In one formulation by a political scientist, Robert Keohane in *After Hegemony* (1984), active leadership by a hegemon may give way to a *regime,* that is, habits and institutions for solving problems and conflicts worked out under the auspices of a benign hegemon. The possibility may be granted, but the historical record offers little support. The Dutch Republic yielded place to Great Britain after three Anglo-Dutch wars in the seventeenth century—the fourth a century later being a much less evenly matched struggle—with Dutch economic leadership leaking away slowly between 1680 and 1730, rather than ending with a bang. British leadership was disguised as a regime of the gold standard, free trade, and balanced budgets, but free trade started to peter out after 1879, balanced budgets ended in World War I, and the gold standard collapsed in two stages in August, 1914, and September, 1931. The gold standard, moreover, in some views, was a sterling standard, just as the Bretton Woods regime was essentially a dollar standard. Signs of British slippage were visible as early as 1870 and increasingly from 1890. The United States' taking over of the economic leadership mantle cannot be seen any earlier than the Tripartite Monetary Agreement of September, 1936, and is generally tied to the lend-lease legislation or the Atlantic Charter of wartime, or to Bretton Woods or the Marshall Plan later. In *The World in Depression, 1929–1939* (1973), I ascribed the length, depth, and width of the depression to the fact that there was no country in charge, as Britain had been more or less in charge from 1850 to 1913. The judgment is debatable and has been debated. It makes the point, however, that transitions are dangerous. Within the United States in the 1930s, Milton Friedman has ob-

served, there was one transition in financial leadership from the Federal
Reserve Bank of New York under Governor Benjamin Strong to the
Board of Governors in Washington, another in the 1932 election from
the Republican Herbert Hoover to the Democrat Franklin D. Roosevelt, each involving or extending a vacuum in decision making. If one
believes that United States economic leadership in the world may be
slipping, the question arises whether a satisfactory regime will replace it,
whether a transition to a new leader will take place with deliberate
speed, or whether the process will be protracted and chaotic.

A major difference with some of the transitions of the past is that
the two logical challengers—the Soviet Union no longer counting—
Japan and Germany, or perhaps not Germany but the European Economic Community as a whole, seem not to be challengers aspiring to
hegemonic, dominant, or even responsible leadership in the world economy. Since defeat in World War II, they have been content under the
U.S. military umbrella, just as the United States was for the most part
quiescent in the protective embrace of the Royal Navy from 1812 to
1922. Influenced or perhaps dictated by American ideas, German and
Japanese constitutions restrain the two countries from military adventure. In the Middle East war, their contribution took the form of treasure, not blood. The fact that the United States sought large monetary
contributions from them is, in fact, one indication of U.S. economic
aging. While both countries are becoming somewhat more assertive, in
Germany *Ostpolitik* overwhelms world economic and political issues,
and did so even before the collapse of the cold war in 1989. German
European policy appears to have been put on hold. Japanese foreign
policy initiatives have picked up of late, especially in the Far East, but
by and large that country has been willing to leave security issues to the
United States while it makes economic hay in the sunshine. It is symbolic
of the unwillingness of both countries to challenge the United States that
they leave the dollar as the world's international money, discouraging
foreign holdings of DM and yen, and even continuing to lend to the
United States in dollars rather than insisting on doing so in their own
currencies, in Roosa bonds, gold, ECU or two- or three-pay instruments. Japanese investment in the United States has switched to a considerable extent from treasury bonds to real estate and direct investment,
both speculative to a degree, although protected against foreign-
exchange risk. There seems to be little short-term prospect of a shift to
another national money as the international unit of account, medium of
exchange, or reserve asset, supplanting the dollar as the dollar sup-
planted sterling, sterling the Dutch guilder, and the guilder the Venetian
ducat and the Florentine florin.

The arguments against a country acting as a hegemon, as a leader, or accepting responsibility for the production of international public goods are powerful. The leader frequently, perhaps inevitably, slips into confusing the international public interest with its national self-interest. Andrew Shonfield once responded to the notion that other countries had been free riders under U.S. leadership by asserting that the United States was a hard and angry rider, ready to kick over the game when it did not have its own way. Early this month at a seminar in Ramatuelle, France, reported in the *New York Times* of September 3, 1991, Roland Dumas, the French Foreign Minister, warned the United States against trying to "rule the world" after the collapse of Soviet power, saying that the United Nations and Europe should counterbalance the one remaining superpower. A week earlier, however, Josef Joffe, the editor of the *Süddeutsche Zeitung* of Munich, wrote in the *New York Times* Op-ed page of August 28, 1991, that Europe lacks a common foreign policy— as demonstrated in the Middle East and in Yugoslavia. The French fall back on "splendid aggravation," the English keep to their favorite place on the fence, and the Germans quietly cultivate their central European garden.

Pluralism is attractive in that it is democratic, but it may not get the job done. Public-choice economists claim that government officials and bureaucrats at home and in international organizations work in their own narrow interests rather than in that of those who employ them, something that some of us who worked nights and weekends in government in the past believe has not always been true, and perhaps need not be.

In fact, public-choice doctrine comes close to taking the position that the production of public goods is impossible without a hegemon. In the first place, to follow the argument of Bruno Frey in *Aussenwirtschaft*, the Swiss journal on international economic relations (45, no. 3 [1990]), Kenneth Arrow's impossibility theorem demonstrates that with three countries and three goals, common or coordinated policies cannot be reached when each country has a different ordering of priorities as among, say, economic growth, stability of prices, and full employment. Leadership is needed to break the deadlock. Second, there is a complex agency problem. The wishes of citizens of a country in whose behalf policies are required must be filtered through their local representatives in government, its representatives at a given international organization, and again through the bureaucrats at that organization. An agency problem exists when each agent pursues his or her own interest rather than that of the principal. With three principal-agent relationships to be penetrated, the chance that international organizations will faithfully serve the interests of a country, Frey maintains, is small (perhaps $\frac{1}{2} \times \frac{1}{2} \times \frac{1}{2}$, or one in eight, to put my numbers on it). When the Swiss were given a chance in 1986 to vote in a referendum on whether or not to join the United Nations, they voted 75 to 25 against it. Frey interprets this as representing an understanding that the United Nations fails to work in the interests of national voters because of the agency problem. Another possibility is that the Swiss, in this as in numerous other instances, are *free riders,* willing to let the rest of the world produce international public goods from which they benefit. Thirdly, there is the *Prisoner's Dilemma,* whether to proceed or hold back without knowing what the other parties are going to do, much as in the ill-fated experiment under President Carter of a G-5 scheme for locomotives to pull the world out of recession, with only two countries—an insufficient number—actually doing much chugging, and hurting their balances of payments in the process. A telling example of ineffectuality in the production of international public goods has been studied by Richard Cooper, who notes that it took eighty years to get the World Health Organization formed and operational, when it was clearly in the interest of all countries to form a body to monitor the spread of disease worldwide ("International Cooperation in Public Health as a Prologue to Macroeconomic Cooperation," in Richard N. Cooper et al., *Can Nations Agree?* Brookings Institution, 1989).

The United Nations is generally regarded as an ineffectual organization, responding in the Korean and Iraq-Kuwait Wars mainly to strong American initiatives. For years the Security Council was paralyzed by Soviet vetos. When power shifted to the Assembly because of this obstructionism, the less-developed countries pushed through vote after vote in their own interest to which the industrial countries refused to respond. Peace in the cold war put an end to Soviet vetos, but the Security Council is now clearly anachronistic, with China and the USSR still holding vetos, along with the declining economic powers, France and the United Kingdom, and no basis for sharing responsibility with Germany and Japan by giving them seats. There is something to be said for unwritten constitutions like the British that can more readily adapt to change. With weighted voting, the World Bank and the International Monetary Fund are in a stronger position to stay relevant, despite Populist attacks on them by developing countries. But international organizations wane as well as wax, often like the typical committee staying on after their raison d'être has evaporated. On the contrary, the Bank for International Settlements, threatened with execution by the United States in 1945, and lacking any clearly defined set of duties or responsibilities, has moved into a number of financial vacuums in the world, creating the swap network in 1961, establishing a protocol in 1975 that allocated responsibility in lender-of-last-resort cases, studying financial innovation, and negotiating the wobbly agreement on the capital requirements of banks. More perhaps than the OECD, the ECE, and, I am tempted to say, the EEC in the financial field now after its early accomplishments, it has the potential for continuing vitality and creativity. This is possibly ascribable to its independence of political direction.

I lack time to explore extensively the pragmatic modes of organization—the G-3, G-5, G-7, G-10, G-30, or the unaligned "77" that numbered several score more the last time anyone counted. The G-7 is the least moribund of these groups, and a spirited defense of it was offered by Undersecretary of the Treasury, David Mulford, in the July/ August, 1991, issue of *The International Economy*, playing down, however, the public relations and photo opportunity aspects of it that led such a politician as President Mitterand to spend his time at the meetings timing his entrances. There are, however, a great many international problems that have little chance of getting on to the crowded and brief agenda of the G-7—terrorism, hostages, the depredations of a Bank of Credit and Commerce International (BCCI), drugs, tax shelters, money laundering, refugees, illegal migration, and economic aid to Eastern Europe. It is possible, perhaps, to revitalize old agencies or create new to deal with particular problems, but often difficult to wind them up after they have ceased to function.

One solution to international organization that seems to be emerging is the regional one. Europe hopes to be an economic unit after 1992, although progress toward this goal may have been slowed down by events in Eastern Europe. The free-trade agreement between Canada and the United States that Mexico may join, in addition, perhaps, Central and South American countries, and Japan's economic initiatives in China, Korea, and elsewhere in the Far East, seem to point in this direction. There are, however, strong reasons against adopting regional blocs as desirable policy. For world political and economic stability, the need is for agreement among the major powers, with the degree of cohesion within each regional bloc much less salient. In exchange rates, for example, the key currencies count, with the peso-dollar rate of local interest only. Many major economic issues, such as the price of oil, cut across regional boundaries. In politics, a regional arrangement would orphan many countries in Africa, the Middle East, Southeast Asia, and elsewhere. Regionalism seems to be making advances, but it is a third- or fourth-best system.

The real fear coming into prominence in the summer of 1991 is a return in the United States to quasi isolationism. The July, 1991, *Atlantic* on the "National Interest" features an article leaning in this direction:

"Interventionism vs. Minding One's Own Business." This debate over whether the Gulf War was in the U.S. national interest has a strong statement of the negative by Christopher Layne. A number of Democrats are reacting to President Bush's foreign policy successes not by suggesting that they should be widened from the military and political fields to the economic, but by urging a return to parochial concerns. As I write, the *New York Times* of September 7, 1991, has an Op-ed piece by Alan Tonelson headlined "Put America First."

There is of course nothing disturbing about attention to the national interest, so long as some considerable room in that goal is left for contribution to a peaceful and prosperous world. In the long run, the international public interest coincides with the national interest. Where there are short-run trade-offs or choices, the answer becomes more complex. One can, to be sure, bite off more than one can chew, taking on the role of world policeman in situations where a certain amount of benign neglect is called for. I am fearful, however, that those who thump the drum for the national interest are in fact urging a return to the isolation that served the United States and the world so badly in the 1920s and 1930s on war debts, tariffs, standing aloof from European banking crises, foreign aid, and the like.

In the long run, countries rise and are overtaken, and in the world economy take on primacy and some responsibility for buttressing the system in critical times and then ultimately give it up. In the warm debate over whether the United States is slipping from preeminence or not, my judgment, not held with much confidence, is that it is aging, becoming sclerotic, losing vitality. It can readily happen that new S-curves grow out of old ones at the top of the curve and pick up speed again. This may happen. I do not bet on it as Nau and Nye do. Rather, I think the prospect is for an extended period of uncertainty. Japan and Germany (or Europe) will remain preoccupied with their own concerns and less and less willing to underwrite U.S. foreign policy leadership, especially in the absence of substantial American economic contributions. We face the threat of a new prolonged transition, with its attendant vacuum of leadership, a transition probably to a primacy of some country not yet singled out. Like the transition from British to American economic primacy, with Britain unable to lead and the United States unwilling, the situation is dangerous. The regime of international institutions established after World War II may get us through the interregnum if that is not too monarchical an expression. I fervently hope so. The years immediately ahead, before the world economy comes to a new steady state, however, I find nervous-making.

CHAPTER 8

Review of Milton Friedman, *Money Mischief:* *Episodes in Monetary History*

Occam's razor—William of Occam was a fourteenth-century English philosopher—holds that one should explain events or outcomes in the most parsimonious manner, with the fewest possible assumptions or causes. Modern chaos theory, in contrast, suggests that everything is more complex than it appears to most people, with few instances where one can say this caused that. Economic theorists, like Milton Friedman, a 1976 Nobel laureate, generally hold to parsimony; in his case, he looks for economic explanations in the field of money. Historians tend to avoid the categorical statements, offering such bromides as: no, that goes back at least 100 years; yes, but not in the South; on the one hand, on the other hand.

"Monetary Mischief" is a collection of papers by Friedman, including a chapter from his 1980 best-seller with Rose Friedman, "Free to Choose," summarizing his theories of money and inflation, and recounting several episodes where chance events or mistakes in policy produced untoward consequences. "Inflation is always and everywhere a *monetary phenomenon*"—a statement found in several places in the book—summarizes his view on the first score.

The mischievous occurrences include the demonetization of silver in Britain in 1816, as he alleges—but an economic historian could make the case that it went back to the gold recoinage of 1774; the "Crime of 1873," when silver was left out of a U.S. act preparing for the resumption of specie payments after the Greenback era of the Civil War, which accentuated the "Great Depression" from 1873 to 1896; and silver purchases by the Roosevelt administration, under the 1933 Thomas amendment, to appease the silver senators, which contributed (but not much) to the defeat of the Chinese Nationalists by the communists.

To those interested in the history of economic thought, the news is

Reprinted from a review of Milton Friedman's *Money Mischief: Episodes in Monetary History* (New York: Harcourt, Brace Jovanovich, 1992) that appeared in the *Boston Globe,* February 9, 1992.

that Friedman has changed his mind and now believes that bimetallism, with both gold and silver as hard money, is a better standard than gold alone.

He does not believe that it is possible to return to bimetallism, or even to the gold standard as recommended by such stalwarts as Jack Kemp, Lewis Lehrman, Jude Wanniski and Robert Mundell. If Britain had not demonetized silver in 1816, the economic history of the nineteenth century would have been different, although how different is not entirely made clear. Prices would have been higher. Silver would not have been demonetized later in the century by Germany, France and the United States.

This approach to history relies on the "counterfactual," what would have happened if; for example, if Cleopatra's nose had been a quarter inch shorter.

Friedman is an adherent of the quantity theory of money, a notion that goes back at least to Jean Bodin in the sixteenth century, but whose modern expositor was Irving Fisher. Friedman says Fisher was "the greatest economist the United States has yet produced." In Fisher's formulation $MV = PT$ (money times velocity is equal to prices times output), output depends on real factors such as the enterprise, industry and ingenuity of people, the extent of thrift, the structure of industry and government. Velocity is a constant in the long run. In consequence, the price level depends on the quantity of money. In a theoretical chapter, this simplistic model, said to be equal in its power to Einstein's $E = mc^2$, is qualified to allow for lags and for short-run effects of money on output. Friedman notes further that monetary institutions evolve in a Darwinian way, and that while money used to consist of only coin, as time went on it was broadened to include bank notes, bank deposits, other liquid assets such as treasury bills, money funds, credit cards, etc. He rejects any notion that inflation may be connected with the labor market, with higher wages being demanded, granted, and then money reluctantly increased to avoid unemployment. In economic jargon, money is exogenous, created independently, outside the system, not endogenous as a response to other factors.

Friedman's conversion from mono- to bimetallism as an international system is based on his belief that bimetallism worked well in France from the 1820s to the 1870s, and more or less automatically. Recent research, however—especially three volumes by Alain Plessis on the Bank of France under the Second Empire—shows that the Bank of England indulged in a lot of manipulation, including swapping silver for gold with the Bank of England, the State Bank of Russia and the Amsterdam and Milan markets, to prevent the system from collapsing under the impact of Gresham's law that bad money drives out good. With the gold discoveries of California and Australia in 1849 and 1851, silver was undervalued and gold overvalued. The Bank had to scramble to get enough gold to pay out lest its silver stock be drawn down completely by arbitrageurs.

A few more quibbles. Friedman believes that hyperinflation cannot occur under a monetary system based on coins. He should look at the debasement of the subsidiary coinage at the start of the Thirty Years' War (1618–1648) in the Holy Roman Empire. He calls the 1948 German monetary reform the work of Ludwig Erhard. That view has been attacked as a myth by German historians and has been put to rest by Otmar Emminger, former head of the Bundesbank, in his recent memoirs. He blames the collapse of silver prices in the 1870s on German silver sales, presumably unaware that $50 million of silver was paid to Prussia by the French as part of the Franco-Prussian indemnity through a German inadvertence—another bit of monetary mischief. The view that bimetallism was the therapy advocated by the masses, against the classes, Main Street against Wall Street, fits U.S. experience, but not that of Germany, where in the 1890s, the aristocratic Junkerfarmers were bimetallist, or even of Britain, where many bankers—probably with landed estates—and including a former governor of the Bank of England, espoused bimetallism.

Economics is full of faddism—ideas that are taken up and pushed by True Believers, often with passion. A number of economists believe in the Kondratieff fifty-year cycle, characterized by Samuelson as science fiction. Jevons thought economic activity was controlled by sun spots. Schumpeter wrote of mono-maniacs, referring, however, to advocates of a silver standard, not gold. As for the passion, note that Karl Helfferich, later a finance minister of the German Reich, in 1899 denounced a bimetallist, one Otto Arendt, with such vehemence that the latter sued for slander.

In 1992, it is well to note the theory of Pierre Vilar, a Spanish historian, that Columbus's voyage was stimulated by the "bullion famine" of the fifteenth century, an endogenous explanation. The evidence is that Columbus mentioned his search for gold sixty-five times in his diary on the voyage.

I have doubt that "Monetary Mischief" will achieve bestsellerdom like "Freedom to Choose." It is interesting, in parts fascinating, especially as Milton Friedman details how he changed his mind. This is not the only 1991 instance of such openness. In the preface to the English translation of "The Golden Franc," memoirs of Emile Moreau, governor of the Bank of France from 1926 to 1930, he states he would now qualify the statement, with Anna Schwartz, in their classic "Monetary History of the United States," that responsibility for the 1929 depression belonged solely to the United States, and admit some blame to France.

In my view, this is better, but still too parsimonious. I may be wrong about the best-seller bit. Complexity may be a winner in academe, but parsimony may still clean up the market.

Part 2

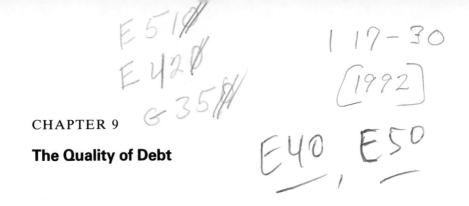

CHAPTER 9

The Quality of Debt

Much of macroeconomic analysis, outside of fiscal policy, runs in terms of the quantity of money. Velocity is assumed to be constant, or to vary only within narrow limits. Control the money supply, the monetarists claim, and you control national income, more or less, but at any rate within a comfortable range.

There are several problems with the monetarist position. First is the question of defining money: does one take currency plus demand deposits, M_1, or add in savings deposits, making the total M_2? There are many more definitions, in some accounts reaching up to M_7. Second, if the market gets the bit in its teeth and "money," properly defined for the recent past is held constant, the market will devise a new medium of exchange, banknotes when money was coin, bank deposits when money consisted of coin and banknotes, and so on. Third, even if one had the right definition of money, the idea that the quantity of money determines national income is highly dubious in the short run, and raises a serious identification problem in the long run. Which is the dependent and which the independent variable? Does a rise in income produce more money, or more money produce the rise in income, with the converse holding for declines in the money supply and in income? There abides the perennial problem of cause and effect, the chicken and the egg.

Some economic analysts seek escape from these dilemmas in calculating the quantity of credit or debt. Henry Kaufman (1986), the Wall Street economist, says "Money matters, but credit counts." Benjamin Friedman (1983), not to be confused with the monetarist, Milton Friedman, the former from Harvard University, the latter emeritus from the University of Chicago, wants to measure the ratio of debt to income, to obtain an analogue to monetary velocity. There are many forms of debt. Money in most of its forms—all except coin—is debt. There are others, of households, nonfinancial firms, financial firms, of governments. If

Reprinted from Dimitri B. Papadimitriou, ed., *Profits, Deficits and Instability* (London: Macmillan, 1992), 189–201.

debt is expanding rapidly, spending and national income are likely to rise; if contracting, to fall. But debt is an *ex post* concept. I once heard Arthur Laffer say in conversation that what we should measure is the unused credit of spending bodies, to get a sense, *ex ante,* of how much debt could expand. John Stuart Mill said something of the same sort for individuals, some years ago:

> The purchasing power of an individual at any moment is not measured by the money actually in his pocket, whether we mean by money the metals or include bank notes. It consists, first, of the money in his possession; secondly, of the money at his banker's, and all other money due him and payable on demand; thirdly, of whatever credit he happens to possess. (*Westminster Review,* 1844, quoted in Jacob Viner, *Studies in the Theory of International Trade,* 1937, 246.)

Mill's focus on the individual underlines that there is an aggregation problem, sometimes referred to as an illustration of the fallacy of composition. The debt or credit of each individual can be measured primarily on the assumption that everything else is unchanged. If the debts of other firms rise, the capacity of a firm to borrow may decline *ex ante.* And the mention of "at any moment" implies that the credit possessed by an individual is conditioned by a host of other factors: the economic outlook, the state of animal spirits (to use a phrase of Keynes) of bankers and other lenders, the fears and hopes of the monetary authorities, including bank regulators, the rate of interest, or perhaps more accurately, the term structure of interest rates.

In addition, the quantity of credit or debt is subject to some of the same definitional difficulties that render the quantity of money problematic. Definitions will vary. Some analysts are interested only in the credit of nonfinancial institutions, and omit interbank loans and deposits, plus what Kaufman (1986) calls "hidden debt, swaps, futures, repos, futures, and a host of other off–balance sheet items." One suggestion of Ian Giddy (1985) is that, for measuring the ratio of capital to debt of a bank, the off–balance sheet items be valued as if they were options, the value of which have been reduced by the financial pundits to a formula. This ingenious suggestion is perhaps too sophisticated to gain widespread acceptance. Should one count domestic debt and foreign debt the same? add household, small firm and large firm debt to one another, dollar for dollar? government debt and private debt?

Like money, debt expands rapidly and elastically with economic euphoria. Adam Smith has a famous passage discussing what is called in the index, but not in the text, the "pernicious practice" of drawing and redrawing bills of exchange. He apologizes for describing it in detail on the ground that it is well known to all men of business. A in Edinburgh draws on B in London, a bill payable two months after date. B in London accepts the bill on the understanding that he can pay it off by drawing a bill on A with a similar maturity. The two are careful to use different banks, and sometimes to bring others into the process, in chains. The Dutch had the same practice with the unpronounceable name of *Wisselruitij*. By such devices credit can be expanded many times on the basis of a small capital base. Sir Francis Baring knew of clerks (about 1808) who were not worth £100 but who were allowed discount of £5000 to £10,000. In 1857 a London accountant claimed to know of firms with capital of less than £10,000 and obligations of £900,000 and held that this was not untypical. Using very different techniques of pyramiding credit on the basis of real estate, one banker, whose suicide was reported in the *New York Times* last summer, owed $475 million but had been jailed because he was unable to raise bail—whether cash or a bond was not stated—of $750,000. As debt rises and falls, its quality varies inversely. Henry Kaufman worries that the volume of debt in the United States approached $8 trillion in 1985; a letter writer to the *New York Times* on 12 August 1988 that it was getting close to $10 trillion. The quantity of debt is a subject of interest in its own right and as a proxy for the quality of debt. It may be useful, however, to approach the quality of debt directly.

By way of a diversionary excursus, I am also interested in the quality of money because of Gresham's law. Innovations producing new kinds of money do not inevitably match old monies in quality, and if bad money drives good money into hoarding or export, the quantity of money can become unstable. This was a crucial issue for the Currency School in Britain in the first half of the nineteenth century that insisted that Bank of England notes be backed, pound for pound above a small fiduciary issue, in gold and silver. It surfaced again in the United States in the twentieth century in the advocacy of 100 percent reserves against bank deposits. I shall come back to these questions later. At the moment, however, I want to mention as part of this parenthesis that the Austrian school of free banking, including a great many non-Austrians, wants to rid banks of all regulation, relying on the opposite of Gresham's law—that is, good money will drive out bad. I am prepared to concede that this is a theoretical possibility, and may even have occurred on one or two occasions. In a seller's market, with goods short, the seller can demand the money of his choice, and will rationally insist on good money. But in buyers' markets, which seem to have prevailed over the last millenium, the buyer chooses the money he spends, and understandably holds back the good.

The quality of money and the quality of debt were considered by economists long before the collection of statistics on financial quantities including national income. Along with the Currency School, the French wanted money as good as gold, and clung to that position down through to the Fifth Republic, as set forth by Jacques Rueff and President Charles deGaulle. The rival to the Currency School, the Banking School, led by the Bank of England and Thomas Tooke, was interested in the quality of debt, wanting bank credit extended only on "real bills," that is, bills of exchange drawn by a seller of merchandise on a buyer, with the goods already moving in transport, and title to the goods represented by a bill of lading often attached to the bill of exchange. The Bank of England in principle discounted only bills of exchange with two good London names, generally those of the seller's bank and the buyer's. The Bank of France wanted three names, and in the crisis of 1848 created Comptoirs d'Escompte (discount offices) to add the third name. (As an aside it may be mentioned that a distinguished international banker, Louis Raphael Bischoffsheim in 1867, told a Commission in Paris investigating monetary practices that he favored one good name over twenty mediocre ones, foreshadowing the famous remark of J. P. Morgan that he loaned not on balance sheets or collateral, but on character. As a still wider diversion, it may be observed that Thomas Ashton has written that Lancashire in the early nineteenth century disliked banknotes as money because of some unhappy experience with failed banks, and used bills of exchange instead, each recipient adding his name, the notes often for odd amounts and bearing ten to twenty names, some of them of bankrupts.) The real-bills doctrine was upheld in the United States by J. Laurence Laughlin of the University of Chicago to 1916 and by my own banking professor at Columbia University, H. Parker Willis, in the 1920s and 1930s.

The Banking School and its real-bills followers had an interest in the quality of credit which was laudable, but disregarded its quantity. They failed to appreciate that as more and more real bills operated as money, they raised prices and made possible the issuance of bills of higher monetary amounts. The process could readily become self-perpetuating, or a positive feedback one, leading to inflation, and in the famous debates in Britain during the Napoleonic War, to depreciation of the exchange rate. They were, moreover, as Hawtrey has indicated, a little severe on some loans not based on bills of exchange: loans to finance inventory, for example, and the process by which bills of exchange became separated from underlying trade shipments was an entirely natural one. As described by the Swedish economic historian, Kurt Samuelsson (1955), the firm of Carlos and Claes Grill in Stockholm would continuously ship goods to their London correspondent and continuously draw bills on him. After a time, particular bills became disassociated from particular shipments, and the Grills drew on London when they needed the money. Real-bills enthusiasts regarded drafts not associated with trade as "finance bills," or even more pejoratively as "accommodation paper," drafts designed to accommodate a borrower in general rather than to promote a given sale. Sometimes finance bills were written for odd amounts to disguise their character. A banking manual of the mid-nineteenth century records a conversation among bank directors in which one director speaks against a loan to a rich client to finance a new house and furnishings, saying that it is not a *bona fide* commercial note that will be paid when due, but accommodation paper! the exclamation point indicating how outrageous it was thought to be.

The contemporary macroeconomist who is concerned with debt structures and the quality of debt is Hyman P. Minsky of the Jerome Levy Economics Institute, New York, whose taxonomy, however, has evoked strong controversy. Minsky divides debt into three categories: hedge finance, speculative finance, and Ponzi finance, the last characterization giving rise to criticism because Charles Ponzi was a swindler. Hedge finance consists in borrowing under conditions where the cash flow in from operations exceeds the payment commitments of the future, including debt repayment. Speculative finance involves payment commitments in excess of cash inflow from operations. These may be banks which expect to continue to receive deposits or nonfinancial firms that roll over their debt or paper. The word *speculative* in the characterization involves speculation primarily on the rate of interest. If a firm needs to roll over debt and interest rates rise, its initial calculations may prove to have been optimistic. Speculative finance as a term, however, seems to imply something more in the way of risk. Ponzi finance, according to Minsky, is a special kind of speculative finance in which cash outflow exceeds cash inflow for an extended period at the end of which, presumably, a surge in cash inflow, such as from the sale of a capital asset under construction, will enable payment commitments to be made good. There are, of course, many normal financial operations of this sort, such as construction loans, and it is misleading to attach the name of a swindler to them. Ponzi paid off initial investors in a fictitious foreign-exchange operation, on which he promised a 45 percent return, with the monies received from new investors—a swindle. I would prefer to call Minsky's categories by less value-loaded names. In any event, the categories chosen are too limited to do justice to the wealth of gradations in the quality of debt.

The quality of debt must be judged by many more variables than the three which go to make up the Minsky scheme, focused on the purpose of the borrowing. Some relate to the terms of the loan, and whether the interest return compensates properly for the risk, the maturity of the debt, the presence or absence of amortization, any claim on assets, or collateral, in the case of liquidation, and sometimes from the point of view of the lender, whether or not it is callable. The size of the debt in relation to the net worth of the borrower is an important consideration, and the size of debt service relative to gross earnings—interest and dividends—of the borrowing corporation. Other considerations are whether or not a debt is guaranteed by a third party, the currency it is denominated in if borrower and lender are in different countries. In the case of financial corporations, an informed depositor should be interested in the capital/deposit ratio, the reserve to deposit ratio, the concentration or diversifications of loans and investments, and the nature of the relationships between bank officers and its borrowers—whether, for example, there are loans to directors, officers or their families in excess of proper business dealings.

These facets of debt evaluation are so numerous and varied that it is impossible in my view to compress them into a single schema. One can perhaps throw light on one and another aspect, however.

Take, for example, so-called junk bonds, bonds sold to the public at high rates of interest that are well short of investment grade, bonds rated AA or better by Moodys or Standard & Poors investment advisory services, because debt service is covered by gross profits of interest and dividends less than several times. These have become popular in the purchase of the equity of corporations being taken over in leveraged buyouts, generally in combination with bank debt raised for the purpose. They bear high rates of interest to compensate for their greater risk, along the lines of the risk return trade-off of the Tobin-Markowitz model for which Tobin received the Nobel Prize. Junk bonds can be diversified through mutual funds which hold various of them and count on the default of a few among them. In one of the first such defaults, that of the REVCO D.S. Inc. drugstore chain in August 1988, which proved unable to meet interest payments of $46 million on $703.5 million of junk bonds, the judge under Chapter 11 bankruptcy proceedings put trade creditors and bank creditors ahead of all other parties, including unsecured creditors, bondholders, and shareholders, should the company ultimately be liquidated.

The *Boston Globe* made the point that Kohlberg, Kravis, and Roberts, who undertook a leveraged buyout of RJR-Nabisco because of difficulty in selling their low-grade bonds, have had to resort to sweeteners of various sorts—what the history of finance calls in French *douceurs*—to get them placed. To the extent that the discharge of the debt requires selling off assets we get close to Minsky's definition of Ponzi finance. A further point should be noted that the announcement of the KKR bond issues drove down the prices of $5 billion of outstanding RJR-Nabisco bonds to such an extent that two insurance companies, Metropolitan and Equitable, sued unsuccessfully to halt the process. The episode makes clear that the quality of debt is not a simple function of the quantity.

Another aspect of the rate of return is whether it is fixed or adjustable, and if adjustable, under what conditions. In a straight fixed rate loan, there are two risks: a default risk that the debtor will be unable to meet his obligation, and an interest-rate risk—that is, the risk of a rise in interest rates which will depress the market value of the loan. The longer the loan to maturity, the greater the interest rate risk for a fixed rate mortgage. It is this effect which has been hard on banks and savings banks in the southwest of the United States in recent years, starting with the sharp rise in interest rates at the beginning of the 1980s. This rise not only knocked down the value of fixed rate mortgages, but lost deposits subject by regulation to a ceiling rate of return as depositors withdrew from banks and thrifts to put their money into unregulated money funds. A shift to adjustable rate mortgages helped at the margin, but did not eliminate the interest rate risk so much as to transfer it from the bank to the borrower, thereby increasing the default risk. Interest rates declined through most of the 1980s down to 1988 when they started up again. What effect adjustable-rate mortgages and the recent popularity of home equity loans which ate up part of the accumulated amortization of many mortgages will have on household capacity to service home debt poses a riveting and important question.

Government deregulation of savings and loan associations in 1986, allowing them to pay higher interest than 5½ percent to hold their deposits, encouraged some, first to offer high rates to attract funds, and then to take on risky loans to earn the requisite returns. Many of the problems of thrift institutions today stem from the one-two punch of first disintermediation and then deregulation. The fact that deposits were insured below $100,000 also proved dysfunctional: a group of deposit brokers came into being, taking sums such as $5 million and spreading it around among risky, high-interest-paying banks in $95,000 bundles to get both the high returns and FDIC insurance.

The complex nature of the quality of debt can be illustrated with the numerous variables affecting an automobile loan. Among the variables are the amount of the down payment, the length of the loan, the net worth of the borrower, his or her employment and its stability, the quality of the automobile, and the extent to which its price holds up in the secondhand market. When the market for automobile loans indulges in overtrading, down payments fall, terms become stretched to four years from the standard two or three. If a bank "securitizes" its automobile loans, aggregating a large number so as to diversify risk, and selling off shares in the pool, this improves the quality of the automobile paper, especially if the bank furnishes an implicit or explicit guarantee against possible individual defaults where the repossessed car has fallen in value below the amount remaining of the loan.

It is of interest in this connection that banks charging high rates on auto loans in recent years have had little trouble, while the automobile companies themselves—pushing sales by 4.9 percent and similar financing over 60 months—have found themselves having to repossess some vehicles from which buyers have walked away with the value of the car depreciated below the remaining loan. In the cases of two companies—Ford and General Motors—write-offs on losses from these bad debts amounted in 1988 to more than $100 million each.

In the home mortgage field, practice in the 1920s was to lend on fixed amount mortgages for terms such as three years. At the end of the period, it was not expected that the loan would be paid off, as in the case of an automobile loan, but that it would be rolled over for an equal period. In some circumstances, if the condition of credit markets had changed substantially, there might be negotiation for a change in terms, largely the new interest rate, but on some occasions the amount of the loan. If markets were tighter, the lender might raise the rate and possibly ask for some reduction of principal. Or with easier money, the debtor might ask for and get a lower interest rate. Like many contracts with fixed periods to run, like those between trade unions and employers, or tenant and landlord, renewal was the rule. In the depression of the 1930s, however, default was so widespread that financial institutions moved to amortize mortgages, with much longer periods, twenty or thirty years. Interest and amortization were paid together at a flat rate, with interest starting high and declining as the debt shrank in size, and amortization picking up gradually. After a stretch of years of accumulated amortization, the owner's equity had built up and the debt fallen, to raise the equity/debt ratio and improve the quality of the obligation. But the attraction of this sort of finance, and its superiority over old flat-rate short-term mortgages have lately been called into question by offers by banks of what are called "home equity loans," loans against the owner's rising equity. These are the equivalent of what used to be known as second mortgages. They clearly reduce the quality of the mortgage, less, to be sure, if the new monies are used for improvements to the property than if they are spent otherwise.

Consumer debt quality is judged by rating bureaus after the fact, on the basis of whether a given household is punctilious in paying off debts or slow pay. There are those who advocate that a young person start out in life by borrowing a substantial sum, put it into a savings account, and pay it back on maturity, regarding the spread between the interest paid and the interest received as a payment for a good credit standing. In many instances, a consumer has to fill out applications for charge account, credit cards and the like, detailing assets, debt, income, employment, and so on. Old-fashioned bankers have difficulty in understanding the thinking of banks that mail out credit cards to lists of people without checking their credit standing. Widespread use of credit cards in the United States is partly responsible for the decline in personal savings, as credit extended to consumers representing dissavings, rises net after pay-downs, each month, some months more, some less. Franco Modigliani won the Nobel Prize for his life-cycle consumption function, in which people save when young, dissave when older. That may have been true once in this country, and may be true today in some countries like Switzerland. For the most part, young people run up substantial debts, for education, house buying and furnishing, and pay them off as they get older and their preoccupation with possessions wanes. Older people do spend, to be sure, on travel and medical outlays, but few of them eat up their savings completely in wasting annuities.

There is also the question of the nature of debt as affected by exchange rates. Under a fixed-rate system, of course, the choice of currency in which the debt is fixed is reduced in importance, although some particularly attractive investments in the 1920s and early 1930s were payable in the creditors' choice among two or three currencies. Debts fixed in gold proved unable to withstand the depreciation of the dollar in 1933. Where debt is denominated in a foreign currency, there may be something akin to the Miller-Modigliani theorem that risks are shifted rather than reduced. In 1932, Colombia had maintained debt service on its dollar bonds until it depreciated the peso. This made the domestic budgetary problem so acute that the government defaulted. In the United States most foreign borrowing has been in dollars, apart from Roosa bonds with an explicit, and swaps with an implicit, exchange guarantee. But if the United States budget and trade deficits keep up much longer, I anticipate that Japanese insurance companies, for one, will become restless in buying U.S. treasury obligations denominated in dollars, and will insist on some sort of exchange guarantee. It is true that the spread between U.S. and Japanese interest rates provides some protection against exchange loss. I should think not enough, however.

Fraud and swindles are a prime source of bad debt. I have written a chapter on the subject in *Manias, Panics and Crashes* (1978), and believe that my judgment then that swindles grow with the boom phase of a cycle of overtrading followed by crash, and peak after the crash, has been borne out by the decade or more of experience since the writing of the first edition. On the upswing, swindles are demand-led. Many people get upset seeing others make money, and blindly rush into dishonest schemes that appear to pay large returns. After the crash, it is a different group that does the swindling, financial people in trouble that try to cheat their way out of it. This follows a supply-led model. Most of these are Ponzi schemes, promising high returns and paying off the early comers with the subscriptions of the late. Collapse seems almost inevitable.

Before turning to what, if anything, to do about quality of debt, I should like to make a point about the predilection for risky investments of latecomers in an industry, thrusting upstarts from the point of view of the Establishment, who try to elbow their way to wealth when most of the good risks have settled into continuing relationships with established banks or investment houses. Examples of such latecomers can be multiplied by the dozen: Jay Cooke, who moved into railroad finance in the 1870s after the profitable roads had been sewed up by other bankers, and was left with the Northern Pacific; Caldwell & Company in municipal finance in Tennessee, Kentucky, Arkansas; the Bank of the United States in third-grade mortgages in New York; the Franklin National Bank in New York in foreign exchange, the Butcher banks in Tennessee, Penn Square in oil exploration . . . one could go on.

Somewhat tangentially related to the newcomer, late-start thruster is a class noted by François Crouzet (1988) in a paper on the Codman Brothers of Boston and Lincoln, Massachusetts, the younger brother of a successful businessman or banker, who brings a firm to the brink of disaster by indiscretions both of high living and poor investments. Crouzet observes that the account of the Codmans may strike some as anecdotal, but he believes that time and again firms have been jeopardized or ruined by lax junior partners. Two prominent historical examples that spring to mind are Jay Cooke's younger brother, Henry, in charge of the Washington office of the firm, and D. W. Chapman of Overend, Gurney & Co., after it had gone public and the Gurneys had retired. Crouzet observes that family relationships have served positive roles in business—nepotism is often a sound practice in a world where a principal cannot trust an agent—but that misplaced confidence or a reluctance to distrust a close relative can end in disaster.

I forbear from trying to outline a comprehensive scheme of the quality of debt, given the number and disparity of the variables involved, but conclude by discussing what, if anything, should be done about it. There are those who say nothing, believers in the efficacy of the market as an evolutionary device to promote the fittest. There are those who advocate free banking, let both the borrower and the lender beware, do nothing beyond the enforcement of contracts and the policing of fraud. Perhaps leave it to the private agencies, the credit bureaus, rating services, print media, to produce the necessary disclosure. Or leave it to the accounting profession to establish standards.

At the other end of the spectrum are the regulators who would enforce a variety of rules to which banks and other financial institutions would have to conform: full disclosure in bond prospectuses, predetermined ratios of reserves of different sorts to deposits of different sorts, set capital ratios, separation of commercial banking and security underwriting, prohibitions against lending more than a certain percentage to any one borrower, limits on loans, to officers and directors. A requirement that banks, for example, "mark to market," write off their loans and investments down from cost to their market valuation, is more often honored in the breach than in the observance; in many cases, say for loans, there is no market, or, as in the case of Third World syndicated bank debt, the market is thin and riddled with air pockets. Mark to market should have been observed more widely in say southwestern United States mortgage lending by thrift institutions, but as a universal rule it is a counsel of perfection. Regulation of all kinds is aimed at promoting customers' confidence and convenience in financial firms' products by certifying the integrity and competence of individual institutions, reducing transactions costs of both financial firms and their clients.

One extreme schema for regulating the quality of debt is that proposed in the 1930s by Henry Simons (1948), the Chicago monetarist. He wanted 100 percent reserves against bank deposits, which he combined with a vigorous attempt to stamp out elasticity of credit throughout the financial system, and not only in banks. This meant restriction of open book credit of nonfinancial firms and of installment loans, limiting government debt to non–interest bearing forms (money) at one end of the spectrum and very long–term debt at the other—ideally perpetual debt or consols. He advocated that all other financial wealth be held in equity form, and would explicitly ban fixed monetary contracts so that no institution that was not a bank could create effective money substitutes. This, he claimed, would especially limit the short-term, nonbank borrowing and lending that made society vulnerable to quixotic changes in business confidence. Movements such as the use of large-scale bank borrowing and the issuance of junk bonds to finance mergers and acquisitions that have added to debt in the United States and shrank the volume of equity held by the market would have been especially anathema.

These views are more royalist than the king, more Chicagoan than the regular Chicago School which has sought 100 percent reserve banking from time to time, but has wanted at the same time to preserve the greatest possible freedom for persons and firms to advance their own interests within a system of what Adam Smith called "magistracy." This then means regulation.

It is not my task to propose an ideal system of regulation to ensure the quality of debt. If I were able to, as I am not, it would be subject to entropy, the propensity of all systems of organization, especially taxation, to lose efficiency over time as loopholes and end runs develop. Institutional organization is a labor of Sisyphus, *perpetuum mobile.* Edward Kane (1988) of Ohio State University has developed a model of financial regulation that resembles a market, with demands for and supplies of regulation, a number of regulators competing with one another, and something of a cobweb in which the regulators lag behind the regulatees. Competition among regulators is justified by the fear of overregulation that he sees likely as a result of a single regulator or a regulatory cartel. It is not clear to me that such a result inevitably follows: there might well develop symbiosis between regulators and regulatees, such as characterized the Interstate Commerce Commission and the railroads, the Federal Communications Commission and the radio and television industry, the Maritime Commission and shipping interests, and perhaps some public utilities commissions and the utilities. A third possibility is that the lag in regulation behind financial innovation lengthens through the inattention of regulators, like the sleep that seems to have prevailed in the control rooms of nuclear power plants. When problems are few, there would likely be a drift of top flight personnel into more challenging fields out of the regulatory agencies, leaving them handicapped when a boom supervenes with its push to reduce lending and investing standards.

It would be convenient if one could devise a numerical measure of debt quality overall, like air or water quality. There are those who say that if you cannot measure something, it doesn't exist. The Harry Trumans of the world don't want a discussion of a problem, with "on the one hand" and "on the other": they want a number.

A valiant attempt at producing a number is Raymond Goldsmith's

(1969) Financial Interrelation Ratio (FIR), representing the volume of all financial assets, including those of financial institutions, household and government bodies, compared with gross national product. Goldsmith's interest was in development, and he determined that this ratio started at about 0.20 in underdeveloped economies and rose with development to about 1.5 when it leveled off. This was an empirical finding published in 1969, when Goldsmith wrote of a "full complement of financial institutions," before the flowering of the Eurocurrency market, credit cards, money market funds, repurchase agreements (repos), negotiable orders of withdrawal (NOW accounts), certificates of deposit (CDs), options, futures, Third World syndicated bank loans, and the like. Debt in the United States grew rapidly from the 1970s, and now runs about three times gross national product. This takes us back to the quantity of debt, as discussed by Benjamin Friedman and Henry Kaufman, an advance over the concentration on the quantity of money, but still short of adequate attention to quality. Rapid increases in quantity are doubtless associated with declines in quality. Kaufman is properly concerned about the substitution of debt for equity—leading away from the stern line of Henry Simons. But Minsky's (1982) concern with debt structures, flawed though his taxonomy may be, calls attention to a critical dimension of an economy's stability or fragility.

Is it proper to call attention to a problem if one lacks all solution except for continuous surveillance and action to contain financial quality when it threatens to get out of hand? I think so. I hope so.

REFERENCES

Crouzet, F., "Opportunity and Risk in Atlantic Trade during the French Revolution," paper presented to the International Symposium in honor of Professor Wolfram Fischer, Berlin (6–7 May 1988).
Friedman, B. J., "The Roles of Money and Credit in Economic Analysis," in James Tobin (ed.), *Macroeconomics, Prices and Quantities: Essays in Memory of Arthur M. Okun* (Washington, D.C.: Brookings, 1983).
Friedman, Milton, *The Optimum Quantity of Money and Other Essays* (Chicago: Aldine, 1963).
Giddy, Ian, "Regulation of Off–Balance Sheet Banking," in Federal Reserve Bank of San Francisco, *The Search for Financial Stability: The Last Fifty Years* (San Francisco, 1985).
Goldsmith, R., *Financial Structure and Development* (New Haven: Yale University Press, 1969).
Hawtry, R. G., *Currency and Credit* (London: Longmans, Green, 1919).

Kane, E., "How Market Forces Influence the Structure of Financial Regulation," paper for the American Enterprise Institute's Financial Market Project (February 1988).

Kaufman, H., *Interest Rates, the Markets, and the New Financial World* (New York: Times Books, 1986).

Kindleberger, Charles P., *Manias, Panics and Crashes: A History of Financial Crises* (New York: Basic Books, 1978).

Minsky, H. P., "The Financial-Instability Hypothesis: Capitalist Processes and the Behavior of the Economy," in C. P. Kindleberger and J. P. Laffargue (eds.), *Financial Crises: Theory, History and Policy* (Cambridge: Cambridge University Press, 1982).

Samuelsson, Kurt, "International Payments and Credit Movements by Swedish Merchant-Houses, 1730–1815." *Scandinavian Economic History Review,* vol. 3 (1955).

Simons, H., *Economic Policy for a Free Society* (Chicago: University of Chicago Press, 1948).

CHAPTER 10

Intermediation, Disintermediation, and Direct Trading

I owe a large intellectual debt to Hyman Minsky who got me to think about instability in financial markets. It may be appropriate in a paper with this title to indicate that I got to Minsky's writings through the intermediation of Martin Mayer, author of *The Bankers* and many other popular works on the economy of our time. I mentioned my interest in financial crises, and Mayer asked whether I knew of Minsky's work. Like many an intermediary, he had, as far as I was concerned, a monopoly of information. After this information had been diffused, I have profited greatly over the years by dealing with Hy in "direct trading."

The concept of intermediation I propose to discuss is primarily economic and financial. Allow me, however, to display my interdisciplinary knowledge by noting that the idea is of greater applicability. Talcott Parsons somewhere wrote that governesses or nannies intermediate between parents and children, especially, I admit, in England. And that in the military, noncommissioned officers intermediate between commissioned officers and privates. To use a different social science, President Theodore Roosevelt intermediated between Japan and Czarist Russia in Portsmouth in 1905, as President Jimmy Carter did between Egypt and Israel at Camp David, and is attempting to do again, as I write, between Ethiopia and its former province, Eritrea, now independent.

Sometimes middlemen are not in the middle, so to speak. Michel Crozier's (1964) *The Bureaucratic Phenomenon* notes that face-to-face communication in governmental hierarchy in France is fraught with tension so that an official at level E will communicate with his superior at D by going above him and dealing through C. More nearly akin to economic and financial considerations is the public relations officer with a monopoly of information who stands between high governmental or business officials and the public.

Reprinted from Steven Fazzari and Dimitri B. Papadimitriou, eds., *Financial Conditions and Macroeconomic Performance: Essays in Honor of Hyman P. Minsky* (Armonk, N.Y.: M. E. Sharpe, 1992), 71–84.

On a macrosociological level, the existence of a large middle class contributes to political stability as it narrows the gap for bright and aggressive members of the lower class to cross as they rise. The middle class also cushions the decline of the elite, including younger sons in a system of primogeniture, and reduces the risk of polarization of society.

To extend the sociological aspects of the subject one iota, observe that when children grow up they no longer need the intermediation of a nanny, if they ever did, and communicate with their parents, in direct trading, often with ruthless bluntness.

But let me narrow the focus to economics and finance. More than a quarter of a century ago, John Gurley and Edward Shaw (1960) produced a path-breaking book, *Money in a Theory of Finance,* which developed the theory of intermediation as the key to monetary and other financial institutions. As they viewed the process, financial structures in an economy developed in evolutionary fashion; from self-financing, to direct financing, to indirect financing through financial intermediaries. Some, but not overwhelming, attention was paid to disintermediation as a pathological process. They did not, however, envisage a further step, relevant today, of a return to direct financial contacts between borrower and lender when the advantage of the banking intermediary has been lost. I have in mind, especially, direct purchases of certificates of deposit and securities issued by large industrial corporations, bought by large pension funds and insurance companies. But first I want to extend the economic theory of intermediation to markets in general, and offer an analogy between goods markets and financial markets, using a bit of the economic history with which I have been keeping myself pleasantly occupied for some years. I will not test your patience by going back millennia in history, but start with such a stapling center as Amsterdam.

Amsterdam happened to be well located, close to the junction between the Atlantic (and the Mediterranean) and the Baltic and North Seas, handy to Britain, and connected by the Rhine and the Meuse to a vast hinterland. After the fall of Antwerp to Spanish attackers in 1585, Amsterdam became an entrepôt center. Its merchants were divided among the First, Second and Third Hand—from which we get these expressions. The First Hand, engaged in "distant trade," brought goods from abroad to the city and took them away again. The Second Hand broke bulk, stored goods, performed other intermediating functions, and repackaged the goods. Repackaging, for example, was necessary if grain from Danzig in Poland was not to explode under the hot Mediterranean sun as a consequence of spontaneous combustion, as it was being delivered say to Leghorn. Wines from Bordeaux were brought to Amsterdam in casks and sometimes bottled there, as free ports do today. The Third Hand sold at retail the small proportion of the total trade that remained in the United Provinces of Holland.

The First Hand had a monopoly of information and of capital; information as to what goods were available where, and what were wanted where. It intermediated by place and risk, and with the help of the Second Hand, by scale. The Second Hand also intermediated by social status, as it traded with the imperious leaders of the Dutch Republic—the First Hand—which clung tightly to power.

Adam Smith wrote the Bible for economists, *The Wealth of Nations,* and it is perhaps impious on my part to take exception to two of his remarks about merchants. In the first, he claimed that a little grocer in a seaport town had all the attributes of a great merchant except capital (1776, 112). This is far from the case as one contemplates the need to learn languages, and to acquire much wider knowledge of accounting, exchange rates, the qualities of goods, their prices, and the markets where they can be bought cheapest and sold at the highest prices. In the second, he stated that the merchant should normally be located at one end of a trade route or the other, in the instant case at Königsberg in East Prussia or Lisbon in Portugal, rather than midway between. But he stayed in Amsterdam and brought his goods there because he was uneasy at being separated from his capital and wanted it under his view, despite the double charges for loading and unloading along with some duties and customs (422). This explanation ignores the functions of intermediating by size and risk, and it assumes that the merchants were, at least in some degree, irrational. By calling attention to the extra charges of handling merchandise in an entrepôt center, however, Dr. Smith made clear the origins of direct trading when the monopoly of information of the great merchants had been dissipated by diffusion, and these costs could be saved.

But intermediation in trade does not persist. When the information monopoly that gave rise to it dissipates, direct trading is substituted for intermediation in goods. Exeter undertook to trade its serges directly to Spain, and Hull its woolen piece goods to Hamburg. London was for long the great exporter of raw materials from the Empire, but in due course, Scandinavia would trade directly with Australia, for example, and British reexports shrank to a small percentage of total exports from figures that previously approached 30 percent. Some intermediation in goods continues, to be sure, where simple processing was called for by the economics of transportation, especially downscaling the final delivery of goods shipped in bulk from the original source. Where it was possible to save handling and the middleman's profit, however, direct trade took over as knowledge of needs and availabilities was widely diffused.

Let me indulge in a bit of Ciceronian rhetoric and say I would enjoy going on discussing intermediation in trade and its replacement by direct trading if space permitted—the Hanseatic merchants, hated by the inland towns on the ground that the merchants set prices at which the towns had to trade and had the power to ruin a country (Moser 1944, 197); Sweden trying to bypass Lübeck in the seventeenth century by selling its copper directly to Amsterdam (Glamann 1971, 456); German and Italian merchants deserting the Lyons fairs at the end of the sixteenth century to exchange goods through the Alpine passes, escaping the heavy taxation of the French monarchy (Boyer-Xambeu, Deleplace, and Gillard 1986, 155); nineteenth-century British merchants who slowed down technical change in cotton yarns and machine tools, telling producers "they don't want them like that" while simultaneously telling customers "they don't make them like that" even though the elimination of the middleman would allow producer and buyer to discuss together and agree on the nature of improved quality and whether it was worth the cost (Kindleberger 1964, 148–49); and, the elimination of jobber and wholesaler by American corporations as they rose in scale from local to regional to national and took the marketing function into the firm for direct buying and selling (Chandler 1962).

Middlemen have long been excoriated and defended. Oscar Wilde said that a publisher is simply a useful middleman between author and reader with no right to express an opinion on the value of what he publishes, while Disraeli wrote "It is well known what a middleman is: he is one who bamboozles one party and plunders the other" (Cole 1989). A newspaper columnist on economics has felt the need to defend middlemen (Warsh 1989). I neither defend nor attack, but observe that intermediaries exist at an early stage of trade, and are usually replaced in due course by direct trade to save transport costs and one layer of profit. The market in the middle may have an artificial monopoly which it guards jealously, as did the Merchant Staplers of Britain selling wool on the continent (Braudel 1986, 448–49), or Danzig with the "privilege of being the only professional middlemen between Polish and West European merchants" (Federowicz 1976, 362). But competition nibbles away at most monopolies in goods, and monopolizing intermediators, as a rule, give way to direct trade.

Our interest, however, is in finance, not trade. Financial centers last longer than trade centers, I hypothesize, because the costs of transport in money—more generally transactions costs—are trivial compared with those in goods. Many trade centers, notably Amsterdam, London, and New York, shifted over from trade to financial intermediation when their informational monopolies in goods eroded and their appetite for risk diminished with rising wealth. But let me proceed more slowly by discussing the various bases for intermediating between borrower and lender.

One ancient basis had to do with social status. Nobles would be contaminated if they dealt directly with commoners, but had less hesitation in doing so through the intermediation of scriveners, notaries, goldsmiths, bankers; in France, *officers* and *financiers* who were holders of particular offices bought from the king. A rapid expansion of intermediary lending can be seen in comparative statics in the rise of the number of scriveners from "several" in the first decade of the seventeenth century to "at least 30 by 1630" (Parker 1974, 537).

One particular form of social intermediation was intimately bound up in risk—lending to the sovereign. The king could not be sued to collect unpaid debts owed by him, so that there was a need for special protection. This included lending on the crown jewels, the grant of a monopoly in the form of a tax, or the collateral of productive assets such as the silver mines of the Tyrol or the mercury mines of Almaden in Spain, both acquired by the Fuggers when their loans were defaulted on. The Spanish *asientos* (a form of loan to the King) were usually accompanied by a permit, which had value, to export silver. Or a member of the king's household, like Sir Stephen Fox in the court of Charles II, would borrow from the public to lend to the king, because the king was unlikely to welsh on a debt to an intimate (Clay 1978). Lionel Cranfield was a courtier of James I who lent to the monarch and borrowed to do so, including once from the merchant and early economic writer Thomas Mun, author of the great book, *England's Treasure by Forraign Trade.* One is surprised to find R. H. Tawney surprised to find that in 1641, financiers called upon to lend to the crown borrowed from others to be able to do so (1958, 107). And of course in France, many of those who paid the court large sums for offices to farm taxes or to take over various monopolies, like that in tobacco, borrowed from the public to obtain the needed capital (Dent 1973).

This antiquarian information has some relevance to the world of today because of the issue of syndicated bank debt by sovereign Third World countries. (This problem was discovered by most of the world in August 1982 when the Mexican debt crisis was revealed, but was apparent to academic observers more than half a decade earlier [see Goodman, ed., 1978]). There is something of a puzzle here that despite an impressive record of default by sovereign debtors, the investing public, including bankers who are presumably sophisticated in such matters, has often taken a childishly optimistic view of foreign government debt. I need not go back to the miserable record of Edward III of England whose defaults were said to have ruined the Bardi, Peruzzi, and Aicobaldi banks of Florence and Lucca (but see Hunt 1990) or to those of Philip II of Spain which undid the Fuggers, Welzers, and the bankers of Genoa. To a world that believes in any degree of rational expectations it is bizarre that French investors were trusting of Czarist Russia in the years from 1888 to 1913. A false analogy presumably was developed between lending to one's own sovereign, who could pay his debts by printing money, and lending to a foreign sovereign who lacks capacity to produce foreign exchange.

After intermediation by social status and to overcome sovereign immunity, I come to intermediation by place. In his classic, *Lombard Street,* Walter Bagehot discusses how the bankers of rich agricultural counties like Somersetshire and Hampshire discounted the bills of the industrial counties of Yorkshire and Lancashire ([1873] 1978, 53), illustrating the process with the testimony of a London bill broker before an 1810 Commission of Inquiry (ibid., 191–93). He claimed, moreover, that the practice still prevailed 60 years later, though in his introduction to Bagehot's *Collected Works,* R. S. Sayers denies it (ibid., 35, 193).

Intermediation by place took other forms. In England, areas with excess savings initially bought bills on places with deficits, through London brokers, but gradually they established a branch in London, or bought out an existing bank there. Banks needing money did the same to obtain funds. London banks in due course established national networks to bring savings efficiently from where they were abundant to where they were needed. For a time, provincial banks with a branch or subsidiary in London could pay depositors at the head office a fixed low rate of interest, whereas the London rate varied with bank rate. In time, the provincial depositors learned to move their funds to London when bank rate went to 4 percent or above. When enough depositors learned this, such a bank as Lloyds of Birmingham learned that it had to maintain a single deposit rate for the entire system (Sayers 1957, 165, 270).

In France, as Jean Bouvier's masterly account of the growth of the *Crédit lyonnais* tells us, Henri Germain started the bank in Lyons, which was heavy with capital accumulated in the silk business, went to Paris in due course to place the monies, and then built a network throughout France. The *Crédit lyonnais* favored those communities with excess savings, at the expense of those that were eager for loans, in order to accumulate funds to use in foreign lending. Deep students of my work on financial centers may remember the riddle: What do the Midland

Bank, the Dresdener Bank, the Bank of Montreal, Bank of Nova Scotia, First Boston Corporation, and the *Crédit lyonnais* have in common? The answer is that the head office of each is located in a different city (or area) than that noted in the institution's name (1978, 67).

Place intermediation, through commercial banks in the United States, has been held back by rules against branch banking, rules now in process of being eased. Savings banks and savings and loan associations, both of which originally provided finance for home building, furnish a good example of the process. In the last decades of the nineteenth century, mortgage markets were regionally segmented by size of city and region, with a spread that ranged from 5.60 percent in cities within 25 miles of New England population centers with more than 100,000 people, to 9.76 percent for banks in the West within 25 miles of towns of 8,000 to 25,000 (Snowden 1988, 278). Such segmentation continued into the early twentieth century for savings institutions. There were some national players like insurance companies that were embarrassed when they felt it necessary to foreclose on farm mortgages in the 1930s, but these were not large enough to close the gap. With a wave of building in the West after World War II, especially in California, a number of thrifts in that state advertised in New York papers for deposits by mail at rates one percentage point or more above rates in the East. Further integration of the market for mortgage money came through Veterans Administration lending and the creation of the Federal National Mortgage Association and the Government National Mortgage Association, known familiarly as "Fannie Mae" and "Ginnie Mae," respectively. When savings bank disintermediation began in the late 1970s and early 1980s, savings banks replaced lost local deposits by borrowing on the national market for CDs. Most recently the packaging of mortgage lending has been undertaken by private as well as government institutions, and some of these packages of diversified mortgages (and automobile loans, installment and credit card paper, and in Britain, export credits) are sold internationally. The intermediation through risk involved in this diversification is discussed below. It is not clear to me whether the private "securitization" of mortgage loans is diversified as to place, like those of Fannie and Ginnie Mae, or are localized.

The securitization of mortgages involves intermediation by size as well as place, and in this instance there is no progression for the small borrower that leads on to direct trading. I do have an illustration of direct trading replacing intermediation in information, if not in mortgage money on houses. In 1974 in discussing the finance of offshore drilling for oil and gas, I asked a banker in Aberdeen whether he would seek information on the subject from his London correspondent who would get it from New York. The answer was that Aberdeen would deal directly with Houston.

Intermediation by size is wider and more commonplace than the foregoing illustration of securitization of mortgages, auto loans, installment paper, and the like. Typically people of small means deposit their savings with intermediaries who lend it in larger volume. This is the essence of the classic function of banks in the "mobilization of loan capital," to use an expression of Ehrenberg ([1895] 1928, 328–29). A strong element of intermediation by risk is involved, because the small saver is typically uninformed about the credit standing of the ultimate borrower and relies on the banking intermediary to lend only to creditworthy individuals and firms. The ignorance of the small depositor, as opposed to the reputed financial sophistication of the large, is of course the basis for limits on governmental deposit insurance in the United States, limits that have been increased with inflation and real wealth from $5,000, originally to $10,000, then $40,000, and now $100,000. There are, moreover, occasions, such as the financial crisis involving the Continental Illinois Bank, when the Federal Deposit Insurance Corporation has guaranteed foreign deposits of more than $100,000 in order to stop a run on a bank, making clear that the purpose of deposit insurance is more to stop runs—the extreme form of disintermediation—than it is to protect small savers. One could perhaps argue that wealthy foreigners may legitimately be more ignorant of the condition of American banks than U.S. residents, but the reasoning is not persuasive. As a classic example of intermediation by size, some years ago it was common knowledge that the Eurodollar market would not take deposits of less than $25,000, nor make loans below $1 million.

Intermediation by size occurs outside of banks in odd-lot houses that break bulk for small investors trading in securities in amounts of less than one hundred shares. At the other end of the scale, trading in lots of thousands of shares is mostly undertaken directly off the floor of the intermediating Stock Exchange, to get the benefit of lower or zero commissions.

Direct dealing between borrower and lender for large loans, cutting out the intermediation of banks, is one of the major innovations in finance in recent years, according to the Cross report (BIS 1986). Pension funds and insurance companies, dealing in large sums of money, are able to judge credit risks through treasurer departments peopled with finance analysts, and to lend with assured safety on certificates of deposit issued by nonfinancial companies or on securities placed directly with them. The banks have begun to miss out on a large portion of industrial loans for the larger companies, and this development is responsible for their intense lobbying for the repeal of the Glass-Steagall Act of 1933 that separated institutions into banks on the one hand, and investment houses on the other, forbidding banks to underwrite the issue of securities. Some of the smaller banks with a deep clientele of middle-size industrial companies with small financial staffs and a need for financial advice that banks traditionally provided, continue to do well. I vividly recall, however, hearing from the chief executive officer of a $400 million-a-year sales company—a big number at the time—that he refused to maintain a compensating balance at his bank, and when the bank president protested and justified such a balance on the ground of providing the company with a variety of services, he interrupted to say that the banks should charge the company for any service it asked for. He not only would not carry a compensating balance, but would, in fact, ride the float and make the treasurer's office in his company a profit center.

The loss of the loan business of large companies has led the banks to seek other sorts of business; some as more nearly "merchant banks," giving financial advice to various kinds of business for fees. Other banks began dealing in financial instruments such as swaps, repos, futures, and the like; still others providing accounting and transfer services to such institutions as mutual funds. In many instances, the loss of the ordinary run of large business loans has led banks to take more risky roads into construction loans, bridge loans for takeover firms, and junk bonds. It is not clear to me whether the surge in Third World debt in the 1970s was related to the shrinkage of ordinary loan outlets or not. In any case, the rise of direct trading between trade and industry on the one hand, and nonbank financial firms on the other has diverted a great many banks from their wonted paths into risky endeavors in which they now find themselves uncomfortable or worse.

The $100,000 limit on deposit insurance led to another form of intermediation by size that was less than salubrious for the economy as a whole; namely, the growth of deposit brokers who took large sums of deposit money and divided them into amounts of less than $100,000 to distribute among weak thrift institutions that had to pay more than standard deposit rates to attract funds. The practice keeps third-rate institutions alive longer than they would otherwise remain. A high deposit rate is normally a sign that the saving bank is in trouble, but the practice of breaking bulk of large sums to provide the weak bank with extra protection is dysfunctional for the system as a whole. It both encourages risk taking and paralyzes the conservative and well-managed thrifts through disintermediation.

Bank competition for deposits led the way, from demand deposits that earned no interest, to Negotiable Orders of Withdrawal (NOW) accounts that did, thus depriving the banks of seignorage. Before the innovation, demand depositors could have been regarded as exploited by banks, which got something for nothing, or very little. Alternatively, demand deposits could be viewed as providing needed liquidity, such liquidity being a service rendered by the bank in time intermediation. Whichever view one takes of non-interest-bearing demand deposits, their demise and the need to "buy" deposits has reduced the earnings of banks on intermediation by size. Foreign banks in Paris which had to buy all their deposits were at a strong disadvantage vis-à-vis domestic banks which attracted the deposits of Frenchmen on which no interest was paid (Koszul 1972). The shift to NOW accounts in the United States has meant that domestic banks had to buy their deposits, as do foreign banks, increasing the degree of international competition.

Banks intermediate not only by place and size of wealth holding, but also by time and risk. For time, it is evident that savers and borrowers have different time preferences. Savers want liquidity, borrowers to have their debts stretched out in time. Banks intermediate by lending long and borrowing short. They can provide liquidity to savers because not all savers will want their money simultaneously—a diversification effect. J. K. Price in discussing British overseas trade historically notes that wholesalers in Britain provided easy credit to exporters who, in turn, gave long credits to their foreign customers. The lengths of credit were equivalent, and most merchants had balance sheets dominated by accounts receivable and debts owed, with little in the way of fixed capital (1989, 278). This reflects a fairly primitive stage in financial development to such an extent that it merits attention.

There was an era in which savings institutions narrowed the gap in time between assets and deposits by requiring notice on deposit withdrawals. Commercial banks made sharp distinctions between demand and time deposits. Fixed terms remain in effect, today, on certificates of deposit, but most savings and time deposits are available on demand. And demand deposits—NOW accounts—earn interest along with time deposits. The threat of disintermediation runs from bank deposits, both commercial and thrift, to money funds, which have the advantage over banks in that there are no legal reserve requirements. Most, too, allow a certain amount of check writing, or easy indirect access to the money on demand. The sharp rise in interest rates at the beginning of the 1980s led to outflows of money from banks to money funds from which it was loaned back to banks again, in certificates of deposits, at higher interest rates. This was not so much disintermediation, perhaps, as reintermediation.

An ironic point is worth mentioning. The small saver in a poor neighborhood generally left his money in savings banks at 5 or 5½ percent interest, without realizing that money funds were available to pay higher returns. The sophistication that produced disintermediation from banks to money funds in prosperous cities and towns was absent in poor neighborhoods. Thus their savings banks, and similar institutions such as credit unions, continued to earn good returns in the 1980s, when the institutions that had been well located in terms of wealth suffered from disintermediation. With higher interest rates they lost deposits and had to borrow in the open market so as not to have to sell their fixed-rate assets—mortgages and bonds—at the lower prices produced by increases in interest rates.

Intermediation by time is still required, but is taking place increasingly through futures markets as opposed to direct dealing. Banks and nonfinancial firms can find that pattern of liquidity that suits them in terms of cash flows in and out through forward contracts that adjust the time profile of anticipated receipts and payments. There remain solvency risks in such contracts, but their use is to fine-tune liquidity. Some years ago I observed that a number of companies would adjust their time preferences as to liquidity through their own intermediation, borrowing long in the Eurobond market when they planned a project, and depositing the funds in the Eurodollar market, so as to have the funds on hand when they were needed. This could be regarded as a form of direct trading within the firm, with the cost of purchasing liquidity represented by the difference between the long- and short-term rates of interest.

Another form of direct trading is the practice of Japanese groups that combine banks and insurance companies with manufacturing and chemical companies so as to be certain to have a source of financing always available. This is a form of vertical integration that applies also in some industries, controlling sources of supply and outlets in order to avoid the risk of interruption from breakdown of the market for inputs or outputs. Where inputs are bulky and difficult to store, as in coal or oil, control through ownership was thought necessary since interruption could not be forestalled by the maintenance of sizable inventories. Some of this vertical integration varied with the business cycle, to be sure; oil companies being readier to own tankers in tight markets and to rely on the market when tanker rates were slack. The move to just-in-time scheduling of materials and components made possible by computers reduces, further, the need to store inputs, just as futures contracts make it less necessary to store cash.

Intermediation by risk is connected with that by time and size. The small saver lends to one intermediary who both accumulates savings for large loans, and diversifies by lending to more than one borrower. The diversification should reduce default risk, although if the intermediary is badly or dishonestly managed, perhaps excessively speculative in its investments, the depositor's presumed gain through reduced default risk from diversification is lost.

In addition to default risk, there is interest-rate risk. With a true time deposit, the depositor has a chance of gain when competitive interest rates decline, an opportunity-cost loss if they rise. The major interest-rate risk in intermediation, however, is that of the bank, as it lends long and borrows short. If its assets are in fixed-rate loans, securities, or mortgages for extended time periods, and interest rates rise, it may both lose depositors and suffer reductions in the value of its assets, even though the latter loss may be disguised by continuing to carry the assets on the books at cost. In recent years, banks and other lenders have sought to escape interest-rate risk by changing the rates paid for deposits on the one hand, and those charged on loans and mortgages on the other. But of course variable rates do not reduce risk overall. They shift it from the bank to the depositor and the borrower.

In one view the role of the intermediary in reducing risk for the lender (or depositor) is less connected with information than with reputation (Terlizzese 1989). The good reputation of a bank or other intermediary rests in the belief of the depositor that the intermediary understands the nature of risks and how to manage them. That view has had to undergo modification when the carefree lending and buying of junk bonds following the 1982 deregulation of the thrifts was exposed to light. But of course information and reputation are closely connected.

International intermediation by reputation has come to attention recently with some striking examples. Christopher Platt has examined the books of the Baring Brothers bank in London in the 1840s and been struck by the fact that gross and net lending by Britain to France differed sharply since much of the French bonds issued in London were bought by Frenchmen. There were elements of size involved, to be sure, as the London bond market was larger than that in Paris, and hence more liquid. But French investors felt safer lending to their own government and new railroads through the City, rather than directly, on the basis that the city's reputation for financial acumen was greater. Later, London issued bonds for the Argentine government bought by Argentinians as well as by British and other investors. There was an element of exchange risk here, as there may have been in European issues of dollar bonds in New York after World War II bought by Europeans. Such risk was minimal in the London-French case of the 1840s given the long-established gold standard. Platt notes that the standard estimates for the British capital outflow before 1914 must be reduced considerably to make allowance for these purchases by the borrowing countries. While this is doubtless true for France and Argentina, there is not, so far as I am aware, evidence that similar differences between net and gross existed for dominion borrowers such as Australia, Canada, and New Zealand.

Somewhat further away from this lending from national creditors to a national debtor through the intermediation of an outside country is that seen by Bacha and Diaz-Alejandro (1982), in their well-known article "International Financial Intermediation: A Long and Tropical View." Here, firms and governments in Third World countries borrowed from U.S. banks at a time when wealth holders in those countries undertook to protect their capital by escaping foreign-exchange control and piling up deposits in U.S. banks, often the same ones. There was no intention on the part of, say Argentine or Mexican, capitalists to lend to their governments through foreign banks; it was nonetheless a form of international intermediation by size and exchange risk.

Still another form of international intermediation by reputation involving the Third World occurred after the OPEC price rise of 1973. One oil expert thought it would have been desirable for the OPEC countries to sell oil to nonoil Third World countries on credit terms (Levy 1982, 245, 266). The producing countries evidently thought otherwise, presumably on the ground that the credit standings of the importers were weaker than those of world-class banks. In consequence they sold only for dollars, with cash on the barrelhead, so to speak. This produced "recycling" as it was then called, but which, in our terms, is international intermediation by reputation, the OPEC countries lending to the Eurodollar market, and the Eurodollar banks lending to the Third World, both oil producers such as Mexico and Venezuela, and the importers.

I have pointed out that the displacement (to use Minsky's term), or exogenous shock, that gave rise to the lending in the first place antedated the November 1973 price rise by a couple of years. In 1970 and 1971, the United States tried to lower interest rates in the interest of President Nixon's reelection campaign at a time when the Bundesbank was tightening interest rates to curb inflation. Money poured out of the United States into the Eurodollar market. As interest rates fell, the world banks sought out new borrowers and found them in the Third World.

Intermediation then, by social status, place, time, and various sorts of risk, whether because of monopolized information or reputation, is continuously threatened by disintermediation, which may be intermediation through a different medium and by direct trading. I hazard the guess that intermediation by social status is a thing of the past, although the point about blue-collar neighborhoods being less subject to disintermediation than white-collar areas suggests a vestigial remnant of the effect. Intermediation by place would seem to be stretched to the limit in a world of ubiquitous computers connected by modems, facsimile machines, and copiers. That by time, and to a certain extent by risk, will compete with new financial instruments such as swaps, options, and the like. The troubles of the junk-bond market would appear to dampen the enthusiasm of some groups for intermediation by default risk, for example in the funds collected by leveraged buyout (LBO) firms to use as bridge loans or equity investment in takeovers.

While intermediation by size changes its form as pension funds and insurance companies achieve a scale where they trade directly with large borrowers issuing notes and securities, that for smaller amounts will doubtless continue. The banking function of providing financial services to smaller companies that choose not to build their own treasurer's department to cover all their financial needs will last. In theory, there should be an advantage in having an outside opinion to guard against intellectual autointoxication, but the herdlike behavior of financial markets in the 1980s raises the question whether outside opinion givers are independent of the waves of financial fashion.

It is likely that the size of companies moving to direct trading will shrink with time, but intermediation as a basic economic function is almost certainly here to stay. At the last minute, however, strong evidence of the loss of business to direct trading at major U.S. banks came with the second quarter of 1990 profit returns, and the efforts of Citicorp and Chase Manhattan to reduce their staffs.

> The need for cost cutting is especially evident for banks like Chase and Citicorp, which have been hurt by a decline in wholesale lending and other financing for large corporations. While the banks still maintain expensive networks of foreign offices, corporate treasurers have learned how to borrow money more cheaply in the securities markets or from foreign banks. (*New York Times* 1990, 29)

An awareness of economic history might have forestalled the buildup now being trimmed down.

REFERENCES

Bacha, Edmar Lisboa, and Carlos F. Diaz-Alejandro. 1982. *International Financial Intermediation: A Long and Tropical View.* Essays in International Finance, No. 147. Princeton, N.J.: Princeton University International Finance Section.

Bagehot, Walter. [1873] 1978. *Lombard Street.* In N. St. John-Stevas, ed., *The Collected Works of Walter Bagehot,* volume 9. London: *The Economist,* 45–233.

Bank for International Settlements. 1986. *Recent Innovations in International Banking.* The Cross Report, prepared by a study group established by the central banks of the Group of Ten countries. Basle: B.I.S.

Bouvier, Jean. 1961. *Le Crédit Lyonnais de 1863 à 1882: Les Années de Formation D'une Banque de Dépôts,* 2 volumes. Paris: SEVPEN.

Boyer-Xambeu, Marie-Thérèse, Chislain Deleplace, and Lucien Gillard. 1986. *Monnaie Privée et Pouvoir des Princes.* Presses de la foundation nationales des sciences politiques.

Braudel, Fernand. 1986. *Civilization & Capitalism, 15th–18th Century.* Vol. 2. *The Wheels of Commerce,* (translated from the French by Sian Reynolds). New York: Harper & Row.

Chandler, Alfred D. 1962. *Strategy and Structure: Chapters in the History of Industrial Enterprise.* Cambridge, Mass.: Harvard University Press.

Clay, Christopher. 1978. *Public Finance and Private Wealth: The Career of Sir Stephen Fox, 1627–1716.* Oxford: Clarendon Press.

Cole, William Rossa. 1989. "Author and Editor Against the Publisher." *New York Times Book Review* (September 3): 1.

Crozier, Michel. 1964. *The Bureaucratic Phenomenon.* Chicago: University of Chicago Press.

Dent, Julian. 1973. *Crisis in Finance: Crown, Financiers and Society in Seventeenth-Century France.* New York: St. Martin's Press.

Federowicz, Jan K. 1988. "Anglo-Polish Commercial Relations in the First Half of the Seventeenth Century." *Journal of European Economic History* 5: 359–78.

Glamann, Kristof. 1971. "European Trade, 1500–1750." In *The Fontana Economic History of Europe: Volume 2, The Sixteenth and Seventeenth Centuries,* Carlo M. Cipolle, ed. Glasgow: Collins/Fontana, 427–526.

Goodman, Stephen, ed. 1978. *Financing and Risk in Developing Countries.* New York: Praeger.

Gurley, John G., and Edward S. Shaw. 1950. *Money in a Theory of Finance.* Washington, DC: Brookings Institution.

Hunt, Edward S. 1990. "A New Look at the Dealings of the Bardi and Peruzzi with Edward III." *Journal of Economic History* 50: 149–62.

Kindleberger, Charles P. 1964. *Economic Growth in France and Britain, 1851–1950.* Cambridge, Mass.: Harvard University Press.

———. 1978. *Economic Response: Comparative Studies in Trade, Finance and Growth.* Cambridge, Mass.: Harvard University Press.

Kozul, Jean-Pierre. 1970. "American Banks in Europe." In *The International Corporation: a Symposium,* C. P. Kindleberger, ed. Cambridge, Mass.: M.I.T. Press, 273–89.

Levy, Walter J. 1982. *Oil Strategy and Politics, 1941–1981.* Melvin A. Conant ed. Boulder, Colo.: Westview Press.

Moser, Justus. 1969. "Some Thoughts about the Decline of Commerce in Inland

Towns." In *European Society in the Eighteenth Century,* Robert and Elborg Forster, eds. (translated by Gerhard Stalling). New York: Walker & Co., 185–89.

Parker, Geoffrey. 1974. "The Emergence of Modern Finance in Europe, 1500–1730." In *The Fontana Economic History of Europe, Volume 2, The Sixteenth and Seventeenth Centuries,* Carlo M. Cipolle, ed. Glasgow: Collins/Fontana.

Price, Jacob M. 1989. "What Did Merchants Do? Reflections on British Overseas Trade, 1660–1770." *The Journal of Economic History* 49: 267–84.

Platt, D. C. M. 1984. *Foreign Finance in Continental Europe and the USA, 1815–1870, Quantities, Origins, Functions & Distribution.* London: George Allen & Unwin.

Sayers, R. S. 1957. *Lloyds Bank in the History of English Banking.* Oxford: Clarendon Press.

———. 1978. Introduction to *The Collected Works of Walter Bagehot,* N. St. John-Stevas, ed., vol. 9. London: *The Economist.*

Snowden, Kenneth A. 1988. "Mortgage Lending and American Urbanization, 1880–1890." *The Journal of Economic History* 4: 273–86.

Tawney, R. H. 1958. *Business and Politics under James I: Lionel Cranfield as Merchant and Minister.* Cambridge: Cambridge University Press.

Terlizzese, Daniele. 1988. "Delegated Screening and Reputation in a Theory of Financial Intermediaries." *Temi di Discussione,* Banca d'Italia, No. 111.

Warsh, David. 1989. "In Defense of Middlemen." *The Boston Globe* (September 3): 33, 38.

CHAPTER 11

The Lender of Last Resort: Pushing the Doctrine Too Far?

I perhaps owe this distinguished gathering an apology for recurring once again to the doctrine of lender of last resort. The late Fred Hirsch brought the subject to the forefront of discussion with a brilliant paper half a generation ago (Hirsch 1977). Hugh Rockoff discussed it earlier in this series honoring Henry Thornton (1986). Governor Carlo Ciampi of the Bank of Italy lectured on the subject in his own country in February of this year (Ciampi 1992). The issue has been pursued in at least two of my books ([1973] 1986, chaps. 9, 10; [1984] 1993, Chap. 15, but esp. 272–78). On this occasion, however, my purpose is not to defend the doctrine in the face of monetarists who believe that the money supply should be fixed, or grow at a fixed rate, rather than be allowed to expand in periods of widespread illiquidity and distress. That issue, to my mind, has been settled in favor of a lender of last resort in financial crisis. Rather, I suggest this evening that the world may have pushed the doctrine too far with deposit insurance for commercial banks and thrifts, the rescue from bankruptcy of such bodies as New York City, some corporations such as Penn Central, Lockheed, and Chrysler Corporation, banks "too big to fail" even though their deposits exceed insured limits by wide margins, and brokerage houses that loaned to such a commodity speculator as Bunker Hunt, who tried to corner the world silver market in the early 1980s. Even now in Japan, government money is called upon to make whole an institution owned by a rich bank, whose troubles were caused by fraud rather than mistakes (*Economist* 1992, 105). Many high-minded principles suffer from entropy or decay over time, and the lender of last resort may be one of them.

The doctrine was first enunciated by Sir Francis Baring and Henry Thornton at the end of the eighteenth century apropos of a series of recent financial crises, especially that of 1793. It was formulated more

---

Based on the 1992 Henry Thornton Lecture presented at City University Business School, London, November 11, 1992.

precisely by Walter Bagehot, at age 22 in 1848, following the 1847 sus-
pension of the Bank Act of 1844. To quote that paper:

> It can be a great defect of a purely metallic circulation that the
> quantity of it cannot be readily suited to any sudden demand. . . .
> Now as paper money can be supplied in unlimited quantities, how-
> ever sudden the demand may be, it does not appear to us that there
> is any objection on principle to sudden issues of paper money to
> meet sudden and large extensions of demand. . . . This power of
> issuing notes is one excessively liable to abuse. . . . It should only
> be used in rare and exceptional cases . . . when the fact of an exten-
> sive *sudden* demand is proved. . . . (Bagehot [1848] 1978, 9: 267)
> (emphasis in original)

The constant repetition of the word *sudden,* and its emphasis in one
instance, makes clear that Bagehot was thinking at an early age in terms
of what is now known as rational expectations, which makes special
allowance for *unanticipated events.* It is also of some mild interest that
Bagehot, in *Lombard Street,* ascribes the origin of the idea of a lender of
last resort to David Ricardo. However modest on his part, the notion
seems far-fetched ([1873] 1978, 75).

I should perhaps mention in passing T. S. Ashton's view that the
Bank of England and the Exchequer recognized well before economists
laid down rules for treatment of crises that the remedy was an emergency issue of some form of paper that bankers, merchants, and the
general public would accept . . . "until men regained trust in one another," and that the Bank of England was already a lender of last resort
in the eighteenth century (1959, 110–12). In *Lombard Street,* written in
response to the Overend, Gurney failure of 1866, Bagehot refined the
concept of a lender of last resort, calling for the central bank to lend
freely at a penalty rate; freely since limited lending on earlier occasions
in the eighteenth century had increased the panic, and at a penalty rate
to fend off merely precautionary borrowers, who were not in dire straits.

In 1793, the Bank of England stated its invariable practice of discounting only two-months commercial paper on two first-class London
names (Clapham 1945, 1:261). Crisis by crisis the rules were breached as
loans were made on important but not first-class names, on mortgages,
on a coal mine, on a West Indian plantation, on a copper works, and to
three American banks in Liverpool whose initial requests had been
refused (Clapham 1945, 1, 2, passim). As panic and bank runs built up
because of an absence of rescuers on the horizon, central banks and
governments everywhere found it necessary to reverse themselves and

provide the sought-for cash, or make ready to do so, which usually relieved the situation by itself. Often, when one institution had promised not to save banks from the consequences of imprudent speculation or lending, when the crash arrived it preserved its dignity by finding another means, such as the Bank of England in 1826 when Lord Liverpool at the Treasury had sworn not to relieve a liquidity crisis through issuing Exchequer bills, and banking guarantees of Barings liabilities in 1890 when Lord Lidderdale of the Bank of England judged that rescues by the bank were becoming so usual that the market counted on them.

As an aside, I may mention that in writing *Manias, Panics and Crashes,* I came across a remark that in some crisis the bank's lending had not been "over nice." I seemed to have lost the reference, so gave none ([1978] 1989, 196). For some purpose undisclosed to me, my colleague, Stanley Fischer, asked where I had gotten the statement, and I diligently searched my notebooks but to no avail. He then turned to his friend Mervin King, Executive Director of the Bank of England, where research revealed that the characterization had been cited by W. C. T. King in his *History of the London Discount Market* (1936). I had accurately remembered the phrase, but failed to note its provenance. Its origin was from the testimony of Jeremiah Harman, director of the bank between 1794 and 1827, governor in 1817 and 1818, before the 1832 Parliamentary Committee of Secrecy on the Bank of England. The evidence dealt with the bank's response to the crisis of 1825, with the expression furnished in an answer to the question in para. 2217—in case any of you share Professor Fischer's curiosity.

In an episode foreshadowing the United States' troubles of the 1980s and 1990s, the Bank of England yielded to the pleas of the three American "W" banks—Wiggins, Wildes, and Wilson—but failed in the effort to save them, and succeeded in liquidating the assets taken over only fourteen years later (Clapham 1945, 2:157).

After World War I, the Bank of England undertook a wider policy of intervention in industry, along with banking, that Sayers called "out of character" (1976, 1:314). The problems lay particularly in steel, which had experienced a boom immediately after the war, when it appeared that German industry would be out of action for a time. The bank started with a private customer of the Newcastle branch, Armstrong Whitworth, the overdraft for which had been increased in 1918. The company then plunged. By 1925 it was clear that it had made a great many bad investments, and the Bank of England loaned it £2.7 million on the construction of a newsprint plant in Newfoundland. In the end, the bank lost only £200,000 capital, and £300,000 in foregone interest on these operations. In 1928, Vickers Armstrong was formed and received a five-year guarantee of its profit, which cost the bank £1 million over five years. Further complex operations in steel took more and more of the bank's and Governor Norman's time, especially after the Hatry crisis of September 1929. In this, and in its dealings in cotton textiles, the bank tried to keep its activities secret, partly so as not to encourage the Labour Party to involve the rescue operations in politics (Tolliday 1987, esp. chap. 8).

Rescue in cotton textiles was necessitated by the troubles of the Williams Deacon Bank, a London clearing institution with its head office in Manchester, and with, at the end of 1928, advances of £3,770,000 to forty cotton companies. The bank first guaranteed these advances up to £1 million. In an interesting exercise that is now called *conditionality*, to preserve secrecy, the Bank allowed Williams Deacon to maintain its dividend, but not to raise it, and required it to reduce its dividend if any other clearing bank were to do so (Sayers 1976, 1:285). When in 1929 the Royal Bank of Scotland took over Williams Deacon, the Bank of England added a sweetener to the deal by throwing in its own Burlington Gardens branch in western London. Sayers explains that the bank had, on the one hand, lost interest in its own profits from private business, and sought to divert public attention away from the real reason for the merger (ibid., 285–86). All in all, the Bank's net loss was £3.2 million, most of which was written off early.

I shift from London to Italy by an easy transition without getting into the 1974 "lifeboat" operation in favor of the fringe banks, about which you know far more than I. Along with steel and cotton, the bank in 1929 led a rescue of the Banca-Italo Britannica, owned and controlled by a British holding company, in which London clearing banks and a British insurance company were involved, along with some Roman and Milanese banks. Banca-Italo Britannica was operated in Italy, where it suffered from the 1926 deflation, some bad investments, a certain amount of malfeasance in the accounts, plus the tightening of interest rates in the Wall Street boom that started in March 1928. Sayers said that the Banca-Italo was widely regarded as a British responsibility, despite its Italian management. As it began to fail, the Bank of England and the three London clearing banks put up most of the funds to keep it going for a while before it was ultimately wound up. The Bank of England's loss of £250,000—its entire contribution to the rescue—is stated to have been "the cost of saving London from threatened shame" (ibid., 259–62).

Secret rescue, or as the Italians call them *salvage* operations, had been under way for a quarter century as the Bank of Italy took over bad assets of leading banks in financial crises of 1907, 1923, 1926, and 1930.

When the full fury of the 1929 depression broke, the Italian government formed the Istituto Ricostruzione Italiana (IRI) to take over these assets from the Bank of Italy in exchange for government bonds, with the thought that they would be worked off over time. IRI was patterned to some extent after the 1931 Reconstruction Finance Corporation (RFC) in the United States, established to make advances to banks and business with liquidity problems, but handicapped by a Democratic Party requirement in subsequent legislation that loans to banks be made public. This last requirement effectively barred its use for banks, which would, by borrowing, announce that their condition was shaky. Substantial loans were made to industry. When the war came, the RFC was converted into the Defense Plant Corporation (DPC) to simplify the provision of credit to defense industry as compared to reliance on the capital market or commercial banks. In due course, with strong recovery during and after the war, RFC/DPC were able to liquidate all these investments, as companies with profits paid off their loans or bought plants to enable debtors to do so. This was a successful workout without a trace of scandal. IRI, on the other hand, was reorganized. The collection of financial and industrial assets was converted into ownership, and IRI operated the companies concerned, largely because of the difficulty of privatization—to use a current neologism—given a weak Italian capital market and the absence of large wartime corporate profits.

Success in working out bad loans and investments, in contrast to writing them off, depends on one or more of several felicitous circumstances: rapid and strong recovery of the economy and asset prices; a buoyant capital market such as that prevailing in the United States in the postwar "golden years"; and buyers willing to take over failed banks, minus government write-offs. In this last connection, valuations placed on good and bad assets in a financial crisis may not hold up over the long run. The cautionary tale is that of the 1929 threatened failure of the Bodencreditanstalt in Austria, rescued by being taken over by the Creditanstalt, which itself collapsed in May 1931, largely as a consequence of the turning bad of the good assets it had acquired from the Bodencredit.

A conservative view of banking is that assets should always be *marked to market,* and that a bank should be closed down and liquidated if its capital is impaired. I confess I do not understand the reasoning of young Henry Thornton, the nephew, in closing down Pole, Thornton & Company in the crisis of 1825 because, while solvent, he was concerned that if he borrowed a second time to gain liquidity, as all the directors of the Bank of England were willing that he should, it would be taken from him by the country banks for which Pole, Thornton served as London correspondent (Ashton 1953, 102–4). The doctrine of marking to market, however, leaves little room for workouts. It fails, moreover, to recognize the distinction between a mutual fund and a bank, or the functions of banks in issuing liabilities that are used as money. If all loans and investments were traded in efficient markets, assets could be marked to market at appropriate intervals, but unless there were a very large amount of capital, liabilities would have to change correspondingly and could no longer serve as money, which has a fixed price. On the asset side, moreover, cash and investments can be valued regularly, but loans cannot. Securitization of mortgages, credit-card liabilities, and in Britain export credits change the balance between assets that can be valued regularly, and those—loans—that cannot.

One must be careful, too, to insist that the markets in which assets are priced are efficient. At the outbreak of the crisis in Third World debt, a few economists insisted that there were market valuations for some of these loans, such as Mexican bonds. But these quotations were largely nominal, and an attempt to sell a substantial quantity would have quickly disclosed their illiquidity. The same is true of many assets that bulk large in balance sheets, even of central banks. Gold is the classic example. Once the United States closed the gold window in 1968, the metal became a commodity and no longer represented money. The liquidity of asset markets is infinitely graded from short-term government bills at one extreme—although in some financial crises it has been claimed that even they cannot be sold at any (meaning any normal) price—and the junkiest of junk bonds at the other. But as Charles Goodhart ([1972] 1986) and Albert Wojnilower (1992) assert, there is a difference in kind, as well as in degree, between investments salable in a market and loans based upon a relationship with a borrower. The latter are not marked to market except in the doleful circumstances of bankruptcy proceedings that have advanced some distance.

Perhaps the largest step in the progressive breakdown of the pure doctrine of the lender of last resort came with the adoption in the United States of deposit insurance. Its origin in the 1933 depression was in what is now called, somewhat ponderously, asymmetric information, the difference in sophistication between individuals of wealth and substantial corporations and the ordinary householder or small business. The former were thought to be able to judge the solvency of a bank, the latter unable. A limit initially set at $5,000 per depositor was thought adequate to divide the two groups. With inflation after World War II, rather than any extension of financial ignorance, the figure was progressively raised, first to $10,000, then to $20,000, to $40,000, and finally to $100,000. I am told that the $100,000 limit was agreed upon in a Congressional conference committee as a compromise between the House and Senate conferees, one set of which had brought in a bill raising the limit from $40,000 to $50,000, the other from $40 to $60,000.

All was quiet during the golden years to 1973, with deposit insurance coming to the rescue of the few banks in trouble. Difficulties were still minimal in the middle 1970s until the second sharp rise in the price of oil in 1979 that threatened inflation. Banks had been forbidden to pay more than 5½ percent on time deposits under Federal Reserve regulation Q. When interest rates rose sharply from 1979 to 1981, widespread disintermediation took place as sophisticated depositors withdrew time and saving deposits from banks to redeposit them in new money funds that paid higher returns because they were unburdened by ceilings. It is a matter of some cynical interest that savings banks in poor parts of cities or poor regions of the country were not disintermediated because their depositors were not conscious of the opportunity to increase their return on idle cash from 5½ percent to 10 percent or more.

Disintermediation was particularly hurtful to the thrift institutions— savings banks, savings and loan associations, and credit unions—which were limited to a few assets, largely long-term fixed-interest mortgages. Squeezed between the high rates they had to pay to replace the withdrawn deposits and low fixed-interest income, the industry pleaded with Congress to remove limits on what they could pay depositors and for permission to make wider and riskier investments. There was also a shift to the adjustable-rate mortgage, but too late to produce substantial change. Deregulation, however, occurred simultaneously with the development of the so-called junk bond, one below investment grade because of the lesser coverage of interest paid by normal income. The consequence was that a wide number of thrift institutions started to pay high rates of interest to attract deposits and to invest in high-paying risky investments to earn the necessary returns. A further development that increased the ultimate burden to be borne by the Federal Deposit Insurance Corporation (FDIC) and its thrift analogue, the Federal Savings and Loan Corporation (FSLIC, pronounced like a patent medicine, Fislick) was the spontaneous development of a new business of deposit brokering. Substantial deposit amounts would be broken up by these brokers into amounts of less than $100,000 and parceled out among a number of high-interest-paying banks, almost certainly weak, in order to qualify for deposit insurance. This was adverse selection with a vengeance. In retrospect, raising the insurance limit from $10,000 or $20,000 per deposit was a mistake, as the transactions costs of placing, say, $5 million among 500 or 250 banks might not have been worthwhile as compared with 50.

As interest rates paid on deposits rose and investments became riskier, the ethics of old-fashioned banking wore thin and a number of bankers slipped into unseemly ways, buying Rembrandts with bank money to decorate their offices; buying yachts to entertain their boards of directors, and possibly their deposit brokers; and hiring salesmen to persuade unsophisticated depositors to switch out of insured deposits into the bank's uninsured (junk) debentures, this to bolster the banks' capital/deposit ratios. Hundreds of such bankers are currently on trial or in jail in the United States.

The ostensible purpose of deposit insurance was to protect the unsophisticated depositor from the odd failure of an individual bank. At a deeper level, the rationale was to prevent bank runs that might spread to other banks and other localities and thus threaten the safety of the banking system as a whole. It was this purpose, in my judgment, that led to the progressive raising of the insured-deposit limit. It was clearly the motive for saving the Continental Illinois, which had bought a great many oil loans from the high-flying Penn Square Bank of Oklahoma, close to the top of the oil market. With its high interest rates, the Continental Illinois had attracted a lot of Japanese depositors, with large amounts of money, who may or may not have been sophisticated. To avoid a precipitous run and a foreign-exchange crisis, the Continental Illinois was rescued without limit with respect to deposit size, and the doctrine that some banks are too big to fail was born or resurrected. In the same vein, the Federal Reserve System urged the New York banks to rescue J. S. Bache and Company, a brokerage house, not a bank, which had advanced hundreds of millions of dollars to Bunker Hunt when he was trying unsuccessfully to corner the world silver market, loans that he was unable to repay on schedule.

There are two types of bank runs, one by public depositors, the outsiders, the second by other banks that become suspicious of an adventurous bank, perhaps a newcomer trying to push its way into the market; after a time they refuse to accept its paper, its exchange contracts, or to lend it federal funds. This was the fate of the Franklin National Bank in 1974, when other New York banks first approached the Federal Reserve Bank of New York to warn it that the Franklin National was on a dangerous course and, when the Federal Reserve seemed to take no steps to correct the situation, finally stopped dealing with it (Spero 1980).

A recent book on financial crises has some curious remarks about depositor runs. It suggests that the depositors who lead such a movement—called *sequentially served depositors*—are helpful insofar as they monitor the performance of banks (Calomiris and Gorton 1991, 120). One wonders whether they would say the same of those who start panics in theater fires. The authors call this source of bank runs *asymmet-*

ric information: some depositors, and presumably bank officials, know more than others, and contrast it with a separate theory based on *random withdrawals,* such as used to occur in the United States in the nineteenth century when bank credit was strained each fall by the necessity to finance the seasonal movement of crops off the farm. Asymmetric information is measured in another paper in the same volume (Mishkin 1991) by the spread in yields between high-quality assets like treasury bills and commercial papers of equal maturity, or between government or triple A bonds and B bonds, both of which spreads widened in financial crisis. Another term for this phenomenon is a *flight to quality,* as sophisticated investors shift assets to higher-grade (and lower-yield) assets as the banking system moves into distress as it approaches crisis.

In the United States, monitoring of bank performance may have been left to a limited extent to sequentially served depositors, but was legally assigned to government regulators, whose performance in the 1980s left much to be desired. In one view the problem lay in the duplication of bank examinations by the staffs of the Comptroller of the Currency in the U.S. Treasury, the Federal Reserve System, and state bank commissions, plus, to some extent, the personnel of the FDIC and FSLIC. "Shared responsibility," said Ludwig Bamberger, a prominent German banker a century ago, "is no responsibility" (Zucker, 1975, 38). Edward Kane, who is more cynical than I deem is warranted, believes that the multiple layers of examination led to bureaucratic competition in deregulation (Kane 1989). Nor have the legal and accounting professions covered themselves with glory in a number of isolated cases where representatives of each have blessed transactions that later have proved to be some distance below the standards of professional probity. Lenders of last resort in my country have brought suit against lawyers and accountants in these circumstances, but have no chance of recovering any sizable part of the losses from malfeasance. The same problem cropped up last spring in Japan, when Toyo Shinkin, an Osaka-based credit union, forged certificates of deposit and ended up with bad debts of ¥ 252 billion. After trying first to push the loss on the creditors, and then on the Sanwa Bank group that owned Toyo Shinkin, both of which resisted, the Ministry of Finance lay the burden on the official Industrial Bank of Japan, an instance of public money used to make good losses from criminal fraud rather than imprudent lending, although the line between the two, in this age, is sometimes hard to draw (*Economist* 1992, 105).

Choosing between workout or write-off presents an agonizing problem for banks in distress, but equally so for the lender of last resort. Sometimes, of course, a bank will embark on one course and then choose or be obliged to change, as Citicorp did in the spring of 1987 after five years of attempted workout, when it wrote off more than $1½ billion of its Third World sovereign debt. Even more perplexing is the task of the Resolution Trust Corporation (RTC), charged with disposing of the assets taken over by the FDIC and FSLIC from banks that are closed, merged, or bailed out. Substantial cyclical recovery might float some of the boats that look wrecked. On the other hand, the longer the RTC waits, the more its losses mount because of accumulating interest. Other questions are whether to sell off the odds and sods of hotels, office buildings, shopping malls, banking quarters, residential housing, golf courses, and the like at wholesale or retail, and if retail, through regular market channels of brokers or by auction. Decision has been made that the government, that is, the taxpayer, bears the loss, now or in future as debt is paid off, rather than the bank depositor and the holder of bank shares, as in 1930 to 1933.

I came late to at least a partial understanding of the issues through reading, a short time ago, Homer Hoyt's book, *One Hundred Years of Land Values in Chicago,* written in 1933. Hoyt has more detail on the separate sections of that city that grew at various rates during the century in question than interests me, but he is superb on the question of real estate bubbles and their bursting. (Parenthetically, I learned about the book when I made up a list of fifty books to be read for enjoyment and instruction by retired bankers, only to have Moses Abramovitz ask why I left off Hoyt.) Hoyt pointed out that stock market booms often spread to real estate, especially in growing cities, but that their respective downside behavior differs. In a stock market collapse, the shakeout of leveraged speculators is wound up in a matter of months. At the time of the crash, speculators in real estate who had been infected by the euphoria in shares congratulate themselves that they are financed by term loans, rather than day-to-day money, and have real instead of paper assets. In the five crashes in Chicago to 1933 and again in 1987, however, it was not possible to evade the liquidation process in real estate. Interest on real estate loans stayed high, along with taxes on the property. Lenders became shy about renewing or extending loans. Buyers suddenly saw the advantage of waiting, rather than carrying out previous intentions. Rents fell as new speculative buildings came on the market, and their owners had difficulty in selling them or finding tenants. When old leases in existing buildings ran out, existing tenants bargained rents down. Instead of liquidation coming to completion in less than a year, it stretched to four, five, or even more years, with devastating effects on owners and lenders, especially banks. It was this experience that produced the FDIC and later FSLIC. Those of you who watched the Olympia and York story unfold in Canada, New York, and

Canary Wharf will understand the prescience of Homer Hoyt, writing sixty years ago.

Despite widespread opinion to the contrary, it was not the decline in the money supply that produced the depression of 1929 to 1933, but the reverse. Ben Bernanke was correct when he wrote (1983) that tight money could lead to depression otherwise than through the money supply. The analysis applied well to the stock market crash of 1987, which made banks leery of lending and produced a delayed but sharp collapse in real estate, bursting the bubble of the 1980s. In 1929, however—at least in my opinion—the effect was felt immediately on commodity prices, as banks in trouble because of illiquid brokers' loans rationed credit to commodity brokers, who were thus unable to clear commodity markets of goods shipped to New York on commission at anything close to prevailing prices. This effect could not recur in 1987 because imported commodities in the United States are bought in the exporting country, not sold on arrival in New York. The major impact in the 1929 depression of falling commodity prices in the first few weeks after the stock market crash has been questioned lately by Barry Eichengreen, who observes that the same mechanism did not operate in London, where brokers' loans were much less substantial than in New York. The reasoning seems not to take into account the fact that if prices of internationally traded goods fall in one market they fall in all (1992, 230).

As lender of last resort, the Resolution Trust Corporation seems still, at the time of writing, to be experimenting with how to handle the disposal of its ragbag of assets. With only a few assets of modest value at any one time, the Bank of England could work off its acquisitions slowly and secretly, covering losses by annual modest charges against profits. In the United States today, the problem is far too substantial to allow such a relatively happy solution. To sell in large batches runs the risk of awarding profits to wealthy capitalists so large as to give rise to an echo of the scandals that contributed to the lamentable problem.

A precedent exists in Italian history, where just after unification in 1860 in which the new kingdom acquired substantial debts from the constituent kingdoms, duchies, and principalities, it seized church lands and a number of large estates. To convert these into cash, it created a private concern, the *Società Anonina per la Vendita dei Beni del Regno* (Corporation for the Sale of Assets of the Kingdom) to sell the collection of "church properties, iron mines on the island of Elba, forests, mineral springs, arsenals, some irrigation canals and common lands, especially sea swamps and mountain tops," administered from 1860 to 1882, with an estimated total value of 1,928 million lire, then approximately $400 million (Clough 1964, 47–54, quotation from 49). Similar disposal problems for which I lack sources with details, were the seizure of church lands and buildings by Henry VIII in Britain and of church and noble lands in France in the revolution, and another large-scale confiscation in Spain in the early nineteenth century. In no case, I gather, was the operation accomplished neatly and without steps forward and back. The problem forcibly dumped in the lap of the RTC will equally become, in the inelegant American expression, "a can of worms."

The central question is who bears the burden of this ill-advised investment and thievery. The list of candidates is substantial:

> the investors and malefactors themselves;
> their creditors;
> bank owners, through the decline in their shares, or their worthlessness, assuming limited liability, leaving aside double liability, such as obtained in many states before 1929, or the unlimited liability that afflicted the Glasgow tobacco lords who lost their estates in 1772 in the failure of the Ayr bank;
> depositors, when banks fail without deposit insurance, or are covered only to a limit, except in those cases where the limit was ignored to prevent a run;
> the central bank, although where central bank profits above statutory amounts accrue to the government and the losses do not reduce profits below this amount, the loss falls on the state;
> the state, through many possible channels:
>> directly, in the case of institutions like the RTC, either the original write-off, or an ultimate one;
>> through tax losses, where the losses of depositors, investors, banks, and others are written off against other taxable income;
>> through the forgiveness of foreign loans, through such arrangements as the Paris club.
> the country as a whole, if bad investments lead to bank runs, collapse, and depression;
> debt holders of all kinds, if the debts acquired by the state in fending off financial crisis are shrugged off through inflation.

Inflation is an unlikely indirect effect of bad investments, though it could occur if a lender of last resort operated with such a lavish hand, failing to shrink the money supply after first enlarging it, that spending got out of hand.

Now that the lender-of-last-resort function has shifted from a rare and infrequent expedient, held under tight control, to one undertaken readily, perhaps too readily, and even lightheartedly, it is well to bear in mind that it has strong features of redistributing income and wealth. Ambiguity as to whether investors or their banks will be saved or not has much to recommend it in order to reduce moral hazard and make nominal caretakers take real care. As in *Candide,* it is well from time to time to cut off the head of a general (let a substantial bank collapse) to "encourage the others."

One appropriate set of losers when a bank fails through ineptitude or worse is the officers, who should lose not only their jobs and the value of their shares, but also any options to buy more at low prices, should the bank and its shares ultimately recover. At the time of the salvage of the Continental Illinois, I was offended that while the responsible officers were sacked, they left by the terms of their employment contracts with golden parachutes in amounts that, in a few cases, exceeded one or two million dollars. When on one occasion at a meeting I expressed this indignation, a lawyer present said that such amounts were inconsequential solace for the lawsuits to which the officers would submit for years ahead. Even so.

The redistribution effects evoke an aspect of last-resort lending and its entropy that I have not stressed, that is, the political dimensions. Recall that Governor Norman wanted to keep his activities in steel and textiles secret so as not to let the Labor Party become involved in the decision making. Lender-of-last-resort help for Austria and Germany in May and June of 1931 aborted when France made them conditional on Austria giving up the Zoll Union with Germany, and on Germany abandoning the construction of the *Panzerkreuzer* (pocket battleship). Japan is holding back in efforts to carry the Commonwealth of Independent States through the current crisis because of the Kurile Islands. In the United States, voting new funds for the FDIC, the FSLIC, and the RTC is embroiled in party politics, which is why the money is voted in spoonsful rather than in an effective dollop, evoking a reminder of Bagehot's "freely." There are strong political arguments against entrusting last-resort operations to independent bodies that might play favorites and discriminate against outsiders in favor of the Establishment. But financial crises often call for decisive and immediate action that central banks are capable of producing, and deliberative political bodies, including such international organizations as the International Monetary Fund, may not be able to deliver.

A sharp observer of financial economics in the United States, Albert M. Wojnilower, senior advisor of First Boston Asset Management, suggested some years ago at the start of the banking crises that since the United States government had to make good in one way or another most of the losses from exuberant and misguided investment in booms and/or bubbles, there might be merit in converting parts of the government into a monopoly bank, making loans and investments, and issuing money, hoping for positive returns and/or seignorage, but ready to absorb unpreventable losses. Ricardo in 1824 proposed a similar idea that all bank notes be issued by the government (Fetter 1980, 109). It is remotely possible that this was the origin of Bagehot's view in *Lombard Street* that Ricardo, rather than Henry Thornton and Sir Francis Baring, first formulated the last-resort doctrine ([1873] 1978, 75).

Rather than move to having government take over the financial system, including banking, I would prefer to try to stuff the genie back in the bottle, reduce the last-resort function to a weapon of rare and occasional use, buttressed by better and more responsible bankers, lawyers, and accountants; stricter bank examinations; and occasional isolated bank failure. I fear this is a counsel of perfection. Communication today is so far-ranging and instantaneous, innovation so institutionalized, emulation so dominant, and independence of thought so rare, that booms and busts are a continuous threat and require that government be constantly prepared to damp down the first and fend off the second. This may be merely the pessimism of advanced years. I fervently hope so.

REFERENCES

Ashton, T. S. 1953. "The Crisis of 1825: Letters from a Young Lady." In *Papers in English Monetary History,* ed. T. S. Ashton and R. S. Sayers. 96–108. Oxford: Clarendon.

Ashton, T. S. 1959. *Economic Fluctuations in England, 1700–1800.* Oxford: Clarendon Press.

Bagehot, Walter. [1848] 1978. "The Currency Monopoly." In Norman St. John-Stevas, ed., *The Collected Works of Walter Bagehot,* 9:235–75. London: The Economist.

Bagehot, Walter. [1873] 1978. *Lombard Street.* In Norman St. John-Stevas, ed., *The Collected Works of Walter Bagehot,* 9:48–233. London: The Economist.

Bernanke, Ben A. 1983. "Nonmonetary Effects of the Financial Crisis in the Propagation of the Great Depression." *American Economic Review* 73: 257–76.

Calomiris, Charles W., and Gary Gorton. 1991. "The Origins of Banking Panics: Models, Facts and Bank Regulations." In R. Glenn Hubbard, ed., *Financial Markets and Financial History,* 109–73. Chicago: University of Chicago Press.

Ciampi, Carlo A. 1992. "Lending of Last Resort." In Banca d'Italia, *Economic Bulletin,* no. 14 (February): 63–69.

Clapham, Sir John. 1945. *The Bank of England: A History.* 2 vols. Cambridge: Cambridge University Press.

Clough, Shepherd B. 1964. *The Economic History of Modern Italy.* New York: Columbia University Press.

Economist. 1992. "Japanese Banks: More Pain." *Economist* 323, no. 7758 (May 9): 105–6.

Eichengreen, Barry. 1992. *Golden Fetters: The Gold Standard and the Great Depression, 1919–1939.* New York and Oxford: Oxford University Press.

Fetter, Frank Whitson. 1980. *The Economist in Parliament, 1780–1868.* Durham, N.C.: Duke University Press.

Goodhart, Charles. [1972] 1986. *The Business of Banking, 1891–1914,* 2d ed. Aldershot: Gower.

Hirsch, Fred. 1977. "The Bagehot Problem." *The Manchester School of Economics and Social Studies* 45 (September): 241–57.

Hoyt, Homer. 1933. *A Hundred Years of Land Values in Chicago: The Relationship of the Growth of Chicago to the Rise in Its Land Values, 1830–1933.* Chicago: University of Chicago Press.

Kane, Edward J. 1989. *The S&L Insurance Mess: How Did it Happen?* Washington, D.C.: Urban Institute Press.

Kindleberger, Charles P. [1973] 1986. *The World in Depression, 1929–1939,* rev. ed. Berkeley: University of California Press.

Kindleberger, Charles P. [1978] 1989. *Manias, Panics and Crashes: A History of Financial Crises,* rev. ed. New York: Basic Books.

Kindleberger, Charles P. [1984] 1993. *A Financial History of Western Europe.* 2d ed. New York: Oxford University Press.

King, W. C. T. 1936. *A History of the London Discount Market.* London: Routledge.

Mishkin, Frederic S. 1991. "Asymmetric Information and Financial Crises." In R. Glenn Hubbard, ed., *Financial Markets and Financial Crises,* 69–108. Chicago and London: University of Chicago Press.

Rockoff, Hugh. 1986. "Walter Bagehot and the Theory of Central Banking." In Forrest Capie and Geoffrey Woods, eds., *Financial Crises and the World Banking System,* 160–80. London: Macmillan.

Sayers, Richard S. 1976. *The Bank of England, 1891–1914.* 3 vols. Cambridge: Cambridge University Press.

Spero, Joan Edelman. 1980. *The Failure of the Franklin National Bank: Challenge to the International Banking System.* New York: Columbia University Press.

Thornton, Marianne [1825] 1953. "The Crisis of 1825: Letters from a Young Lady." In T. S. Ashton and R. S. Sayers, eds., *Papers in English Monetary History,* 96–108. Oxford: Clarendon Press.

Tolliday, Steven. 1987. *Business, Banking and Politics: The Case of British Steel, 1918–1939.* Cambridge, Mass.: Harvard University Press.

Wojnilower, Albert M. 1990. "Financial Institutions Cannot Compete." Pamphlet. New York: First Boston Management Corporation.
Wojnilower, Albert M. 1992. "Markets and Relationships." Pamphlet. New York: First Boston Management Corporation.
Zucker, Stanley. 1975, *Ludwig Bamberger: German Liberal Politician and Social Critic, 1823–1899,* Pittsburgh, Pa.: University of Pittsburgh Press.

CHAPTER 12

Why Did the Golden Age Last So Long?

As the first speaker, it falls to my lot to welcome Sir Alec into the Club of Nonagenarians. Some of you may protest that he has become merely an octogenarian. I cling to the view that he is completing his eighth and entering into his ninth decade. Join the Club, Alec. Eighty is a good round number; 81, coming up, is a square number. If you regret leaving 79 which was a prime number, take comfort from the fact that when you reach 83 you will be in your prime again.

We met in 1943 or 1944 through the kindly office of Bill Salant, late brother of your friend and mine, Walter Salant. As intermediary, Bill invited me to lunch with you. With my present enfeebled faculties, I am unable to recall who, if anyone, produced trenchant or particularly witty remarks, but I have strongly in memory that it was a very pleasant occasion. And our friendship, started perhaps forty-eight years ago, goes on. We are currently engaged in a genial competition in hypergraphia, to see which of us, as aging overachievers, will produce more acres of print. I cheat in one way, by publishing old letters and books. You enlist collaborators, such as Nita Watts and Barry Eichengreen. Nor do I know how to score edited books, such as your magnificent *Robert Hall Diaries,* volumes 1 and 2. Both of us count our medals back to the Second World War and its German aftermath. But if you will permit me a personal note, my father-in-law, a professor of English, once produced a paper for a small literary group on "Shakespeare's Old Men," and irritated his white-haired auditors by emphasizing how cranky and tiresome Shakespeare's old men all were. You provide a brilliant counterexample.

The original program for this happy occasion was entitled "The Legacy of the 1960s," and this paper was to be on "Why Did the Boom Last So Long?" I apologize for taking the liberty of altering my title to "Why Did the Golden Age Last So Long?," and for leaving out any reference to the 1960s. I, for one, am glad to have seen the 1960s go.

Reprinted from Frances Cairncross and Alec Cairncross, eds., *The Legacy of the Golden Age: The 1960s and their Economic Consequences.* (New York and London: Routledge, 1992), 15–30.

OPEC, that got us into so much trouble, was founded in 1960, although on my earlier showing that may belong to the 1950s. The 1960s themselves were a turbulent period socially, with the free-speech movement in Berkeley in 1963, the assassinations in the United States in 1963 and 1968, the Notting Hill Gate riots, the Vietnam War which drove President Johnson from office and the so-called events of May–June in Paris which did the same for President de Gaulle, not to mention Woodstock in 1969.

Rather than limit myself to the 1960s, I propose to deal with what has been called the "Golden Age," from around 1950 to 1973, a quarter century in economic history just as 1815 to 1914 was a century, not in the decimal system starting with the birth of Christ, but in the economic phenomena that interest our profession. The period was first called the golden age in 1944 in a discussion of postwar planning by Sir Richard Hopkins of the U.K. Treasury who urged the Chancellor of the Exchequer to concentrate his budget speech on the transitional period which "is what matters to most people," with only brief remarks on the "golden age" that might follow (Cairncross and Watts 1989: 86). The term has been adopted in the 1980s by that consummate statistical analyst of economic growth, Angus Maddison (1982: ch. 6) and by a group of leftist economists (Glyn *et al.* 1990) who are thought by one of their number to have originated the term (Singh 1990: 239). A somewhat more refined characterization is provided by Herman van der Wee, who calls the 1960s a "golden age," but the 1950s a "silver" one (1986: ch. 2). Gold and silver are both precious metals, and I adopt the Alfred Marshall program of symmetalism, but inflate the name to "golden."

I might have entitled this talk "Why did the Golden Age Come to an End?" When positive feedback, or a self-reinforcing mechanism which has lasted for a considerable period, comes to a halt, the question as readily arises why the virtuous circle broke down as why it was so virtuous over such a distance. It is difficult, perhaps impossible, to separate the two. *Pace* Alfred Marshall, Nature, at least in its social-science manifestation, seems to have made a jump, or at least suffered a fall.

How did the Golden Age happen to last for roughly 23 years? On one showing I could claim that the period was half of a Kondratieff cycle, and that these are 50 (or 55) years in length, and half of 50 is 25, which is more or less 23. I shall not do so. I come to the Kondratieff explanation later but not to accept it. A preferable explanation, in my judgment, runs in terms of a start, a self-reinforcing mechanism, and an end of the boom. I also propose to dwell to some extent on the height and the spread of the boom, as well as its length. An abundance of theories have been put forward on these issues, by no means mutually exclusive, and the analysis runs the risk of overdetermination, with more equations than unknowns, of the sort that I have recently encountered dealing with the British economic crisis of 1621, where observers list causes running up to eight or more, and as many as eight remedies.

A preliminary word on the spread and the height. I confess to some surprise that Britons think of the 1950s and 1960s as a period of boom. My recollection of the time runs in terms of (1) league tables in which the United Kingdom (and the United States) stood at the bottom of the list; (2) stop-go, or more accurately go-stop, with the British authorities obliged to slam on the deflationary brakes every few years after the economy had picked up speed, in order to prevent the balance-of-payments deficit running up too sharply; and (3) books such as Lord (Nicholas) Kaldor's *Causes of the Slow Rate of Economic Growth of the United Kingdom* (1966) and Wilfred Beckerman's *Slow Growth in Britain* (1979). The reasons for focusing on slow growth then, and a golden age now, may well be a change in the field of vision, from comparison with other industrial countries in the immediate postwar period (table 12.1) to that with the historical British performance later. Past United Kingdom figures—though the early numbers are somewhat shaky—show the 1950–73 British performance to have been an outstanding one (table 12.2).

Let me first attempt to dispose of the notion that the Golden Age was simply the fourth Kondratieff downswing in prices (or in some versions upswing in GDP) in a system that has been reproducing itself since 1790 (Rostow 1978: ch. 10, especially pp. 109–10), or in one version since 1495 (Goldstein 1988). In Rostow's formulation, upswings (1790–1815, 1848–73, 1896–1920, 1935–51 and 1972 onward) occur when the population outgrows foodstuffs and raw materials, especially energy, whereas downswings (1815–48, 1873–96 and 1920–35)

TABLE 12.1. Growth of Output (GDP at constant prices) per Head of Population, 1950–73

Country	% Annual Average Compound Growth Rate
Japan	8.4
Germany	5.0
Italy	4.8
France	4.2
Canada	3.0
United Kingdom	2.5
United States	2.2

TABLE 12.2. Growth of United Kingdom Output (GDP at constant prices) per Head of Population 1700–1987

Period	% Annual average compound growth rate
1700–1820	0.4
1820–1870	1.5
1870–1913	1.0
1913–1950	0.9
1950–1973	2.5
1973–1979	1.3
1973–1987	1.5

Source: Maddison 1982: 44; figures for 1973–87, Maddison 1989: 35.

are intervals when primary product prices are falling along with interest rates. Rostow calls 1941–72 a downswing but notes that it was a period of endemic inflation that shares some but not all of the characteristics of previous downswings.

I find no persuasive explanation for the periodicity of complete Kondratieff cycles of fifty to sixty years, or for upswings and downswings of roughly half that length. At first view the upswings seem to occur in major wars—the Napoleonic Wars and the First and Second World Wars, with perhaps the Crimean War, the American Civil War and the Prussian Wars against Denmark, Austria and France responsible for the upswing from 1848 to 1873. Such wars are presumably extrinsic to economic behavior, although Goldstein's rather tortured model makes them endogenous. Maddison expresses some sympathy with Rostow's characterization of the Golden Age as part of a Kondratieff, though he is uncomfortable with calling it a downswing (1982: 80), and finally rejects the Rostovian analysis on the ground that prices are an inadequate substitute for an aggregate such as GDP. Jay W. Forrester is also a follower of Kondratieff, but with a different central driving force—industrial investment, rather than the relationship between population and resources.

I choose to dismiss the Kondratieff hypothesis without further treatment, believing with Samuelson that it is science fiction (Goldstein 1988: 21). Kitchin, Juglar and Kuznets cycles have intuitive explanations in inventories, industrial investment and housing respectively. Intuitive explanations for the fifty-five-year cycle are superabundant beyond the Rostow population-resources relationship and Forrester's long-term investment. They involve technological breakthroughs, including Fordism (Mensch 1979), and overshooting plus correction in capital markets

(Berry 1991). Each is single-valued. None is persuasive. I proceed with the Golden Age of 1950–73 without the Procrustean bed furnished by the eminent Russian statistician.

Opposed to the notion that economic activity moves in repeating fifty-five-year cycles of which this golden age is a recent half is the leftist view that the golden age was a historical aberration (Singh 1990: 240), "the product of a *unique economic regime*" (Glyn *et al.* 1990: 40; emphasis in the original). The regime arose from a mixture of four elements: (1) a macroeconomic structure in which wages followed productivity growth, profits held up and investment stood high along with consumption—a positive feedback mechanism ran from profits to investment to rising productivity to profits again; (2) a system of production emphasizing large-scale units, and labor satisfied because of an expectation of rising income; (3) coordination of domestic policies affecting wages, prices and governmental policies, both monetary and fiscal; and (4) a benign international monetary system under United States hegemony, with stable money, low trade barriers, progressively lowered still further, and trade growing faster than output (Glyn *et al.* 1990: 40ff.). All this began to unravel in the late 1960s before the first OPEC price hike of 1973. Wages kept on rising, but this time faster than productivity, prices underwent inflationary increases and the international system fell apart, beginning in 1968 when President Nixon closed the gold window, and very evidently in 1971 when the dollar was devalued, before being following in 1974 by floating. The emphasis is on uniqueness on the one hand and the hint of underconsumption on the other. As far as it goes, the analysis carries conviction, though I think it leaves out one or two important elements.

Nor do mainstream economists lack a variety of explanations of the Golden Age, emphasizing real economic variables, sociological variables and policy choices. There is a wide difference of opinion between those who ascribe the boom to policy decisions and others who emphasize institutions and chance events. The span as a whole can be divided into the initial propulsive forces, the positive feedback mechanism and finally, though that word is too strong, the reversal. I will offer lists of theories and their authors, by no means mutually exclusive, before coming to my preferred combination. I hasten to add that I do not feel dogmatic about the list of factors, nor the weights that should be assigned to them, though I am made uneasy by those like the ambitious Edward Denison (1967) who try to disaggregate the various forces and measure their contributions exactly.

The main theories of the Golden Age divide somewhat along the following lines: initial recovery from war, followed by "catching up" (Abramovitz 1986, 1990; Dumke 1990); governmental policies (Maddison 1964, 1982, 1989; Heller 1966); sociological theories (Postan 1967; Olson 1982); and eclectic theories (Denison 1967; Matthews *et al.* 1982; van der Wee 1986). A second group assume that the boom has somehow started—whether by catching up, governmental policy or other means—and concentrate on the feedback mechanisms. These include export-led growth as the boom in leading countries spills over into imports (Lamfalussy 1963) and elastic supplies of labor (Kindleberger 1967). On the forces that brought the Golden Age to an end there are exogenous factors like the Russian wheat crop failures of 1971 and 1972 that raised the cost of living, the OPEC shock of 1973, the breakdown of the Bretton Woods system, the exhaustion of positive stimuli under catching up and the exhaustion of the positive feedback mechanism.

Recovery can be said to have been achieved when economic output had reached the prewar level. We need not deal with the contribution to that recovery of the Marshall Plan, monetary reform (in Germany), currency devaluation from overvalued levels and the like. Following Maddison (1982: 93) it can be said that recovery was complete by 1950. Catching up then begins and has to do with investment in productive capital—not housing—at the level of the most technologically advanced country. In discussing investment in the United Kingdom, Matthews takes the very high rate of investment in historical terms as "exogenous," but it can be regarded, following Abramovitz and Dumke, as catching up to the United States level. A wide gap had resulted from the two World Wars in which American technology made rapid advances while that of Europe did not. Some catching up may have taken place in the 1920s, but little in the 1930s when technological progress, despite Schumpeter, was limited.

Catching-up theory postulates convergence, that levels of technological proficiency have an inherent tendency to reach the same point. Abramovitz notes that fifteen countries which, on the average, had levels of productivity about 45 percent of that of the United States in 1950, had reached more than 65 percent in 1963, and continued to advance to 75 percent by 1979. Among the catching-up countries, convergence was demonstrated by the fact that the coefficient of variation among the fifteen declined from 0.37 in 1950 to 0.15 in 1973 (Abramovitz 1990: 3, Table 1). That the fifteen industrial countries caught up to the extent they did, while the less developed countries still lagged behind, is ascribed to his belief that to close a technological gap a country needs "social capability." This concept is unmeasurable, but a proxy for it may be found in years of popular education, or in political, commercial, industrial and financial institutions (Abramovitz 1986: 388).[1] Abramovitz asserts that economic catching up is self-limiting (1990: 9), although he notes the Matthews view that the closer one gets to the technological leader the easier it should be to close the gap. Indeed there is no necessary limit at full convergence since the country that is behind but rapidly advancing technically can, as Japan illustrated, surpass the level of the country originally serving as the standard. Abramovitz further notes that a theory postulating convergence as a normal tendency fails to explain the past century and a half when Britain opened up a wide gap from 1760 to 1850, and later was overtaken by Germany in a number of industries and overall by the United States.

Dumke's investigation of recovery and catching up for Germany presents a great deal of analysis and econometrics, on the latter of which I beg to be excused from comment. He shows a graph (Dumke 1990: 457, Figure 2) in which there is a sharp drop after the war from the 1930 trend, which trend is shortly regained. The recovery after the Second World War, however, was not matched after the First World War. On that occasion, long-run growth did not recover to the prewar trend line, but moved parallel to it, at a lower level. I ascribe the difference in the two postwar recoveries to widely different social conditions, along lines noted by Mancur Olson.

Catching up goes a long way to explain why rates of investment were so high in the Golden Age, but surely not all the way, nor is the process helpful to our understanding of the end of the Golden Age. A technological gap remained in 1973, and there is no reason to think that Germany and Japan will cease to make technological progress at a rapid pace when they reach the general U.S. level.

Government policy, and especially Keynesian control of demand, was a favorite explanation for the supergrowth of the 1950s at least, even if the model looks a little less robust in the following decade. In his earliest book Maddison (1964) looks almost exclusively to demand rather than supply. Two years later, Walter Heller's Godkin Lectures at Harvard proclaimed the arrival of a new look in economic policy and process, with the countercyclical focus of the 1950s discarded in favor of

---

1. The case of Sweden in the middle of the nineteenth century may be cited as an illustration of "social capability." This was a country at a fairly low level of economic development, but with a high degree of literacy and the foundations of an efficient banking system. With the British repeal of the Corn Laws in 1846 and later the timber duties, exports of oats for British horses and lumber for building, carried in Norwegian and Swedish bottoms after the repeal of the Navigation Acts, produced very rapid export-led growth (Sandberg 1979).

gap closing and growth (1966: vii). In a passage verging on *chutzpah,* Heller asserted:

> The doubling of our growth rate in the last five years—moving it up from the bottom to the top of the ladder among advanced countries—has strengthened not only the dollar, but our strategic position in dealing with our free world partners. What a change from 1961 when President Kennedy "ordered" me not to return from an international economic meeting in Paris until I had discovered the secret of European growth! What satisfaction he would have found in the "reverse lend-lease" of ideas which now finds European nations studying and borrowing some of the techniques of what President Johnson has called "the American economic miracle." (1966: 11)

Pride went before a fall. American Keynesian economists recommended a tax increase in 1967 to reverse the reduction finally achieved in 1964—to mop up the purchasing power that heated up the economy as the Vietnam War went on—but President Johnson was unwilling to present such a proposal to the Congress, lest his Vietnam policies be challenged. A bit later in Britain, Matthews (1968) denied that the high level of investment in Britain had been the result of demand policy manipulated by government, since the Britain budget on current account was in surplus practically all through the past decade, a conclusion that was subsequently challenged by an economist who called attention to the government's deficit on capital account. Matthews also rejected the possibility that the British economy had been stabilized by the balanced-budget multiplier, holding that the expansionary effect of high government taxation and spending was smaller than the restrictive bias of the current-account surplus. He admitted that the great investment boom was stimulated to a degree by tax policy, but claimed that its main cause was the scope for investment provided by the low level of the capital stock—catching up at the investment if not at the technological level—and not to government policy. Somewhat distinctly related to the balanced-budget multiplier is Minsky's (1986) view that the much larger role of government in the total economy dampens the business cycle because of built-in stabilizers, and thus permits continuous growth. But in this case the relationship of government spending and taxation to GDP cannot be ascribed to any particular policy to achieve growth.

Another government policy which requires mention is planning.

French planning, pushed by Jean Monnet,[2] went back to 1947, when the first four-year plan set goals for a limited number of strategic sectors, and continued into the 1960s. At the height of enthusiasm for planning a spate of books appeared explaining how it worked (Hackett and Hackett 1963; Bauchet 1964). One enthusiast claimed that economic planning extended all over Europe, except for the United Kingdom, including even the Federal Republic of Germany where the emphasis on *Sozialmarktwirtschaft* was on *sozial* rather than on *markt* (Shonfield 1966). In the United Kingdom, moreover, a start at planning was made in 1962 with the establishment of a National Economic Development Council that finally produced a plan in 1965. This never got off the ground, however, as a conservative government tried to convert it from growth into a means of restraining inflation against trade union pressure. In due course France lost its appetite for *planification* which gradually gave way to *déplanification*. Planning would not work, the alibi ran, in a single country bound with others in a Common Market; it was necessary to plan for all, and others would not go along. The real reason was that business firms preferred to be guided by profits rather than by government indication of the path to be followed.

One more possibility for government policy guiding economic growth rests in monetary policy—though Cairncross and Watts (1989: ch. 14) make clear that, at least before 1961, the Bank of England did not always see eye to eye on monetary policy with the economic section of the Cabinet or the Treasury. Maddison resists Harry Johnson's claim that well-behaved management of money will automatically produce full employment (Maddison 1982: 132). I suspect that if Harry were with us today he would decline to claim that monetary policy was responsible either for the boom when it was overshadowed by Keynesian fiscal policy or for the letdown after 1973 when monetary policy came into intellectual favor.

I now turn to sociological theories. The most ambitious relates to the spread of growth rates between Japan and Germany on the one hand and the United Kingdom and the United States on the other. Slow growth was blamed on what Mancur Olson called "distributive coalitions," or, in more usual American parlance, vested interests. These protect their narrow welfare with ferocity without regard to the common weal. Each group seeks to ensure that it bears no or a minimal share of the burdens of society, whether from reconstruction or, in

---

2. Paul Streeten used to say that "the love of Monnet is the root of all evil." Let me also record his dictum that "if Russian planning was imperative and French planning indicative, British planning was surely subjunctive."

the 1920s German case, reparations, fending off taxes and raising prices to push inflation on others. Deadlocked distributional coalitions block the national agenda and slow down overall decisions. In Olson's view defeat in the Second World War destroyed the groups in Germany and Japan that had power to look after parochial concerns. An illuminating comparison lies between Germany after the First World War and West Germany after the Second World War. In the first case, Junkers, peasants, industrialists, trade unionists and civil servants all survived relatively intact to hold on to political power and to block action against them, with the result that reconstruction and reparations led to hyperinflation. After the Second World War, these groups had been destroyed—trade unionists, peasants and civil servants during the Nazi rule, and Junkers by the loss of territory in the east—and while industry survived, its prestige did not. The way was cleared for a far-reaching monetary reform in 1948 to restore incentives to work and invest, a process aided by the fact that the country was governed by occupying powers which took responsibility for the necessary heroic measures. After the Marshall Plan had restocked the economy, the *Wirtschaftswunder* took off. In Postan's (1967) analysis, most of Europe after the Second World War, but not the United Kingdom, was led by "new men" in government and industry after the failures of occupation and defeat.

There is an important issue here as to whether it would have been possible to have the monetary reform of the Second World War after the First World War or whether it would have been blocked and resisted. To my mind there has not been enough discussion of the failures of monetary reform in France, where the question was raised but never properly discussed, and the weak monetary reform in a country like Belgium. The issue is very relevant to what is happening now in Eastern Europe.

A crucial aspect of the German experience was the fact that after having been cooped up in autarky during the 1930s and the war, businessmen looked abroad more and more, with the more vigorous among them choosing to sell in foreign markets. High rates of investment, first for recovery and then for catching up, drove up national income which then spilled abroad from the leaders in the league tables to other countries, not as import surpluses but as rapidly rising gross imports. West Germany and Japan in fact had strong export surpluses in a world of declining import barriers and discrimination. The openness of the world economy, fostered by the Bretton Woods institutions, the General Agreement on Tariffs and Trade (GATT), economic assistance—initially to Europe and later to the Third World—plus convertibility, made possible mutually supporting high growth for countries engaged in catching up.

How did the Golden Age last so long? My explanation runs in terms of positive feedback, much along the lines of Glyn *et al.* (1990), with profits leading to investment leading to increased productivity, higher wages, higher consumption, higher profits and so on. The process is self-reinforcing so long as wages do not squeeze profits by rising faster than productivity. Where I differ from Glyn *et al.* is in the mechanism that restrains wages to the rate of productivity increases. They emphasize labor's expectations of continued growth in real income, and presumably self-imposed restraint. That may have played a role in West Germany when it had a weak trade union movement, and perhaps even in French coal mining in the early 1950s when Communist unions, cooperating with the government, held wages down. I cling, however, to my old view that wages were held down by an elastic labor supply (Kindleberger 1967). West Germany was blessed by a steady inflow of expellees and refugees from the East—labor with high levels of "social capability," to return to Abramovitz's phrase, easy to absorb because educated to more or less the same degree as the existing West German population, German speaking, and avid to restore their wealth, income and social status, and hence willing to work hard. Following the Germans from the East were the so-called guest workers, initially largely from Italy, then from Spain, Portugal, Yugoslavia and Turkey. These were at first readily absorbed, as they were mostly skilled, single, young and content to live in barracks, consume little and save a lot to remit to families at home. Later, when parts and whole families joined the movement, the economic benefits of immigration declined; it was necessary to provide more adequate housing and other social overhead capital, especially hospitals and schools.

The real limits to immigration, however, proved to be social, rather than economic. When foreign workers reached one-third of the Swiss labor force, the flow was cut off as the Swiss voters felt their Swiss identity threatened. Similar social unhappiness arose in West Germany, which closed off those urban areas where the guest workers and their families reached 12 percent of the local population.

Let me say parenthetically that this positive feedback process (or Marxian or Lewis model of growth with unlimited supplies of labor) will probably not apply to the 1990–91 movement of ethnic Germans and others westward after the November 1989 collapse of the Wall. The original Lewis model helped the receiving country by holding wages down and profits up, *permitting*, but *not* inevitably leading to, high reinvestment of profits. At the same time, it stimulated growth in the country of emigration by draining off underemployed workers, raising the share of rent and bringing the marginal revenue product of remaining labor up to the point where it more nearly approximated the wage rate, thus stimulating investment there as well. In today's world I fear that westward European migration may inhibit growth in both sending and receiving countries: in the sending countries by leaving gaps in the balance of skills and making some towns and firms inefficient as they lose necessary professional and skilled workers; in the receiving countries in the West by diverting capital from productive uses to infrastructure, at a time when pressures on savings to provide aid and capital for reconstructing and cleaning up the environment in the East and buying off the Russians are already great.

I must not rely too heavily on the expellee-refugee stream plus the guest workers in the Golden Age. There were other sources of surplus labor: unemployment left over from the 1930s and the war; migrants from the countryside to the city, especially in countries like France and Italy with rapidly rising productivity in agriculture; natural population growth after emigration had been cut off, in a country such as the Netherlands, for example, which no longer shipped a stream of colonists to the East Indies. It is significant, however, that British agriculture was already efficient and had little surplus population to send to factories, and that British labor unions beat off the attempt of government to admit as immigrants Polish miners reluctant to return to their country. Miners were clearly needed in Britain after the wartime Bevin-boy experiment failed and when many of the soldiers from mine districts, like the Durham and Northumberland Light Infantry, failed to go back to the mines.[3] Britain did experience considerable immigration from former colonial possessions, directly or, in the case of some Indians and Pakistanis, via other former colonies. This supply was ultimately cut off because of social disturbances, but seemed meanwhile to have moved into service industries rather than mining or manufacturing. There may well have been a question about its social capability.

Britain had very low unemployment up to 1965, and even acute shortages of labor in the booms of 1960 and 1964, especially of skilled labor but to some extent of labor in general (Matthews *et al.* 1982: 85–

---

3. In many European countries, coal mining had been the lowest-paid occupation in the inter-war period, but leaped to become one of the highest after the Second World War. What had been a non-competing group became assimilated into the total labor force, with the result that the disagreeable character of the work required wage premia. A sociological parallel phenomenon occurred in France in the First World War. Before the war, the major coal mining areas of the Pas de Calais and the Nord had birthrates much higher than that of the rest of France, breeding, in fact, more or less like animals (Zola 1885). The First World War and the reconstruction of the northern battleground afterwards integrated the miners into the French labor force and brought the birthrate down to the national level (Ariès 1948: 202–63).

93). This was partly because management treated labor as an overhead rather than a variable cost, preferring to shorten hours when demand slackened rather than lay workers off, for fear that in a recurring boom it would not be able to rehire (ibid.: 90, especially Figure 3.4).

The gilt of the Golden Age was beginning to wear thin in the late 1960s. The widespread notion that the boom was stopped by the price rise in all of OPEC in November 1973 overstates the matter considerably. This shock put punctuation to the Golden Age, perhaps as the *coup de grâce* to an already wounded boom that was slipping into stagflation. Various elements that earlier contributed to positive feedback were weakening. In the Netherlands wages had been held down and profits held up by a deliberate incomes policy that collapsed as early as 1961. A further inflationary element was the "Dutch disease," a general rise in wages to match those in the Dutch North Sea gasfields. Productivity figures are on the whole crude, and calculated over long periods, such as the Golden Age as a whole rather than year by year (Maddison 1982: ch. 4; 1989: Table 7.2 and 7.3). I nonetheless hazard a guess that U.S. productivity increases slowed down with the outbreak of war in Vietnam and the program of space exploration that followed the Soviet Union's launching of Sputnik in 1957 and the American landing on the moon in 1969. One student of technological history states that the break in American technological advance came in 1971 when the Congress refused to allocate funds for a supersonic transport proposed to match the Concorde (Gimpel 1976: 2).

It is generally recognized that military research in the Second World War stimulated civilian productivity increases, especially in airplanes, electronics and computers. More recent military and space research in the United States seems to have yielded fewer innovations of civilian importance, with Teflon coming to the mind of most people looking for examples. With productivity slowing down and expectations of real-wage growth continuing, the United States slipped into an inflationary mode, compounded by failure to reverse the 1964 tax cut as the economy heated up. Depreciation of sterling in 1967 called for restrictive macroeconomic measures, which led to rising unemployment after the long years below 3 percent, a level which had been regarded as "full employment" during the postwar planning stages. When the French students rioted in May of 1968 they were joined by trade unionists at the Renault plant in Villancourt outside Paris, necessitating the Accord de Grenelle between the unions and the government. This raised wages sharply, much like the Accord de Matignon of June 1936 when the Blum government yielded to the strikes that brought the Popular Front to power.

There is perhaps no need for me to recite the gradual breakdown of the Bretton Woods Agreement, but I would like to make two or three points, with emphasis on my disagreement from the conventional opinion on particular matters. First, I disagree with Triffin (1960) who thought the dollar system was a disaster because he measured balance-of-payments disequilibrium on the liquidity definition, which I believe is appropriate for most countries in the world economy but not for one that acts like a world banker. Bankers are in the business of lending long and borrowing short, and doing so does not constitute disequilibrium. Second, the system was doomed by the fact that more and more individuals and national monetary authorities hoarded the base money of the system, borrowing dollars (or selling assets for them) and converting the dollars to gold, encouraged by the publicly lamented fears of U.S. authorities from Eisenhower to Reagan about the so-called deficit. Benign neglect was a mistake made later under President Reagan; it was a desirable policy in the 1960s. Third, a critical mistake was made in 1971, when the Federal Reserve System lowered interest rates in the United States at a time when the Bundesbank was trying to repel imported inflation by tightening. With the two capital markets joined through the Eurocurrency system, the inconsistent policies poured dollars abroad, lowered world interest rates, set international banks looking for loans and started the wave of Third World borrowing that has produced such difficulty since 1982, this well before the OPEC price rise of November 1973. I used to call the Board's action "the Crime of 1971"; now I prefer, with Talleyrand, to believe it was worse than a crime: it was a blunder.

I return to my subject: how did the Golden Age last so long? Which Golden Age: the British in comparison with a century and a half earlier, or the world's, largely the industrial countries, led by the miracles of Japan and Germany? For Britain, I would emphasize the growth of exports, catching up (investment) and, despite Matthews, government policy which time and again pulled back from impetuous forced-draft tactics.[4] There were a number of economists at the time—I fear I have forgotten whom—who advocated pushing ahead when the balance of payments turned adverse, on the theory that more growth with economies of scale would lower costs, expand exports and right the balance of

---

4. "Direct injections of demand by fiscal or monetary policy or public-sector investment were not responsible for the unusually high level of activity. . . . It is possible, however, that government policy in a broader sense did contribute to the high average level of activity, partly on account of the devaluations of 1949 and 1967, partly by the timing of fiscal and monetary measures, partly by effects on confidence. Within the postwar period there was a trend towards more expansionary policies up to the mid-1960s" (Matthews *et al.* 1982: 313).

payments through growth. "Damn the torpedoes: full speed ahead." This may work on occasion but not, I think, with unemployment hovering around 1 percent.

I do not know enough about Japan to pronounce on its economic miracle. Unemployment decreased from a high of 2.5 percent of the labor force in 1955 to a steady 1.1–1.3 percent through the 1960s (Maddison 1982: 208, Table C6(b)). Labor productivity per man hour in 1970 relative prices went up almost sixfold between 1950 and 1975 compared with only double or triple for most other advanced countries (ibid.: 212, Table C10). This was catching up, and surpassing with a vengeance.

When I started this paper I did not think I would find myself in agreement with Glyn *et al.* (1990)—in fact I did not know of the existence of their work. If they will allow me to incorporate in their analysis the Lewis model of growth with unlimited supplies of labor—and after all it derives from Marx—I will go along happily. Let us hope that future depression and wartime gaps do not open so widely again as to encourage a catch-up process to start, nor that millions of people will be driven from their homes to depress wages where they are taken in.

Perhaps you will let me go beyond my brief. If I choose not to believe in the Kondratieff cycle, and hesitate to predict that a new Golden Age will never recur, I am committed to the S- or Gompertz curve as a general truth in economic life. Chaos theory suggests that growth movements begin as mutations which, if they take root, start slowly. Many wither. Those that grow do so slowly at first and may later pick up speed. In due course, however, they meet with some obstacle, decay in entropy, in any event slow down. If one fits a trend and plots deviations from it, the S-curve may be reduced to cycles, but the essence is in the S itself, not in the derivative, and there is no reason why the deviations should be of a given length. That catching up carries within it the seeds of its own leveling off or decline seems to me a general truth akin to the population of fruit flies in a jar, the life cycle of the individual and, I suspect, the life cycle of people in the aggregate or society. The S-curve is useless for prediction because new S-curves may emerge from others as new mutations occur. But the top of the long S-curves in British and American history may help explain why the United Kingdom and the United States were on the bottom of the league tables.

REFERENCES

Abramovitz, M. (1986) "Catching up, forging head, and falling behind," *Journal of Economic History* 17 (2) (June): 385–406.

——— (1990) "The catch-up factor in postwar economic growth," *Economic Inquiry* 18 (January): 1–18.

Ariès, P. (1948) *Histoire des populations françaises et leurs attitudes devant la vie depuis le XVIIIe siècle,* Paris: Philippe Ariès.

Bauchet, P. (1964) *Economic Planning: The French Experience,* New York: Praeger.

Beckerman, W. (ed.) (1979) *Slow Growth in Britain,* Oxford: Oxford University Press.

Berry, B. J. O. (1991) *Long-Wave Rhythms in Economic Development and Behavior,* Baltimore, MD, and London: Johns Hopkins University Press.

Cairncross, A. (ed.) (1989, 1991) *The Robert Hall Diaries,* vol. 1, *1947–1953;* vol. 2, *1954–56,* London: Unwin & Hyman.

Cairncross, A. and Watts, N. (1989) *The Economic Section, 1939–1961: A Study in Economic Advising,* London and New York: Routledge.

Denison, E. F. (assisted by Poullier, J.-P.) (1967) *Why Growth Rates Differ,* Washington, DC: Brookings Institution.

Dumke, R. H. (1990) "Reassessing the *Wirtschaftswunder:* reconstruction and postwar growth in West Germany in an international context," *Oxford Bulletin of Economics and Statistics* 52 (2): 51–91.

Gimpel, J. (1976) "How to help the United States age gracefully," unpublished memorandum, pp. 1–24.

Glyn, A., Hughes, A., Lipietz, A. and Singh, A. (1990) "The rise and fall of the Golden Age," in S. A. Marglin and J. B. Schor (eds.) *The Golden Age and Capitalism: Reinterpreting the Postwar Experience,* Oxford: Clarendon Press.

Goldstein, J. H. (1988) *Long Cycles: Prosperity and War in the Modern Age,* New Haven, CT: Yale University Press.

Hackett, J. and Hackett, A.-M. (1963) *Economic Planning in France,* Cambridge MA: Harvard University Press.

Heller, W. W. (1966) *New Dimensions of Political Economy,* Cambridge, MA: Harvard University Press.

Kaldor, N. (1966) *Causes of the Slow Rate of Growth of the United Kingdom,* Cambridge: Cambridge University Press.

Kaplan, J. J. and Schleiminger G. (1989) *The European Payments Union,* Oxford: Clarendon Press.

Kindleberger, C. P. (1967) *Europe's Postwar Growth: The Role of the Labor Supply,* Cambridge, MA: Harvard University Press.

Lamfalussy, A. (1963) *The United Kingdom and the Six: An Essay on Economic Growth in Western Europe,* Homewood, IL: Irwin.

Lewis, W. A. (1954) "Economic development with unlimited supplies of labour," *The Manchester School* (May).

Maddison, A. (1964) *Economic Growth in the West: Cooperative Experience in Europe and North America,* New York: Twentieth Century Fund.

——— (1982) *Phases of Capitalist Development,* Oxford, New York: Oxford University Press.

———— (1989) *The World Economy in the 20th Century,* Paris: OECD.

Matthews, R. C. O. (1968) "Why has Britain had full employment since the war?" *Economic Journal* 77 (311) (September): 558–69.

Matthews, R. C. O., Feinstein, C. H. and Odling-Smee, J. C. (1982) *British Economic Growth, 1856–1973,* Oxford: Clarendon Press.

Mensch, G. (1979) *Stalemate in Technology,* Cambridge, MA: Ballinger.

Minsky, H. (1986) *Stabilizing an Unstable Economy,* New Haven, CT: Yale University Press.

Olson, M. (1982) *The Rise and Decline of Nations: Economic Growth, Stagflation and Social Rigidities,* New Haven, CT: Yale University Press.

Postan, M. M. (1967) *An Economic History of Western Europe, 1945–64,* London: Methuen.

Rostow, W. W. (1978) *The World Economy: History and Prospects,* Austin, TX: University of Texas Press.

Sandberg, L. C. (1979) "The case of the impoverished sophisticate: human capital and Swedish economic growth before World War I," *Journal of Economic History* 39 (March): 225–41.

Shonfield, A. (1966) *Modern Capitalism: The Changing Balance of Public and Private Power,* New York: Oxford University Press.

Singh, A. (1990) "Southern competition, labor standards and industrial development in the North and South," in Bureau of International Labor Affairs, US Department of Labor, *Labor Standards and Development in the Global Economy,* pp. 239–64, Washington, DC: US Department of Labor.

van der Wee, H. (1986) *Prosperity and Upheaval: The World Economy, 1945–1980,* Berkeley, CA: University of California Press.

Zola, E. (1885) *Germinal,* Harmondsworth: Penguin, 1954.

CHAPTER 13

Rules vs. Men: Lessons from a Century of
Monetary Policy

Introduction

The problem that Knut Borchardt tackled with his "Constraints and Room for Manoeuvre in the Great Depression of the Early Thirties"— to use the title in English[1]—is a pervasive one that permeates many aspects of economic, political, and personal life, and has a critical bearing on both efficiency and ethics. I choose to condense the issue as "rules vs. men," since it often appears in that guise. Most generally the question is when do circumstances of an extreme nature call for breaking rules and regulation, even the law, surely commitments made to others without force of law, when to depart from established principles or, to express it more pejoratively, ideologies to serve pragmatic ends. In bureaucratic organizations it is sometimes posed as when should an outranked official or a staff expert giving advice on what he or she is convinced is the right course to follow and is overruled resign, instead of subsiding quietly. The questions posing the issue are usually complex, intelligent and responsible persons can readily divide.

I offer two introductory examples: one close to a disaster, the other a success. With the integration of East with West Germany, no clear rule told how to handle the currency. The simple-minded political view, a mark is a mark, ran contrary to the advice of the Bundesbank and proved mistaken. In August 1982, on the other hand, as the Mexican debt crisis exploded, the Federal Reserve System, contrary to all rules and regulations of which I am aware, advanced $1 billion to the Mexican

---

Reprinted from Christoph Buchheim, Michael Hutter, and Harold James, eds., *Zerrissene Zwischenkriegszeit: Wirtschaftshistorische Beiträge* (Baden-Baden: Nomos Verlagsgesellschaft, 1994), 157–75.

1. Borchardt, K., Constraints and Room for Manoeuvre in the Great Depression of the Early Thirties: Toward a Revision of the Received Historical Picture, in: Borchardt, K.: Perspectives on Modern German Economic History and Policy, translated by Peter Lambert, Cambridge 1991, pp. 143–60.

government as payment against future deliveries of oil to the Strategic Oil Reserve of the United States, maintained in salt mines in Louisiana. After the second sharp rise in the price of oil engineered by OPEC in 1979, oil was clearly valuable collateral as well as a strategic commodity and wide understanding of this fact doubtless helped to quell any potential objection. There was no objection. Men had set aside the rules and met an emergency.

I come in due course to the question whether Heinrich Brüning, the German Chancellor in 1931 and 1932, was justified or not in pressing on with deflation and in putting the goal of bringing a halt to reparations ahead of tackling the issue of the rapid increases in unemployment in Germany in those years. Central to the issue is whether he had a choice or whether the commitments under the Dawes Plan, the Young Plan, the statutes of the Reichsbank and the like rendered any alternative course impossible. In the interest of full disclosure I should perhaps immediately confess that I am more or less on the side of Carl-Ludwig Holtfrerich's position that there were alternatives to deflation that promised better outcomes if Brüning had been forceful enough to break through the constraints upon him.[2] To regard the final end of reparations at the Lausanne Conference in the summer of 1932 as the successful culmination of Brüning's policy, even though he fell 100 meters from the goal by being voted out of office in May of that year, strikes me like Charles Lamb's recipe for roast pig which consisted in burning a house down around the animal.

To keep the discussion more general and to honor Knut Borchardt with whom I have collaborated and whom I greatly admire, I propose not an exercise dealing with an episode in economic history, but an essay in politico-economic behavior, using a number of historical examples.

I. *English and French Examples from the 19th Century*

Let me begin by citing a number of British authorities who have pronounced on the issue more or less concisely:

"There are times when rules and precedents cannot be broken; others when they cannot be adhered to with safety."[3]
"I am satisfied that laying down a 'hard and fast rule'—on whether

---

2. Holtfrerich, C.-L. Alternativen zu Brünings Wirtschaftspolitik in der Weltwirtschaftskrise? Historische Zeitschrift 235, 1982, pp. 605–31.
3. Joplin, T.: Case for Parliamentary Inquiry into the Circumstances of the Panic, in: A Letter to Thomas Gisborne, Esq., M.P., London after 1832.

bankers' deposits at the Bank of England can be lent out—would be very dangerous; in very important and very changeable business, rigid rules are apt to be often dangerous . . . no certain fixed proportion of its liabilities can in present times be laid down as that which the Bank ought to keep in reserve . . . The forces of the enemy being variable, those of the defense cannot always be the same."

"I admit this conclusion is very inconvenient . . . unhappily, the rule which is the most simple is not always the rule which is most to be relied upon. The practical difficulties of life often cannot be met by very simple rules; those difficulties being complex and many, the rules of countering them cannot be single or simple. A uniform remedy for many diseases often ends by killing the patient"[4]

Bagehot does not dismiss the rule on bankers' balances entirely:

"The idea that bankers' balances ought never to be lent is only a natural aggravation of the truth that these balances should be lent with extreme caution."[5]

Bagehot entered into this discussion in his first published paper which appeared in 1848, commenting on the controversy between the Banking and the Currency Schools of British monetary policy, over whether the money supply should be relatively fixed by being tied up to the Bank of England's bullion reserve, or elastic so as to move up and down with the expansion and contraction of commerce:

"The currency argument is this: it is a great defect of a purely metallic circulation that the quantity of it cannot be readily suited to any sudden demand; it takes time to get new supplies of gold and silver, and, in the meantime, a temporary rise in the value of bullion takes place. Now as paper money can be supplied in unlimited quantities, however sudden the demand may be, it does not appear to us that there is an objection in principle to sudden issues of paper money to meet sudden and large extensions of demand. This power of issuing notes is one excessively liable to abuse. Such a power ought only to be lodged in the hands of government. It should only be used in rare and exceptional cases. But when the fact of an

---

4. Bagehot, W.: Lombard Street (1873), in: St. John-Stevas, N. (ed.): The Collected Works of Walter Bagehot, vol. IX, London 1978, pp. 207–8.

5. Bagehot, *Lombard Street*, p. 207.

extensive and *sudden* [Bagehot's emphasis] demand is proved, we
see no objections, but decided advantage, in introducing this new
element into a metallic circulation."[6]

The distinction between the rule for normal times and that in a time of a
sudden demand for money complicates the case for rules, especially as it
carries the implication that men are needed to "prove" the existence of
"an extensive sudden demand." The emphasis on suddenness brings up
a qualification in the theory of rational expectations that unanticipated
shocks may modify the rule that markets should be left alone to find
their equilibria without government intervention. One emerges with two
rules, one for ordinary times, say on trend, and another for financial
crises when lender-of-last-resort action is needed. Historical revealed
preference suggests that a normal rule, either let the market handle it, or
supply money to the system at a regular rate of growth, is often set aside,
at least briefly. Much depends on the nature of the shock—whether the
bursting of a speculative bubble, or the outbreak of what promises to be
a prolonged war.

One of the most powerful advocates of a fixed rule for supplying
money, Milton Friedman, who would even go so far as to abolish central
banks to get rid of their men who may be tempted to exercise judgment
and adjust policy to circumstances, had considerable sympathy with the
existence of two rules, when in his "Monetary History of the United
States," written with Anna Jacobson Schwartz, he or they note that a
financial crisis is like an avalanche, a slide of unstable earth previously
held back by a rock that comes loose.[7] Quoting Bagehot's prescription
that a financial crisis is like neuralgia, and one must not starve it carries
the implication that the money supply at times must be elastic.[8]

Sir Robert Peel, the British prime minister in 1844, demonstrated a
profound understanding of the dilemma posed by the choice between
rules and men in commenting on the Bank Act in a letter of June 4,
1844:

"My Confidence is unshaken that we have taken all the Precautions
which legislation can prudently take against the Recurrence of a
pecuniary Crisis [i.e. have drawn up a proper set of rules]. It may
occur in spite of our Precautions; and if it be necessary to assume a

---

6. Bagehot, W.: The Currency Monopoly (1848), in: Collected Works, vol. IX
p. 267.
7. Friedman, M./Jacobson Schwartz, A.: A Monetary History of the United States,
1867–1960, Princeton 1963, p. 419.
8. Friedman and Schwartz, Monetary History, p. 395.

grave responsibility, I dare say Men will be found willing to assume such a Responsibility."[9]

Before the passage of the Bank Act of 1844, the Bank of England had come to the rescue of financial markets on numerous occasions, and broken its internal rule on discounting which was to rediscount only two-months' commercial bills with two good London names. In various crises it loaned on out-of-town names, on mortgages, including some on unimproved land and one on a West Indian plantation, on the securities of a copper company through which it acquired in bankruptcy a copper works.[10] According to the testimony of Jeremiah Harman of the Bank of England it loaned in the panic of 1825 "by every possible means and in modes we have never adopted before in short, by every possible means consistent with the safety of the Bank, and we were not on some occasions over-nice."[11]

With the passage of the Bank Act of 1844, a Machiavellian device helped to regularize the handling of financial crises. As lender of last resort the Bank of England broke the rules limiting the issue of banknotes to the small (at that time) fiduciary issue against government bonds, plus gold in the Issue Department, but only after receiving a Letter of Indemnity from the Chancellor of the Exchequer stating that it would not be prosecuted for its violation of the law. This preserved the principle, but granted the exception. As is widely known, the Letter of Indemnity in 1848 and 1866 at times of crises so calmed the market that there was no need of an excess issue, and that in the crisis of 1857 the excess was very small.

The Letter of Indemnity was by no means the only device available for meeting a financial crisis. One might have returned to the issuance by the government of Exchequer bills, made available to merchants against the collateral of commodity inventories, and discountable at the Bank of England. This technique had calmed the roiled financial waters of the canal mania in 1793. It was not available in 1825, however, because when meeting with a deputation of merchants asking for Exchequer bills, Lord Liverpool, the Chancellor of the Exchequer, hoping to quell the agitated speculation, publicly refused, saying he would resign first. When panic ensued in 1825 in spite of his effort to forestall it, the Bank of England found a little breathing room to meet the run on its

---

9. Great Britain, Parliamentary Papers: Monetary Policy, Commercial Distress (1857), Shannon 1969, vol. 9, p. xxix.

10. Clapham, J.: The Bank of England. A History, vol. 2, Cambridge 1945, pp. 206–7.

11. Bagehot, Lombard Street, p. 73.

notes in a swap of silver against gold with the Bank of France, and a chance discovery of a box of one-pound notes that had been retired on its way to the resumption of the gold standard in 1821. More was needed, however, and the government ordered the Bank to lend £3 million to merchants against the collateral of commodity stocks, in effect, cutting out the intermediation of the Exchequer. The Court of Directors of the Bank seriously considered a motion to refuse to comply with the request, but ultimately went along, "the sullen answer of driven men" as Sir John Clapham put it.[12]

Lord Liverpool's refusal, of course, rested on his concern that repetition of a breach in standard practice would set a precedent, and constitute a change of rule. The same worry that continuous setting aside of rules would vitiate them led Lord Lidderdale, Governor of the Bank of England in 1890 at the time of the Baring crisis to refuse to accept the offer of a Letter of Indemnity from the Chancellor, Viscount Goschen. He turned instead to another device, a guarantee of liabilities of the Baring bank. Similar guarantees had been used in 1857 in Hamburg, and twice in the 1880s in France, once half-heartedly in 1882 in the collapse of the *Union Générale,* to save the brokers in the bankruptcy but not the principal, and again, more seriously in 1888 when the *Comptoir d'Escompte* failed because of the collapse of the scheme of its president, Denfert-Rocherau, to corner the world copper market.[13] Both in 1857 in Hamburg, and in 1890 in London, but not in Paris in the 1880s, the guarantee of bank liabilities was combined with a foreign loan, in the earlier episode, the *Silberzug* (silver train) from Austria,[14] in the Baring crisis, two loans from the State Bank of Russia and the Bank of France.[15] One further alternative, which might be characterized as a policy, is to take no action, either because of procrastination, the fall of policy leaders into a catatonic state, or an ideological conviction that it is best to let the fire burn itself out and the victims take their medicine. Among the last group are persons who think that markets are always efficient. The number of those in the latter category tends to shrink when crisis actually arrives, and most governmental authorities and central bankers—occasionally also private bankers—feel a responsibility to take some action to correct or dampen a crisis.

While the Bank of England in the middle of the nineteenth century was settling into an orthodox routine, across the channel the Bank of France was confronted with a new political position following the Revo-

---

12. Clapham, Bank of England, vol. 2, p. 108.

13. Bouvier, J.: Le Krach de l'Union Générale, 1878–1885, Paris 1960, chap. V.

14. Böhme, H.: Frankfurt und Hamburg: Des Deutschen Silber- und Goldloch und die Allerenglischte Stadt des Kontinents, Frankfurt 1968, pp. 255–68.

15. Clapham, Bank of England, vol. 2, pp. 329–30.

lution of 1848 and the *coup d'état* of 1851. Both central banks had been established in wartime to assist government finance, the Bank of France in 1800 to promote Napoleon I's military adventures. The takeover by Napoleon III in December 1851 posed new problems for the Bank as the Emperor had been infected by Saint-Simonian doctrine that believed in vigorous promotion of economic activity by the state. The Bank was called upon to assist in a debt conversion to reduce interest rates from 5 to 4 percent, and to promote the lagging building of the French railway network by making advances on bonds issued by some railroads.[16] While these measures were carried through after an agreement between the Bank and the government on March 2, 1852, many of the Regents were worried and expressed the view that the Bank of England would not have made loans on the collateral of railroad bonds.[17] Starting on March 15, the Bank began to lend on the railroad bonds, many of them a new type, devised by Isaac Pereire, with a low rate of nominal interest, but sold at a deep discount so as to leave room for capital appreciation.[18] In signing the agreement a number of the regents asserted that it was their moral obligation to assist, but some felt they were directly feeding speculation. On March 25, the Bank went still further and agreed to make advances on the debt of the City of Paris, but absolutely refused to do so for Marseilles and Bordeaux.[19]

Intense speculation in railroad securities, spurred by the rivalry of the Rothschilds with the Pereires, with whom the Emperor had now fallen out, led him to decree an end to the formation of new railroad companies. The Bank of France continued to make advances for companies with unfinished construction products. Almost 600 million francs of advances were later made in the four years 1858–1861. Two directors were vigorously opposed, especially Lafond, who had quit the wine trade at age 45 "to join the upper classes."[20] Lafond asked whether the resumption of the advances to railway companies was legal, and received the reply from the Governor that it was legal in the spirit of the law if not the letter.[21] Much of the support for the railroad bond policy came from the iron and steel regents, especially Eugène Schneider of the

---

16. Plessis, A.: La Politique de la Banque de France de 1851 à 1870, Geneva 1985, chap. ii, esp. pp. 89–108.
17. Plessis, La Politique, p. 91.
18. Cameron, R.: France and the Economic Development of Europe (1800–1914), Princeton 1961, p. 128.
19. Plessis, La Politique, pp. 105–6.
20. Plessis, A.: Régents et gouverneurs de la Banque de France sous le Second Empire, Geneva 1985, p. 144.
21. Plessis, La Politique, p. 287.

Schneider-Creusot steel company. After 1861, the Bank halted its "exceptional aid" to companies.[22] Plessis goes on to discuss new advances to the government to assist Fould in a new bond conversion to bring the interest rate down from 4½ to 3 percent. He remarks that aid to the Treasury was often dealt with discretely, was not discussed in the full Council of Regents but only in the Committee of Discounts. Little mention of the Bank's relations with the Treasury appears in the Minutes of the Bank as the question was left to the governor and the most influential regents.[23]

This somewhat cavalier disregard by men for law, principles of central banking, precepts and widely accepted practice opened up the possibilities for malfeasance and trouble, and there was of course some. Apart from the crisis of 1864 caused by the fall in the price of cotton at the end of the Civil War in the United States, however, the period of the Second Empire from 1851 to 1870, dominated by men rather than rules, and by men often locked in antagonistic battle with one another, were on the whole continuously prosperous, in considerable part because of the railroad boom financed by the Bank of France.

II. *The Crisis of the Bank of France in 1924*

I deal with one major incident of the 1920s before moving on to the Great Depression following 1929. At the end of the First World War, the French government had accumulated a substantial debt to the Bank of France for short-term advances—some 24 billion francs, which greatly enlarged the money supply and was regarded as highly inflationary. French experience with inflation, going back to the Mississippi bubble of John Law and the Assignats during the French Revolution had produced a hypersensitivity to that form of monetary pathology, and politicians of all stripes thought steps should be taken to head inflation off. In consequence, a convention was concluded between the Chamber of Deputies and the Treasury to reduce the debt by 2 billion francs a year, starting in 1921, with the goal of wiping it out entirely in twelve years. In addition, this so-called François-Marsal convention set a ceiling (*plafond*) on the Bank of France's note issue. The prospect at the time was that the Treasury's debt would ultimately be paid off through the receipt of reparations from Germany, and that the franc would be returned to prewar par.

The prospects of 1920 proved illusory, however. In 1921, the full

---

22. Plessis, La Politique, pp. 288–89.
23. Plessis, La Politique, p. 293.

two billion of Treasury debt was paid down but in 1922 only one billion, and in 1923 only 200 million.[24] Already a bright civil servant in the Treasury, Pierre de Mouÿ, began to agitate for change. In the first place, he pointed out that the attempt to control the money supply through Bank of France notes and its advances to the Treasury was futile because of the existence of the large short-term Treasury debt in the form of *Bons de la Défense Nationale,* billions of which matured every month, and which were equivalent to cash, since the Treasury had to pay off those that were not rolled over. The skittishness of the public made any attempt to refund the Bons at long term hopeless. Nor would political conditions permit a large increase in taxes, either a capital levy, as the Socialists wanted, or a tax on income under conditions in which the existing income tax was widely evaded. Proposals for taxes brought down the government, and called for a new cabinet. De Mouÿ, in March 1923, the director of the *Mouvement général des fonds* (public debt), wanted the government deficit—albeit a decreasing one—financed by the Bank of France; there was no other way to meet governmental expenditure—taxes, bond issues, or illegal borrowing from the major banks.[25] In his view the paranoia over inflation was a chimera. A limited increase in Bank advances to the Treasury and increase in the ceiling on the note issue, openly announced and explained, was the safest course. Already the Bank and the Treasury were undertaking extraordinary measures to disguise the amount of money in circulation, which had to be reported weekly in the Bank's statement, moving excess notes of a given branch to another branch as its day in the week to report came up. De Mouÿ's recommendation found no response.

In early 1924 an opportunity to straighten out the position came with an attack on the franc by financial interests in Holland, Austria and Germany, against which after yielding some depreciation, a bear squeeze, engineered by Lazard Frères with the help of a $100 million loan from J. P. Morgan & Co., brought the franc back above the level at the start of the attack. No advantage was taken of the respite, however, to take any fundamental steps through either increased taxes, reduced spending or debt refunding. The franc struggled along but with the books of the Bank of France heavily doctored. Advances to the government were made in contravention of the François-Marsal convention, but indirectly,

---

24. Jeanneney, J.-N.: Leçon d'histoire pour une gauche au pouvoir. La faillite du Cartel (1924–1926), Paris 1977, p. 33.

25. Schuker, S. A.: The End of French Predominance in Europe: The Financial Crisis of 1924 and the Adoption of the Dawes Plan, Chapel Hill 1976, p. 50.

by making advances to the commercial banks which loaned to the government. It was a time of lying.[26]

In mid-October 1924, one James LeClerc, an undergovernor of the Bank of France, regarded by the governor, Georges Robineau, and his secretary-general, Aupetit, as an outsider, discovered that the Bank's statements had been falsified. He went to the Finance Minister, Etienne Clémentel. There he was offered another job outside the Bank, but he refused. Clémentel felt himself exposed as he had promised the Chamber of Deputies that he would not "make inflation," i.e., evade the ceiling. He called Robineau and Aupetit to a meeting with the premier, Edouard Herriot, where possible alternative courses of action were discussed, not the recommendation of de Mouÿ for making a clean breast of it, citing the impossibility of the circumstances of 1924 of meeting the commitment of 1920, and openly borrowing on advances from the Bank, but what Jean-Noël Jeanneney calls various "silly ideas," reducing to minimum levels the balances from which the Treasury paid its bills, undertaking an intensive campaign to induce the public to make its payments by check instead of banknotes, issuing a new money in Madagascar and the Saar to replace Bank of France banknotes, which could then be cancelled.[27] Robineau told the Regents of the Bank of France on the eighteenth of December, and found them stupefied, fearful of being compromised. Herriot kept stalling for time, unable to decide among left-wing measures such as the capital levy or the right favoring cuts in spending, repeal of the 1918 ignored decree for the registration of exported capital. New ideas cropped up as the franc sank in the exchange market: a new Morgan loan and new squeeze, or the sale of 500 million francs worth of copper, stored in the Bourges arsenal. In March of 1925, François de Wendel, a right-wing Regent, told the government that unless an accurate balance sheet of the Bank was published by April 9 he would resign publicly. Herriot faced defeat either way: by announcing his deception or trying to levy new taxes. He hesitated further and then chose the taxes.[28] The political lives of the cabinet and the leadership at the Bank of France were numbered, and expired in mid-1926 after a long and agonizing struggle.

There is, of course, no assurance that if the policy of Pierre de Mouÿ offered in June 27, 1924 and repeated in October had been followed—announce that the government and the Bank were unilaterally to denounce the convention with the Chamber of Deputies, and the

26. Jeanneney, Leçon d'histoire, pp. 77–78.
27. Jeanneney, Leçon d'histoire, p. 83.
28. Jeanneney, Leçon d'histoire, pp. 90–110.

reasons why such a heroic measure was inescapable—matters would have worked out differently. It is virtually certain that the right wing—the so-called Wall of Money—would not have condoned it. Whether the public at large would have done is problematic. In any event, it is clear that the "men" involved—Herriot, Clémentel and Robineau—failed to rise to the occasion. The fate of the advocate of forthrightness followed classical lines: in the crisis month of December 1924, de Mouÿ was "kicked upstairs," to the position of director of customs, from which he retired six years later to join a bank at the age of 43.[29]

As an aside, I mention a postwar instance of a messenger with truth to convey who was not applauded for it. Emilio (Pete) G. Collado, director of the Office of Finance and Development in the Department of State in 1945, went to the meeting of heads of state at Potsdam in July and August with his superior, William L. Clayton, undersecretary of state for economic affairs, travelling by air. At Potsdam they caught up with the Secretary of State James F. Byrnes and President Harry S. Truman who had come by naval vessel, the U.S. battleship *Missouri.* In a first meeting with Clayton and Collado, Secretary Byrnes mentioned that he and the President had decided to cancel immediately the Lend-Lease program of assistance to the Allies in the European theatre. Each had been a senator at the time of the passage of the Lend-Lease legislation in 1941, when the Roosevelt administration had promised that the program would not be continued beyond the end of the war. Collado, who was deeply informed about the details of lend-lease operations, protested to the Secretary, listing a series of problems of importance which would require lend-lease financing for an extended period. My memory is weak, but I recall one example, the need to lend-lease a hospital ship to Brazil to enable that country to return its wounded in Italy to their own country. The Secretary grew impatient and repeated: we have cancelled Lend-Lease. Collado returned to his list of problems. The Secretary grew irritated, and turning to Mr. Clayton, said, pointing to Collado, "I do not want to see that man again." In their postwar memoirs Truman and Byrnes acknowledge that the abrupt halt to Lend-Lease had been a mistake and each inferentially blamed the other.

III. *Examples from the Great Depression*

Matters are complicated in my first example as there were at least two sets of men, one in Washington and some of the regional Federal Reserve Banks outside of New York, members of the Federal Reserve

---

29. Schuker, End of French Predominance, footnote, p. 50.

Open-Market Committee Conference, recommending "rules" to the Federal Reserve Board which issued them to the Bank in New York, and the other carrying out operations in the financial capital in New York, face to face with financial conditions and in touch with foreign central banks. The balance between the two sets had been altered in October 1928 by the death of Governor Benjamin Strong, an experienced and authoritative central banker. His neophyte successor, George L. Harrison, was less well-placed to contest policy decisions he thought misguided. When the New York Stock Market crashed on October 24 and 29, 1929, Governor Harrison proceeded immediately to buy $160 million of U.S. government bonds in open-market operations to provide the money market with liquidity in contravention, as widely thought, of the Open-Market Conference Committee instruction of August 1929 which authorized the New York Bank to operate on its own initiative only within a limit of $25 million a week. In addition, the New York Bank encouraged member banks to discount freely. The Bank claimed that its open-market operations were not bound by the Conference Committee limitation as it had a residual right to operate on its own initiative as a matter of general credit policy. The Board of Governors on the other hand took the view that the Bank's action was close to insubordination. On November 12, the Open-Market Committee Conference, with Governor Harrison presiding, recommended abandonment of the $25 million a week limit, and fresh purchases of $200 million. The Board's response was that the position was too unclear to formulate a long-run policy at the time, but in sudden emergency, when consultation was difficult, it would not object to purchases by the New York Bank.[30] With this less than whole-hearted support, the New York Bank proceeded to buy $160 million of government securities during the rest of November.

Tension between the Board and the Open-Market Committee on the one hand and the New York Bank on the other was muddled by the fact that the members of the Board of Governors were not unanimous and that some governors of the other regional banks took strenuous opposition to the New York view. The episode runs in sharp contrast to the stock market crash of October 19, 1987, when the Chairman of the Board of Governors, Alan Greenspan, and the President of the New York Federal Reserve Bank, Gerald Corrigan, moved instantly to flood the financial market with reserves through open-market purchases, and offered to support any banks in temporary difficulty. Friedman and Schwartz on the whole favor a fixed money supply or one growing at a regular rate, but support the Harrison view of the October 1929 re-

---

30. Friedman and Schwartz, Monetary History, p. 363.

sponse to the crash on lender-of-last-resort grounds, as noted earlier, making a distinction between an internal drain which must not be starved, and an external one which calls for higher interest rates.[31]

After a series of bank failures in the Middle West and South-Central part of the country in November 1930 came the important failure of the Bank of the United States in December. The New York Fed kept advocating open-market operations but was resisted by the Board in Washington. Because so many banks had run out of commercial bills eligible for rediscounting, the New York Bank urged the Board to allow it to discount ineligible paper.[32] This was turned down. The Federal Reserve Bank of New York with the support of the State Superintendent of Banks in the state sought to put together a guarantee of the Bank of the United States liabilities through members of the New York Clearing House. At the last minute some of the leading banks refused to go along. The refusal is regarded by Friedman and Schwartz as based on discrimination against an outsider Jewish group.[33] A contrary view has been offered by Peter Temin that the Bank of the United States was too far gone with bad loans to speculators and its own offices to constitute a suitable candidate for rescue.[34]

The crisis then shifted to Europe. The failure of the Credit-Anstalt Bank in Vienna on May 11, 1931, which in some eyes, though not mine, marked the beginning of the international phase of the Great Depression, provided another example of rule breaking in the first instance, followed by second thoughts. The Credit-Anstalt was the largest of the Austrian banks with 53 percent of the deposits in the commercial banking system, a system that had been weakened by a banking crisis in 1924 when a number of Austrian banks had suffered heavy losses in speculation against the French franc, and again in 1929 when the second largest bank, at that time, the Bodencreditanstalt, failed, with many of its problem assets absorbed at overvalued levels into the Credit-Anstalt. The announcement of the failure was accompanied by a plan for reconstruction of the bank in which the Austrian government, the Rothschild interests in Austria and the Austrian National Bank would make up the bank's losses and contribute new capital. There was a heavy run on the Credit-Anstalt and the other leading banks in Vienna, which the Austrian National Bank met by discounting freely. In the absence of sufficient commercial bills called

---

31. Friedman and Schwartz, Monetary History, p. 395.

32. Lucia, J. L.: The Failure of the Bank of the United States. A Reappraisal, in: Explorations in Economic History 22, 1985, p. 412.

33. Friedman and Schwartz, Monetary History, p. 309 note.

34. Temin, P.: Did Monetary Forces Cause the Great Depression?, New York 1976, pp. 91–94.

for by its regulators, R. Reisch, the Austrian National Bank president, liberally discounted finance bills, called by Aurel Schubert promissory notes. In four days, the panic run was brought to a halt.[35] To end the external drain the Austrian National Bank raised its discount rate and sought a loan from the Bank for International Settlements in Basle, which had opened the year before. The loan was provided but proved inadequate on several accounts: too small, too late, and carrying with it conditions that proved impossible for the Austrian government to meet and survive. After the initial successful spurt of domestic discounting, moreover, dissension developed within the Austrian National Bank, with the president wanting to continue discounting on terms which departed from the rules, but the vice-president and the director-general opposed. Inevitably the resulting hesitation was felt at home and abroad, the external drain continued, and the country was forced to impose control on foreign withdrawals.

As is well known the crisis spread to Germany and Britain. One could perhaps make a case that the Second Labour (MacDonald) government in Britain should have defiantly ignored the recommendations of the May Committee published in July 1931 that called for balancing the budget through cutting the dole (payments to the unemployed), but there were also the conditions to borrowing from official and private banks in the United States and France that the conservative policies of the May Committee be adhered to. A split developed in the Labour Party between those who called the May recommendations and the foreign conditions a "bankers' ramp" (in American English "racket"), and those who wanted to stay in power and operate within the constraints. The Labour government fell and was succeeded by a National government, with Ramsay MacDonald still as Prime Minister and Philip Snowden still Chancellor of the Exchequer. The government proceeded to reduce wages and the dole. A cut in Navy pay led to demonstrations by sailors in the naval base at Invergordon on September 16, regarded on the Continent of Europe as a mutiny, signifying a breakdown in one of the two traditional bulwarks of the British Empire, the Royal Navy and the Bank of England. Withdrawals of capital picked up speed. On September 21 the pound sterling gave up adherence to the gold standard. There was no real discussion of alternatives. A recent book on MacDonald characterized him as overworked and dispirited, abandoned by the Labour Party, welcoming the National government as a group of

---

35. Schubert, A.: The Credit-Anstalt Crisis of 1931, Cambridge 1985, chap. 2, esp. pp. 13, 147.

individuals with no set views rather than party politicians, and hence able to take hard decisions.[36] In the event, the movement from the formation of the National government to the forced depreciation of the pound which was not controlled in any way looked more like one of drift. The 30 percent depreciation of the pound (40 percent appreciation of the dollar, franc and Reichsmark) put sharp downward pressure on world commodity prices and accelerated deflation outside of the sterling area.

Depreciation of the world's key currency raised questions for all sorts of countries, questions which are still debated in those countries that did not follow the pound. Jürgen Schiemann has examined the controversy in Germany and concluded that such a course for the Reichsmark, assuming it had been possible, would have dampened the deflation somewhat but was unlikely to help the balance of payments.[37] Knut Borchardt thinks on the whole that public opinion would not have allowed Germany to abandon the parity achieved with difficulty in 1924. He further adduces technical reasons why such a course was undesirable, not all of which seem fully cogent. The international trade accounts were in surplus, but then sharp deflation reduces imports more than exports and leads to an export surplus; it would be unfair to German external creditors with claims in Reichsmarks, and would raise the Reichsmark equivalent of debts owed in foreign currencies (notably dollars), though these debts were not being serviced under the Standstill Agreement.[38] In the end he comes down to two powerful reasons, both of which, with the advantage of hindsight, seem to be based on faulty economic reasoning. Depreciation of the Reichsmark was regarded as inflationary, after the analogy of the early 1920s when inflation led to depreciation. But in severe depression some inflation, if it were true that depreciation would raise prices and incomes, was highly desirable. In addition the general public regarded depreciation as the policy of the

---

36. Williamson, P.: National Crisis and National Government. British Politics, the Economy, and Empire, 1926–1932. Cambridge 1992. I have not been able to see the book, but derive this account from a review by Daniel F. Calhoun in the Journal of Economic History 53, 1993, pp. 173–75.

37. Schiemann, J.: Die deutsche Währung in der Wirtschaftskrise, 1929–1933. Währungspolitik und Abwertungskontroverse unter den Bedingungen der Reparationen, Bern 1980.

38. Borchardt, K.: Could and Should Germany have Followed Great Britain in Leaving the Gold Standard?, in: Journal of European Economic History 3, 1984, pp. 471–97. See also Borchardt, K.: Zur Frage der währungspolitischen Optionen Deutschlands in der Weltwirtschaftskrise, in: Borchardt, K./Holzheu, F. (eds.): Theorie und Politik der internationalen Wirtschaftsbeziehungen, Stuttgart 1980.

extreme right, the National Socialist Party, so that adherence to gold was considered a bulwark against Hitler. Even Oberregierungsrat Wilhelm Lautenbach, whose Keynesian views well before the publication of *The General Theory of Employment, Interest and Money* (1936) were intensely debated in Germany in 1931 and 1932, was persuaded that "in the matter of currency the utmost correctness is necessary."[39] But there was no discussion of the positive experiences of other countries like Sweden which followed the pound off gold. Their histories and constraints, to be sure, were different from those of Germany, but their experience raises questions about the economic arguments, especially the fear of inflation, that seemed to count for so much.

Depreciation of the pound sterling called directly and indirectly for policy decisions in many countries. In one instance, the smaller countries of Europe which had lost part of their reserves held in sterling, immediately turned and withdrew their dollar reserves in gold, followed at a more leisurely and dignified pace by the Bank of France. This posed a problem for the Federal Reserve System. The classic response to an external drain, according to Bagehot, as Friedman and Schwartz note, is to raise interest rates. On the other hand, the United States had responded to the gold inflow of the early 1920s by sterilizing it, selling off government bonds so as not to let commercial bank reserves rise. A symmetrical policy in response to the gold outflow would have been to leave interest rates (the rediscount rate) unchanged and offset the loss of gold reserves by buying government bonds.[40]

The New York Bank voted to follow the classic prescription and on October 6, 1931 voted to increase the discount rate from 1½ to 2½ percent. It informed vice-president W. Randolph Burgess, en route to Europe by ship, with an assistant, Emile Despres, of its decision. Despres urged Burgess to ask the Bank to delay long enough for them to send a message, and drafted one which Burgess sent, arguing strongly against the step. Friedman and Schwartz record that at the October 8 meeting in New York:

"The only discordant note was a cablegram from Burgess, who was in Europe on a mission from the Bank, recommending no action that would bring about higher money rates in the United States. The cablegram was read at the meeting, then disregarded."[41]

---

39. Borchardt, Should Germany have Followed Britain?, p. 498.
40. Friedman and Schwartz, Monetary History, pp. 395–96.
41. Friedman and Schwartz, Monetary History, p. 381.

In the introduction to his collected papers, Despres writes: "Our sole accomplishment was to delay by all of one day what was perhaps the most disastrous policy decision of the Great Depression!"[42]

The Federal Reserve Bank of New York (and the Board which confirmed its recommendation) may have been, and in most judgments were wrong in raising the discount rate in October 1931, but the New York Bank continued to argue for expanding the money supply through open-market purchases of government bonds. Because of the gold losses, there was a problem, or at least what some officials of the system perceived as a problem, that of "free gold." With the stock-market collapse of 1929, a worldwide sharp decline in commodity prices occurred, as banks in the United States, loaded with illiquid brokers' loans, rationed credit to other borrowers, as recently explained by Ben Bernanke.[43] This affected especially commodity brokers in New York who needed credit to buy primary products shipped to that market on consignment to be sold on arrival. Without credit, commodities were dumped on the market and their prices plunged. The fall in price reduced the value of United States imports and the supply of eligible paper available for discount. The Federal Reserve Act of 1913 stipulated that the Federal Reserve liabilities, notes and deposits, had to be backed by gold up to a 40 percent minimum, with rediscounts for the remaining 60 percent, but that gold in excess of 40 percent, so-called free gold, could be substituted for rediscounts. The sharp decline in foreign and internal trade and the consequent fall in eligible paper made it necessary to use free gold as backing for the system's liabilities. If government bonds could have been substituted for commercial bills there would have been no problem. Without such authority, which was finally provided in the Glass-Steagall Act of February 27, 1932, open market operations which would have enlarged the liabilities of the Federal Reserve System might have run against a limitation because of a shortage of free gold. Friedman and Schwartz dismiss the problem with a long list of reasons: the Fed might have bought more bills if it had increased the interest rate it paid; commercial banks under the regulations could discount finance bills collateralized by government bonds; concern about free gold was by no means unanimous and came mostly from those who were advocating an enlarged program of open-market purchases; etc. Perhaps the most telling reason they give is that when the Glass-Steagall Act finally permitted the substitution of government paper

---

42. Meier, G. M. (ed.): International Economic Reform. Collected Papers of Emile Despres, New York 1973, p. xii.

43. Bernanke, B. S.: Nonmonetary Effects of the Financial Crisis in the Propagation of the Great Depression in: American Economic Review 73, 1983, pp. 257–76.

for rediscounts, six weeks went by before the System began its massive buying program, not too little, as in so many instances, but too late.[44] Thirty-some years later it seems to this reader that Friedman and Schwartz push too hard. Free gold was, if not a solid obstacle to a determined policy of monetary expansion, at least perceived as such. Dynamic leadership, which President Hoover and his Board of Governors did not provide, would have gone to Congressional leaders and announced that the provisions of the Federal Reserve Act regarding the need for commercial bills, and the exclusion of governments as backing for the System's liabilities, were archaic, interfering with policy flexibility, and would be set aside. Legislation would be sought in due course but in the meantime it was necessary to act. But by this time President Hoover was committed to his particular panacea, the Reconstruction Finance Corporation, which came into being December 1931, and in addition was becoming catatonic.

Conclusion

It is, I hope, clear from the foregoing that I do not find Borchardt's conclusion that Brüning had no alternatives to this policy of deflation completely persuasive. To some degree his analysis resembles the form of argument that finds objections successively to paths A, B, C, D, and E, and having dismissed each in turn, concludes that that leaves F. Secondly I find him insufficiently critical of Brüning's strategy—to concentrate on reparations first and then on such other foreign-policy successes as the *Zollunion* and the *Panzerkreuzer* to each of which objection could be and was made, as opposed to domestic employment. Third, I was deeply impressed by the debate over the Lautenbach memorandum at the Reichsbank on September 16 and 17, 1931 (to the published transcript of which Borchardt contributed a lucid introduction and explanatory footnotes), which showed that the forces of a spending program, financed by Reichsbank credit, had important support not only in a few academic circles, but widely there and inside and outside government otherwise.[45] The record of the secret debate recently uncovered in the files of the Mt. Pelerin Society is highly moving, as in a Shakespearean drama, especially with the agonized interventions of Reichsbank president Hans Luther, fearful that his institution was to be molested. It is ironic that both in the free-gold case in the United States

---

44. Friedman and Schwartz, Monetary History, p. 391.
45. Borchardt, K./Schötz, H. O. (eds.): Wirtschaftspolitik in der Krise: Die (Geheim-) Konferenz der Friedrich List-Gesellschaft im September 1931 über Möglichkeiten und Folgen einer Kreditausweitung, Baden-Baden 1991.

and the Lautenbach program, rejected proposals were adopted later and abundantly, if too late, with tragic economic consequences in the United States, and a benign economic but malign political outcome in Germany.

The dilemma posed by a choice between rules and men largely begs the question. There are, to be sure, times when rules, constraints, commitments, contract or treaty provisions stand in the way and should be transcended because of *force majeure,* acts of God, some *deus ex machina* that makes clear that all bets are off. The classic example, of course, is the outbreak of war. But many times the thrust of the rules is muddy, or there are two or more rules running in opposite directions, between which rational men may differ as to which should apply in particular circumstances. I have a strong propensity for citing the difficulty of choosing between "Look before you leap," and "He who hesitates is lost." The issue on whether or not to raise the rediscount rate of the Federal Reserve System in October 1931 after the gold drain to Europe stresses the ambiguity inherent in many economic conditions. The classic therapy may well call for meeting an external drain with a rise in interest rates, but when a number of small central banks panic, when world commodity prices have just been forced lower by the appreciation of the dollar, the French franc and the Reichsmark, and when there was little or no chance that the central banks in question would respond to a higher rate by reexchanging gold for dollars, the classic therapy might have been deemed to have no chance of working.

If one relies on men of responsibility to make the right choice in crisis among conflicting rules, or to follow an altogether different course for which no precedent exists, there is a danger of creating new precedents and new rules, which may be applied mistakenly under different circumstances. This is the inconvenience that Bagehot found in concluding that "the forces of the enemy being variable, those of the defense cannot always be the same." "Anything goes" as a slogan leaves room for authoritarian rule, such as Charles I's Stop of the Exchequer in 1672, or Philip II's unilateral conversion of short-term collateralized *asientos* into long-term *juros,* bonds denominated only in money in the late sixteenth century, or forced government loans to finance extravagances. British experience in financial crises in the nineteenth century seems to me to have combined the right mixture of an evidently temporary expedient—the Letters of Indemnity—with stern resistance to letting such action freeze into precedent on which markets could count.

The alternative to rules—men, which of course includes women—begs another question. Men have different responsibilities, principles, understandings, interests. Like Justices of the Supreme Court in the United States, highly trained successful men and women, deeply versed in the law, they frequently differ in close decisions, five on one side, four on the other. As widely noticed and sometimes derided, economic experts from time to time offer diverging advices. One should also note the thought of the American humorist, Mr. Dooley, that the Supreme Court follows the election returns, so that public opinion is involved. With strong and cohesive leadership, near unanimity of experts and understanding or pliant followership, men can be trusted in crisis to perform better than rules. I judge the Marshall Plan to have been such a case, though a revisionist view is not lacking.[46] In the ordinary crisis, however, if that is not an oxymoron, the need may be not only to choose between rules in general and more flexible decisions by men, but between the antithetical injunctions, each right in its time and place: (this to the catatonic) "Don't just stand there; do something," and (this to the hyperactivist) "Don't just do something; stand there."

---

46. See, for example, Milward, A.: The Reconstruction of Western Europe, 1945–51, London 1984, esp. chap. I.

CHAPTER 14

The Economic Crisis of 1619 to 1623

Introduction

F 32

The first quarter of the seventeenth century, up to and through the beginnings of the Thirty Years' War with the defenestration at Prague in 1618,
has been widely described as a period of crisis. The crisis was particularly
acute between 1619 and 1623; sometimes and in particular localities it was
described as a "commercial crisis," sometimes as a "joint crisis in commerce and industry," but usually as a "currency crisis" and in one instance
as a "monetary crisis and panic" and even "a monetary corner."[1] Moreover, it was set within a deeper structural crisis covering 100 to 150 years
of transition from medieval to modern times. The period has been vari-
ously described as a movement from feudalism to capitalism; from a
feudal to a nation-state society; from the political and economic ascen-
dency of the South (Italy and Spain) to that of the North (the United
Provinces of Holland and England); from a "natural economy" based on
the self-sufficient household and barter to the use of markets and money;

Reprinted from *Journal of Economic History* 5, no. 1 (March 1991): 149–75. Copyright © The Economic History Association. Reprinted with the permission of Cambridge
University Press.

Several scholars have been helpful in referring me to and sending me copies of
papers not readily accessible in Cambridge. Thanks are due to Rondo Cameron, Wolfram
Fischer, Christopher Friedrichs, Geoffrey Parker, and Mark Steele. Professors Fischer and
Friedrichs also commented on an early draft, as did the members of the Washington Area
Economic History seminar. I have also benefited from the revision suggestions of two
anonymous referees and Peter Lindert.

A bewildering number of coins of varying worth is mentioned in this article, but in
general the subsidiary coins of the Holy Roman Empire comprised the silver gulden (or
florin) of 60 kreuzer, the groschen of 3 kreuzer, and various other duodecimal denominations such as the 6, 12, and 24 kreuzer, the batzen of 4 kreuzer, and the penny, four to a
batzen. The 1559 standard for higher denominations included the silver Reichstaler (in
Dutch the *rixdaler*) of 1 florin, 4 kreuzer, and the gold ducat of 3 florins.

1. Supple, "Thomas Mun"; Supple, *Commercial Crisis;* Spooner, *Monetary Movements in France,* 32; Romano, "Italy," 193; and Shaw, *History of Currency,* 102.

from separate deals to continuous trade on bourses; and from the polynuclear system of European cities to a mononuclear one with its core in Amsterdam.[2] Other disruptive factors were the Eighty Years' War from 1572 to 1652, between Spain and the Netherlands, and the Thirty Years' War from 1618 to 1648. Many accounts assign a major role to the falling off of silver imports to Europe from Spanish America after about 1600 or 1620, inadequately compensated for by the gradual rise of credit—but the data on which this judgment is based have lately been questioned.[3] Jan de Vries indicated that, while no single event between 1600 and 1750 ushered in the new phase in European economic history, a good candidate for such a role would have been the trade crisis of 1619 to 1622.[4]

My interest in that crisis does not concern its potential role as a catalyst of modern economies, but rather its function in the mechanism for the spread of primarily financial crisis from one part of Europe to another. This is an interest I have explored elsewhere under very different institutional conditions in the crisis of 1720, 1873, 1890, and 1929.[5] My focus here is on the Holy Roman Empire (largely Germany) and Poland and the period of gradual debasement of the currency between 1600 and 1618, followed by a rapid phase from 1619 or 1620 to 1622 and 1623, when the currency was more or less stabilized. I propose to discuss the idiosyncratic phrase by which the episode is known, the *Kipper- und Wipperzeit,* relate it to the particular monetary conditions of the period, and suggest one or two broad comparisons with the inflations in Germany in 1923 and 1947. Finally I draw some conclusions relevant to the concept of unregulated banking advocated today in a number of economists' quarters in Europe and the United States.

The Kipper- und Wipperzeit

The term *Kipper und Wipper* was seventeenth-century slang. The economic historian Friedrich-Wilhelm Henning identified the *Kipper* part with "clipping," easily perpetrated on coins before the introduction of milled edges in Britain later in the century; the practice was discussed at length by Thomas Macaulay in his *History of England.* Geoffrey

---

2. Hobsbawm, "Crisis"; Trevor-Roper, "General Crisis"; Rapp, *Industry and Economic Decline;* Heckscher, *Economic History of Sweden,* chap. 4; Parker, "Emergence of Modern Finance"; and van der Wee, "Industrial Dynamics."

3. Attman, *American Bullion.*

4. de Vries, *Age of Crisis,* 115.

5. Kindleberger, *Manias;* Kindleberger, "International Propagation"; and Kindleberger, "Panic of 1873."

Parker, leaning heavily on the word *Wippe,* offered "seesaw" for the second half.[6]

Fritz Redlich explained the combination as deriving from the actions of money exchangers who kept their scales moving to befuddle the innocent onlookers whose good money was being exchanged for bad.[7] *Kippen* is "to tilt," and while *Wippe* is in fact a seesaw, *wippen,* the verb, is "to wag." *Kipper- und Wipperzeit* was analogous to Cockney rhyming slang such as hurley-burley. The words even generated offspring in such expressions as *Kipperei* (the act of debasement), *Kippergeld* (*Geld* meaning money), and *Kippermünze* (*Münze* being coins and also mints). *Auswippen* meant to select out good coins to hoard or export. Redlich explains that *Kippergeld* was not clipped so much as debased by altering its denomination, weight, metal, or fineness. Most of the trouble arose not from "crying up" existing coins with higher denominations but from hoarding and reminting good coins and minting new ones of lighter weight, baser metal, or both.

Supplies of Precious Metals

Even without the extended wars and the malversation of mint masters and their higher authorities, getting the currency right in this period posed difficulties because of rapidly changing relative supplies of gold, silver, and copper and the opportunities this gave to exercise Gresham's Law. It would have been impossible to have a monometallic money. Gold was needed for large international transactions, after clearing as many payments as possible through bills of exchange. Silver was used for purchases in the Baltic, the Far and Middle East, and for large payments in domestic trade. There was virtually no problem with the larger gold and silver coins at this time. The trouble lay in the subsidiary coinage, starting out as silver—gulden, groschen, kreuzer, batzen, and even pennies—and ending up as vellon or billon, silver with varying amounts of copper up to 99 percent, and pure copper, sometimes weakly whitened. Germany has been said to have been on a de facto copper standard from about 1621 to 1623.[8]

Supplies of these precious and semiprecious metals varied. Upon the discovery of the New World in 1492, there was an initial flow of looted gold. In about 1540 the silver mountain Potosí in Peru was discovered; it was rendered highly productive after about 1570. Much, perhaps

---

6. Henning, *Das vorindustrielle Deutschland;* Macauley, *History of England,* vol. 4, 181–201; and Parker, *Thirty Years' War,* 90.

7. Redlich, *Die deutsche Inflation,* 17–21.

8. Ibid., 11.

most, of the silver arriving in Spain left Europe afterward—some to the Baltic and through Russia and Poland farther east, some to the eastern Mediterranean, but most to India and China directly around the Cape of Good Hope.[9] In 1613, King Gustav Adolphus began to increase production of and export copper from the Stora Kopperberg in Sweden to ransom the fortress at Alvsborg from Denmark. The Swedes raised the ransom by borrowing in Amsterdam against the collateral of copper, marketing new supplies through Hamburg and Amsterdam rather than Lübeck. Other copper came to Europe from Japan, and the price fell almost by one-half. In Germany, nevertheless, copper came to be in short supply as German mints used more and more: musical instruments, kettles, pipes, gutters, and even church bells and baptismal fonts, some of them stolen, were dumped into the melting pot.[10]

These surges in the supply of first one metal then another changed their relative prices and, as mentioned, created severe Gresham's Law-type problems in Europe. The drying up of New World gold supplies and the spurt of silver imports ruined the silver mines in central Europe that had produced for mints such as that of the Slick family in Joachimstal (from whence came *thaler,* later transmogrified into "dollar"). The bulge in the supply of copper led Spain, exhausted financially by war and drained of silver, seriously to debase its currency. From 1599 to 1606, the Spanish monarchy coined 22 million ducats in vellon, a copper alloy. The bankruptcy of the Spanish treasury in 1607, which destroyed its credit and led to the failure of the Fuggers and a number of Genoan bankers, elicited a royal promise to the *Cortes* to coin no more copper—a promise kept for ten years. In 1617 to 1619, the monarchy obtained permission of the *Cortes* to resume and coined five million ducats in copper. Two years later another 14 million were added. Spain experienced financial crises at the level of the monarchy in 1557, 1575, 1596, 1607, 1627, and 1647—though not, on this showing, in 1619 to 1623. That it avoided the latter crisis may have been a benefit of the truce with Holland that lasted from 1607 to 1621, easing the strain on the budget. In the private sector, however, a continuous squeeze was felt. In the mid-sixteenth century there were 50 or 60 operators importing silver in ingots. By 1615, only eight were left, four of which went bankrupt shortly thereafter; by 1620, only three remained. Redlich mentions that the Spanish monarchy's crisis of 1627 was an echo of the *Kipper- und Wipperzeit.*[11]

---

9. Kindleberger, "Spenders and Hoarders."

10. Heckscher, *Economic History of Sweden,* 79, 85, 105; Spooner, *Monetary Movements in France,* 46; and Langer, *Kulturgeschichte,* 30.

11. Spooner, *Monetary Movements in France,* 38; Ehrenberg, *Fuggers,* 334; Parker, *Thirty Years' War,* 77; Vilar, *Gold and Money,* 141; and Redlich, *Die deutsche Inflation,* 12.

The Monetary Porosity of Small States

Metallic standards, of course, have an inherent potential for divergence between the nominal value of a coin and its actual value as metal. Moreover, coin passed readily over the borders of states and through the gates of cities despite attempts of kings, princes, dukes, counts, and the like to control it. The result was, in most jurisdictions, a mishmash of coins of varied origins. A century and a half after the time in question, in his digression on banks of deposit and especially the Bank of Amsterdam, Adam Smith drew a distinction between large and small states.

> The currency of a great state, such as France or England, generally consists almost entirely of its own coin. Should this currency therefore be at any time, worn, clipt or otherwise degraded below its standard value, the state by a reformation of its coin can effectively re-establish its currency. But the currency of a small state, such as Genoa or Hamburgh, can seldom consist altogether in its own coin, but must be made up, in great measure, of the coins of all the neighboring states with which its inhabitants have continual intercourse. Such a state, therefore, by reforming its coin will not always be able to reform its currency.[12]

A modern German historian of the Thirty Years' War made the same point, expressing the view that the Austrian hereditary lands and perhaps Bavaria and Brandenburg were "big and compact enough" to use independent minting for their own domestic purposes. Similarly, a nineteenth-century writer referred to small states as "monetarily pathological border states" (*münzkranke Grenzlande*). But if Smith's remark was meant to apply to the early seventeenth century, he was too optimistic about France's ability to make its own coin dominate its monetary circulation—and perhaps about Britain's as well. Spooner makes clear that France had no single monetary unit but was instead a series of economic zones, dominated in the west by silver reales from Spain and in Burgundy and Champagne by billon, another copper alloy, from Germany.[13] In England, a sharp distinction was made between foreign coin and coin of domestic minting. For example, it was recommended that the East India Company be allowed to export only foreign, not domestic

12. Smith, *Wealth of Nations,* 446.
13. Schöttle, "Münz- und Geldgeschichte," 82; Opel, *Deutsche Finanznoth,* 216; and Spooner, *Monetary Movements in France,* 4, 9.

coin (nor silver bullion). Foreign currencies had circulated freely in Sweden ever since money had come into general use. A century later there were as many as 50 different, mainly foreign, coins, 22 gold and 29 silver, circulating in Milan. Still later, in 1816, at least 70 coins—from Holland, France, Belgium, and various German states—circulated in the Rhineland, and Prussian coins were rarely seen despite the efforts of Prussian officials to enforce rules against the use of older and foreign coins.[14]

Transactions in various types of coin required a unit of account into which the various monies could be translated and compared. This was often an "imaginary money," in the sense that it need not be coined and circulated: the pound and shilling in England were long imaginary units of account, as were the livre tournois in France, and the livre or lira in Milan. Imaginary money that served as a unit of account was a public good: in Einaudi's words, "a splendid instrument for performing certain tasks of public policy."[15] While Reichstalers were widely coined in the "mosaic Germany" made up of many states, they were mostly hoarded during the period in question so that they became an imaginary money for calculating the debasement of the subsidiary coinage (in German, *Scheidemünze*).

The larger coins of gold and silver, used for international trade where bills of exchange had not yet penetrated or to settle balances where they had not cleared evenly, were frequently weighed and tested, though not always with complete honesty, as the word *Wipper*—"to wag (the scales)"—indicates. Subsidiary coins, used for retail trade and wages and by the ordinary person in payment of rents, dues, and taxes, more frequently were reckoned at their nominal value, whether from ignorance or to save transactions costs. This lends some slight support to Georg Knapp's monetary theory, which said that the value of money was determined by the state.[16] Whenever there exist, side by side, coins of the same nominal worth but of different weight and fineness, profit is to be made by exchanging debased for good coin and melting down the latter or exporting the metal. Base money was imported and good money exported as early as the thirteenth century, well before the time of Sir Thomas Gresham, Queen Elizabeth I's exchanger. It has been suggested that Aristotle was aware of the tendency; it was clearly enunciated by Nicholas Oreme, Bishop of Lisieux, in his *De Moneta* of about

14. Thirsk and Cooper, *Economic Documents*, 11, 211, 214; Einaudi, "Imaginary Money," 242–43; and Tilly, *Financial Institutions in the Rhineland,* chap. 2, esp. 20–21.

15. de Roover, *Gresham*, 32, Spooner, *Monetary Movements in France,* 20; and Einaudi, 244, 260.

16. Ellis, *German Monetary Theory.*

1360, and it was well known to Copernicus in 1525.[17] The theory continues to be known as Gresham's Law, however, because it, like so many false historical terms, has proven impossible to change once adopted.

Controlling Gresham's Law

None of the methods that have attempted to combat the workings and effects of Gresham's Law has met with great success. Forbidding the import of bad coin and/or the export of good has failed even when accompanied by dire penalties such as death by burning, mutilation, confiscation of all goods, and banishment. Smuggling coin through city gates in bundles of produce was virtually impossible to stop, especially on market days.[18]

Another method has been to adjust the denominations of existing coins by "crying up" good coins, or raising their denomination to reduce the metal content of a stated value, or "crying down" the bad. This adjustment can be made by separate states or by a number of states via treaties. As early as March 1609, a mint treaty among Mecklenburg, Schleswig-Holstein, Hamburg, and Lübeck was concluded—in anticipation, Shaw says, of approaching disorder.[19]

Alternatively, the entire coinage may be called in and reminted at the old standard weight and fineness, thus imposing a loss on the sovereign, or at lower weights, reduced fineness, or higher prices, thus shifting the burden to the holders of money.

A more sophisticated method is to establish banks of deposit requiring wealthholders, and especially merchants, to deposit their holdings of currency above certain minimums in a bank where the coin would be assayed, weighed, and recorded on the books at its metal content. Merchants may then be required to deposit receipts in international trade above a certain minimum and make similar payments against those accounts. This last function, related to bills of exchange (*wechsel* in German, *wissel* in Dutch), stabilizes the metallic value of bills of exchange, which in turn reduces transactions costs. Adam Smith noted that the exchange rate on the Bank of Amsterdam generally stood at a premium of about 5 percent over the specie rate because of the greater certainty about the value of the money.[20] Deliberations leading to the establishment of the Bank of Amsterdam started about 1606 in the early days of

---

17. Feaveryear, *The Pound Sterling,* 11; and Wolowski, *La question monétaire,* 15, 90–91.
18. Schöttle, "Die grosse deutsche Geldkrise," 50.
19. Shaw, *History of Currency,* 104.
20. Smith, *Wealth of Nations,* 451.

the *Kipper- und Wipperzeit,* before depreciation had gone far; the Bank was created in 1609. Its success in achieving its goal is reflected in the statement that "Ten years later, Hamburg led to a fixed exchange rate against the fluctuating money of other states."[21] Similar banks were established in Middleburg (Holland) in 1616, in Hamburg and Venice in 1619, and in Delft and Nuremberg in 1621—these last at the height of the debasement. With the stabilization of 1623 began a falloff in the establishment of deposit banks, lasting until 1634. The Swabian Circle proposed the establishment of a bank of deposit in the fall of 1619, but the project was converted into a bank to buy silver for the local mint in such centers as Genoa, to overcome the shortage in southern Germany. It was quickly closed down.[22]

A further method of control is to decree and enforce minting standards by means of official coin-testing days and the administration of oaths to mint masters and selected assayers. As with most of the other methods, success in holding to standards over a wide territory was limited. In the sixteenth century, the Holy Roman Empire sought to standardize the coinage of the Empire in decrees issued in 1524, again in 1551, and at Augsburg in 1559. The rules were laid down with little comprehension of the difficulty of maintaining a fixed relationship between the stated values of gold, silver coins, and copper at a time of significant shifts in the supplies of these precious metals, or of the difficulty of providing an adequate supply of subsidiary coins, which, according to the Augsburg Ordinance, were to be of silver. The Empire administered oaths to all mint masters, and there was one proposal to extend them to mint workers. Redlich calls this 1615 proposal "senseless," saying it should have been extended to the diemakers. Coin-testing trials, too, were hardly efficacious: one General Assayer Rentzsch, describing the debasement of the coinage in the Lower Saxon Circle and particularly in Pomerania, the Saxon dukedom, and the Harz dynasty, claimed that the mints kept a supply of good groschen on hand to show the General Assayer on his visits.[23]

The primary difficulty, however, was the absence of effective central authority. The Holy Roman Empire consisted of a variegated collection of Electoral states, principalities, duchies, other states, cities, bishoprics, and the like, organized into circles (*Kreise*), one of the tasks of which was to implement decisions under the Imperial Mint

---

21. Kellenbenz, *Sephardim an der Unteren Elbe,* 254.

22. Schöttle, "Münz- und Geldgeschichte," 85.

23. Wuttke, "Zur Kipper- und Wipperzeit in Kursachsen," 120–21, 136; and Redlich, *Die deutsche Inflation,* 51.

Ordinances. Circles formed something of a crazy-quilt pattern, stretching obliquely from southwest to northeast in a number of cases, though many were called "Upper" and "Lower" or "Northern" and "Southern." The Swabian, Frankish, and Westphalian circles were formed along ancient tribal boundaries.[24] Bohemia and Moravia lay within the Empire but were outside the system of circles, as were Savoy and most of Switzerland. The Empire, moreover, included parts of what are now France, Belgium, Italy, and of course Austria, as shown on the map in Figure 14.1.

Most German literature on the *Kipper- und Wipperzeit* deals with a single circle, especially with Upper and Electoral Saxony and with Swabia.[25] Maria Bogucka has at least one article in English on the experience in Poland.[26] Writing on Bohemia, Arnošt Klíma asserts, contrary to my hypothesis, that the inflation in Bohemia in the early seventeenth century (1621 to 1623) was *unconnected* (his emphasis) with the general European economic situation of the time but had special features evoked by the uprising of the Czech Estates of 1616 to 1620 and their defeat.[27] Shaw has twice dealt with the question generally, without giving much attention to either the propagation mechanism or the 1622-to-1623 stabilization.[28] Writing on French currency problems of the period, Spooner looks over his shoulder at the Germany (and Spanish) inflationary disorders.[29] The considerable literature on the commercial crisis in Britain at the time debates the extent to which it resulted from the debasement of German subsidiary coinage.[30]

Currency debasement and the Thirty Years' War

As is true of so many financial crises transmitted from place to place, it is virtually impossible to pin down a unique geographic origin. The mechanism is clear enough and has been described in a chapter appendix on coin debasement by Jacob van Klavaren.[31] A prince (duke, bishop, abbot, city) with the right to coin money foresees troubles arising from the

24. Wuttke, "Zur Kipper- und Wipperzeit in Kursachsen," 123.
25. Ibid.; Redlich, *Die deutsche Inflation;* Gaettens, *Geschichte des Inflationen;* Schöttle, "Die grosse deutsche Geldkrise"; and Schöttle, "Münz- und Geldgeschichte."
26. Bogucka, "The Monetary Crisis."
27. Klíma, "Inflation in Bohemia," 375–86.
28. Shaw, *History of Currency;* and Shaw, "The Monetary Movements of 1600–21."
29. Spooner, *Monetary Movements in France.*
30. Gould, "The Trade Depression of the Early 1620s"; Feaveryear, *The Pound Sterling;* Supple, "Thomas Mun"; Supple, "Currency and Commerce"; Supple, *Commercial Crisis;* and for documents, Thirsk and Cooper, *Economic Documents.*
31. Van Klavaren, *General Economic History,* appendix to chap. 13.

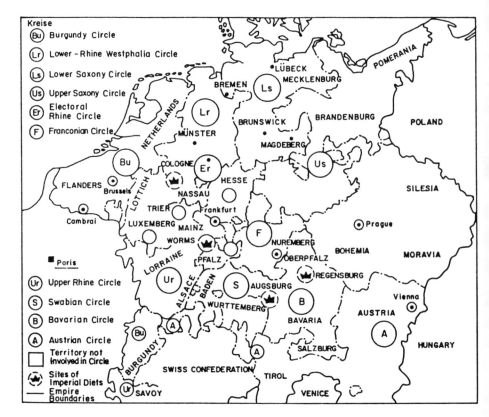

Fig. 14.1.   Division of the Holy Roman Empire into circles, 1512.
(Source: dtv, *Atlas*, vol. 1, p. 218).

Reformation and the Counterreformation that led to the Thirty Years'
War. A war chest is needed and, after war breaks out, soldiers (who are
increasingly mercenaries) have to be mobilized and strong points forti-
fied. Adam Smith holds forth to this subject, too, but in connection with
debt rather than debasement.[32]

Apart perhaps from Spanish Flanders (Antwerp), Holland (Amsterdam), and Spain, the last of which continually overborrowed, governmental capacity to borrow in the first half of the seventeenth century in
Europe was limited by the absence of efficient capital markets and competent officials. France raised money through the sale of offices, a
means not open to the many small states of the Empire. Taxation of
commodities would have had to be uniform to prevent arbitrage from

32. Smith, *Wealth of Nations*, 861–62.

state to state, an integrative step for which the Empire was far from ready. One way to prepare financially for war was for the separate principalities, duchies, cities, and the like to seek greater seignorage by coining more money. Many states were interested in raising seignorage within their own boundaries, but it was soon discovered that debased money could be taken abroad and exchanged for good money, which could in turn be brought back and recoined with greater seignorage. Those engaged in exchanging debased money for good included northern Italians and Jews, but people from all walks of life and even women participated. Glib dealers went abroad to set up exchange booths, exploiting as best they could pastors, millers, and peasants.[33]

And so the neighboring principality finds itself flooded with bad coin and losing good. To retain the latter, it raises the price of the metal in its coins, thus crying them up. With the higher prices it begins to attract good coin and export bad. The process builds up. Some princes lease mints to entrepreneurs, who need to add their profit to the seignorage of the prince specified in the leasing contract. At the old prices mints find that the higher price of silver and rising wages make it unprofitable to produce standard subsidiary coins.[34] Thus honorable mints stop producing subsidiary coins altogether.

The price of the good Reichstaler kept rising in terms of debased groschen (see Table 14.1) at an interesting rate until 1619, and especially rapidly in 1621 and the first months of 1622, a period characterized by Shaw as the peak of monetary panic and crisis.[35] These figures seem to be averaged across many states, though some higher ones in 1622 are pinpointed for Nuremberg, Augsburg, and Vienna. In general, according to Opel, northern German states such as Westphalia, Luneberg, Pomerania, Mecklenberg, and the Hanseatic cities experienced less depreciation of their subsidiary coinage than did those in the south. In July 1622 the Reichstaler went to 15 gulden in Nuremberg; with the help of the death penalty, the city council got it down to 10 gulden. But the various sources fail to agree narrowly on rates, not unexpectedly given a country with a primitive transport and communication network.[36]

A historian of the Swabian experience and its central city, Ulm, suggests that the first invasion of debased money came from Italy and especially Switzerland as early as 1580. The entry point for the northern

---

33. Langer, *Kulturgeschichte,* 29; and Opel, "Deutsche Finanznoth," 222.

34. Wuttke, "Zur Kipper- und Wipperzeit in Kursachsen," 126, 132; and Gaettens, *Geschichte des Inflationen,* 74.

35. Shaw, *History of Currency,* 102.

36. Opel, "Deutsche Finanznoth," 229–31.

TABLE 14.1.   Quotations of the Reichstaler on Specific Dates, in Florins and Kreutzers

Date		Florins	Kreutzers	Date		Florins	Kreutzers
1582		1	8	1621	Jan.	2	20
1587		1	9		Feb.	2	24
1590		1	10		March	2	30
1594		1	11		April	2	36
1596		1	12		May 25	2	48
1603		1	14		May 31	3	15
1604		1	14		June	3	6
1605		1	15		July	3	15
1607		1	16		Aug.	4	0
1608		1	20		Aug. 10	3	15[a]
1609	June 15	1	22		Sept.	4	30[a]
	July 7				Oct.	5	0[a]
	Dec. 19 }	1	24		Nov.	5	30[a]
1610		1	24		Dec.	6	30[a]
1613	Sept.	1	26		Dec. 20	3	15
1614	Aug.	1	28	1622	Jan. 18	7	30[b]
1615	March	1	28		Jan. 27	4	30
	Nov. 1	1	24		Feb. 10	10	0[c]
	Nov. 17	1	30		March	10	0[c]
1616		1	30		March 12	6	0
1617		1	30		June 16	3	15
1618		1	32		Oct.	5	0
1619	Oct.	1	48		Nov.	6	0
	Dec.	2	4	1623	April	1	30[d]
1620	June	2	8				
	Nov. 9	2	20				

Source: Shaw, *History of Currency,* 103. Shaw observed that similar quotations of the gulden, thaler, and the gold gulden for the empire at large are available. They are set out in Shaw, "The Monetary Movements of 1600–21," 209.

Note: 60 kreutzers equals 1 florin.

[a] Nuremberg

[b] Augsburg

[c] Vienna

[d] Value was fixed at this last figure until 1669.

Italian noble counterfeiters and those of Graubunden in Switzerland, especially the Bishop of Chur, was at Lindau on the Bodensee (Lake Constance). The same account, however, records that three upper circles—Swabia, Franconia, and Bavaria—found the counterfeiting of the Upper Rhine Circle that included Strassburg to be particularly insolent.[37]

As the agio on the Reichstaler rose slowly during the seventeenth

37. Schöttle, "Münz- und Geldgeschichte," 78–80.

century, more and more mints were established or leased by princes and nobles, both secular and ecclesiastical, as well as by cities. Some were even rented by the week. An early attempt had been made in 1603 and 1604 to limit the number of mints to no more than three or four to a circle, except for those having silver mines. The move was opposed by six cities with mint privileges, all located in the lower Saxon Circle: Lübeck, Hamburg, Rostock, Bremen, Brunswick, and Magdeburg. This successful opposition allowed other towns with minting privileges to establish more mints; even those without the privilege began minting.[38] Mints sprang up "like mushrooms after a warm rain"[39] and debased coinage "poured from them in avalanche proportions."[40] Brunswick had 17 mints in 1620; by 1623 there were 40, including a convent that in the course of a few months converted itself into a mint employing 300 to 400 workers.[41]

One widely noted operation was the lease by the Emperor Ferdinand II himself to a consortium of which only five names are known. These included Prince Carl von Liechtenstein and Albert Wallenstein, a general, later Duke of Friedland and then of Mecklenberg, who was murdered in 1634. Wallenstein had married an elderly widow in 1609 and inherited her fortune when she died in 1614. This he enlarged with the mint lease covering Bohemia, Moravia, and Lower Austria. With these monies he bought close to 60 estates in Bohemia belonging to Protestants after the Catholics had won the battle of the White Mountain in November 1620 and either confiscated the estates or bought them at imposed prices with debased coinage. These fortunes enabled Wallenstein to finance his own army in Thirty Years' War battles at a time when other armies had to rely on booty just to feed their troops.[42] The consortium's final contract in January 1622 specified a payment of 6 million gulden of 60 kreuzers to the Emperor, with substantial profits to its members. The terms of the lease are known but not the names of most of the leaseholders, who may have chosen to be anonymous. The cartel later took over a lease of the mint of the Bishop of Breslau in Silesia.[43]

Because most of the literature describes single circles, or at most two or three, little speaks to the geographical spread of the debasement.

38. Gaettens, *Geschichte des Inflationen,* 75.

39. Langer, *Kulturgeschichte,* 30.

40. Schöttle, "Münz- und Geldgeschichte," 84.

41. Langer, *Kulturgeschichte,* 80, Further mint numbers are given by, among others, Opel, "Deutsche Finanznoth," 226–27.

42. Redlich, *De Praeda Militari.*

43. Gaettens, *Geschichte des Inflationen,* 86–87, 97–98; and Klíma, "Inflation in Bohemia," 378–79.

Indeed, Opel says that it is impossible to give a full account of the territorial spread of the *Kipper und Wipper*. Of particular interest is its spread from the German states to Poland, possibly through Danzig at the instance of the Dutch who were said to have dominated that port and dictated its prices and exchange rates. Alternatively, it may have moved along the coast from Pomerania, one of the worst debasers in the Lower Saxon Circle, or via Cracow, which was the center for the export of Polish coins to Silesia and the Czech lands. Another route was via Leipzig, which paid the highest prices for silver in all of Germany, so that silver poured into it. Leipzig was also a central city for coins, its fair specializing in trade with the east, including Poland, a country with minting troubles of its own at that time. The larger coins depreciated more slowly in Danzig than elsewhere because of the Polish export surplus, mostly rye and timber, which the Dutch paid in silver. But Poland also had import surpluses, not only with central Europe but also with the Near and Far East, and considerable amounts of coin left the country eastward by way of Lvov. It is difficult to reconcile the various statements about Polish money: Bogucka claims Poland was flooded with foreign coin, whereas one earlier source on Germany notes that good Reich coins left the country and light Polish, Dutch, Spanish, and Hungarian coins flowed in. The same account elsewhere notes that all groups in Brandenberg—merchants, hand laborers, peasants, retailers, daily workers, and serving people—sold to Poland, along with Mecklenburg and Pomerania, in order to acquire precious metals.[44]

The British Commercial Crisis of 1621

Britain's economic crisis, in contrast, was more commercial than financial and did not involve currency debasement at domestic mints. Much of it was ascribed to the loss of wool exports to the Continent resulting from the undervaluation of the German and Polish currencies: prices rose less than the metal value of coin—at least subsidiary coin—declined. But contemporary documents present long lists of reasons for the decline in income and rise in unemployment in Britain: (1) the shortage of money in the country as a result of the export of coin and bullion, partly through the East India Company to pay for pepper and calico but also to the Baltic for timber and naval stores; (2) the abortive

---

44. Opel, "Deutsche Finanznoth," 228; Braudel, *The Wheels of Commerce,* 255; Wuttke, "Zur Kipper- und Wipperzeit in Kursachsen," 113, 136; Bogucka, "The Monetary Crisis," 141–43; Gaettens, *Geschichte des Inflationen,* 83; Redlich, *Die deutsche Inflation,* 14; and Opel, "Deutsche Finanznoth," 216–37.

Alderman Cockayne project of 1615 to hold back woolens from the Continent for finishing in England; (3) the clumsy adjustment of the prices of gold and silver relative to the ratio in Amsterdam: first in 1606, when the silver content of coins was lowered more than gold, and again in 1611, when the price of all gold coins was raised[45] to bring a large volume of silver to the mint from 1601 to 1611, and none from 1611 to 1630; (4) the trial in the Star Chamber in 1617 and 1618 of 18 foreign merchants for smuggling coin out of England to the fantastic extent of £7 million, which may have been a blundering attempt to stop the flow of interest payments to Holland but also possibly led to a halt in Dutch lending to London and contributed to the financial crisis there in 1621.[46]

The loss in exports of woolen cloth gets special stress in the contemporary documents, as exports fell from 127,000 pieces in 1614 to 45,000 in 1640 after having risen from 100,000 pieces in 1600. Further causes of the "spectacular British crisis of the 1620s" have been adduced: bad harvests, plague, and the disastrous loss of 11 ships, some filled with silver, in the Far Eastern Dutch-British war of 1618 and 1619. The many causes (and remedies) cited suggest that the crisis was overdetermined in the minds of contemporaries, so it is difficult at this remove and in the absence of sufficient financial data to form a solid judgment. Feaveryear suggests that the Gresham's Law undervaluation of silver was more important than the decline in cloth exports, because the continued inflow of gold to the mint implies that the balance of payments cannot be blamed.[47] The exchange of an equal value of silver for gold was a blow to the "*effective* monetary circulation" because of the far greater use of silver than gold in ordinary transactions.[48]

I have some difficulty in accepting the analysis that the debasement of German and Polish coins led to the English commercial difficulties, because the debasement affected primarily the subsidiary coinage and not those of larger denomination such as the silver Reichstaler or the gold ducat normally used to settle balances in international trade. These coins may have been so widely hoarded, however, that the effective exchange rate ran to the gulden (or florin) rather than to the

45. Feaveryear, *The Pound Sterling*, 88–89.

46. Barbour, *Capitalism and Amsterdam*, 122–23. Among those convicted and fined was Philip Burlamachi, a royal exchanger of Italian stock, who was born in France, began his career in the Netherlands, and arrived in England in 1605. See Judge, "Philip Burlamachi."

47. Thirsk and Cooper, *Economic Documents*, chaps. 1, 5, 6; Wilson, *Transformation of Europe*, 53; Chauduri, *English East India Company*, 60–61; and Feaveryear, *The Pound Sterling*, 89.

48. Supple, *Commercial Crisis*, 173, italics in the original.

higher units of account. As I have already noted, and as has been recently analyzed for later inflations, inflation can be accompanied by export surpluses at a stage frequently encountered when the external depreciation exceeds the rise of domestic prices.[49] Evidence from the Swabian Circle, at a considerable distance from the seacoast, indicates concern over local export surpluses. Ulm, Biberach, and Überlingen restricted the export of foodstuffs, hay, cattle, and yarn and confined sales to local markets following a "policy of supply," the rationale for which was developed in Italy in the eighteenth century.[50] Closer to the time I am concerned with, Biberach clad its civil servants in uniforms of Meissen cloth rather than the English cloth that "had become too dear, and must be paid for in ducats, doubloons, Rose Nobles and other hard talers, all of which required a larger agio."[51] Shortages in Swabia became so acute that the authorities on one occasion commandeered a shipment passing through on its way to Switzerland and sold the goods on the local market.

The Incidence of Debasement and Inflation

Many people in this period became very rich: often through minting, as was partly the case of Wallenstein, and sometimes through corruption. The Duke of Lerma, who managed Spain for 20 years until 1618, when he was attacked for malfeasance, amassed a fortune of 44 million thalers, equivalent to the entire income of Phillip III of Spain for five years. Earlier the Duke of Alva, a Spanish general in the Netherlands war with no reputation as a rich man, had died in 1582 with 600 dozen silver plates and 800 silver platters. In Poland magnates, nobles, and well-to-do burghers hoarded jewelry, luxury plate, and coin by the ton, according to Bogucka, who notes that Duke Januz of Ostrog left a sum of 600,000 ducats, 290,000 different coins, 400,000 crowns (gulden), and 30 barrels of broken silver. Similar treasures are recorded in the inventories of other decedents. The members of the Prague consortium made their profits by selling silver to the mint at exorbitant prices and in large volume. Hans de Witte, who operated the mint, sold silver at a low price but in such volume that he received 31,240,000 gulden. Klíma also mentions the case of Albrecht Jan Smiřký, who at the time of the uprising of the Protestant Estates in 1618 deposited 300,000 gold ducats and three

49. Hoszowski, *Les prix à Lwow*, 64. For a modern statement, see Bernholz, "Currency Competition."

50. Schöttle, "Die grosse deutsche Geldkrise," 41; and Stuart, *Free Trade in Tuscany*.

51. Schöttle, "Die grosse deutsche Geldkrise," 41.

TABLE 14.2.   Prices of Selected Foodstuffs, Augsburg, 1618–1624

	Pennies per Bushel					Pennies per Pound				Pennies per Quart	
Year	Rye	Barley	Oats	Peas	Rice	Pepper	Cheese	Carp	Grease	Honey	Milk
1618	787	756	473	1006	21.0	196	35.0	24.5	21. 0	84.0	3.50
1619	952	892	544	n.a.	21.0	189	35.0	24.5	n.a.	96.7	3.50
1620	1153	1036	552	1428	19.0	203	38.5	25.0	24.5	100.6	3.50
1621	2636	1771	1337	1720	20.0	420	84.0	70.0	70.0	129.5	3.50
1622	6516	4755	3729	6065	n.a.	560	224.0	126.0	n.a.	369.2	2.65
1623	2357	2065	1271	2895	26.2	140	52.3	52.5	52.5	121.0	2.67
1624	1938	1370	1054	1568	21.0	157	52.5	42.0	42.0	108.0	3.01

Source: Elsas, *Geschichte der Preise*, vol. 1, 595, 602, 623.
Note: n.a. indicates not available.

tons of gold jewelry in Frankfurt am Main.[52] There is less anecdotal evidence of huge fortunes in the German circles, perhaps because many of them were dissipated in the Thirty Years' War.

If the rich in some cases benefited from the currency debasement of the *Kipper- und Wipperzeit,* the poor suffered, especially salaried workers in cities without a plot of land or animals for meat. That prices of basic foodstuffs rose on the order of five to eight times during the inflation is indicated by data gathered from (rather unreliable) hospital records; those of Augsburg are shown in Table 14.2 and inflation for rye is shown in Figure 14.2. The latter also indicates daily wages for journeyman masons and for farm laborers engaged in the harvest.

Although we lack cost-of-living indices for that portion of the population using market than natural or barter economies, a crude estimate of real income is possible using journeyman masons' daily wages and the price of rye in Augsburg. The rough correlation of food prices in Table 14.2 provides some limited justification for taking the price of rye as a proxy for the cost of living; it is likely, too, that bread constituted approximately 50 percent of the cost of living. The data of Table 14.3 suggest that real wages of market participants in Augsburg fell by more than half from 1619 to 1621 and perhaps to a third in 1622. Recovery after stabilization was of course impeded by the Thirty Years' War. The table provides a comparison with real wages for building labor in Southern England as calculated by Phelps Brown and Hopkins, and makes clear the far greater loss in Germany than in Britain.

---

52. Parker, *Thirty Years' War,* 49; Braudel, *Structure of Everyday Life,* 463; and Klíma, "Inflation in Bohemia," 376, 381.

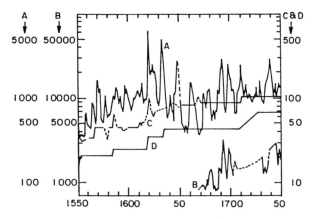

Fig. 14.2.   Prices and Wages in Augsburg, 1550–1750. *A* equals price of rye in pennies per bushel; *B* equals price of wheat in pennies per bushel; *C* equals daily wage of journeyman masons (summertime) in pennies per day; *D* equals daily wage of farm laborers (reapers) in pennies per day. All series are on semilog scales. (*Source:* Elsas, *Geschichte der Preise,* vol. 1, p. 784. The data are taken from hospital records.)

TABLE 14.3.   Relatives of Real Wages in Augsburg and Southern England for Specified Years 1611–1627 (1601–1610 = 100)

Year	Augsburg	Southern England
1611	77	100
1612	82	90
1613	105	85
1615	78	85
1617	129	88
1619	118	95
1621	52	102
1622	34	90
1625	55	80
1627	68	95

Source: For Augsburg, calculated from daily summer wages of journeyman masons and the price of rye by Elsas, *Geschichte der Preise,* vol. 1, 731–32, 395; for southern England, calculated from Phelps Brown and Hopkins, "Seven Centuries of Prices," 312–13.

Perhaps more damaging than the gap between wages and prices was the widespread breakdown of trade between town and country. Peasants refused to deliver produce to the town or city unless they were paid in Reichstalers or received outrageous prices in coin. Everywhere was evidence of what is called today "private compensation" (organized barter) and the trading of town dwellers' household possessions for country dwellers' food. Craftsmen such as shoemakers, potters, saddlers, and rope makers kept their goods at home, and the baker, butcher, and fishmonger stopped bringing goods to the market.[53] The available literature does not discuss the impact of the debasement/inflation on merchants in the Hanseatic ports or the major trading cities, but judging by the pressures in the former for stabilization and for deposit banking, the adverse impact on merchants there was probably substantial.

In the first stages of the debasement there was a boom, felt all over Europe.[54] Bit by bit the pace of debasement and inflation accelerated in 1620 and especially in the summer of 1621 and the first quarter of 1622, when it became manic.

> As soon as one receives a penny or a groschen that is a bit better than another, he becomes a profiteer. . . . It follows that doctors leave the sick, and think more of profits than of Hippocrates and Galenus, judges forget the law, hang their practices on the wall and let him who will read Bartholus and Baldus. The same is true of other learned folk, studying arithmetic more than rhetoric and philosophy; merchants, retailers and other trades—people push their businesses with short goods, which are then marked with a mint stamp.[55]

Even nobles danced around the golden calf.[56]

The 1622 quotation is perhaps evocative of the 1980s' interest in financial manipulation, but especially echoes a 1650 quotation from a Spanish source: "Agriculture laid down the plow . . . the arts disdained mechanical tools. . . . Goods became proud."[57]

At first the uneducated masses could not tell the difference between

---

53. Wuttke, "Zur Kipper- und Wipperzeit in Kursachsen," 148; Schöttle, "Die grosse deutsche Geldkrise," 41; and Langer, *Kulturgeschichte*, 31.

54. Glamann, "European Trade," 481; and Gaettens, *Geschichte des Inflationen*, 88.

55. Quoted in Ibid., 89.

56. Redlich, *Die deutsche Inflationen*, 89.

57. Vilar, *Gold and Money*, 168–69.

good and bad money, so authorities in Ulm forbade exchanges of money against money—but to no avail. In some cases, as understanding spread, peasants were forced to take bad coin and pay in good. This slowness to understand was echoed later, when it took months for the masses to realize that good money had come back. The literature stresses that the exchangers "enticed" the general run of people, provoking "giddiness." One particularly debased coin was called a "snare" (*Schlinger*). In time, as domestic trade broke down, the differences became all too apparent. In Hameln, the glittering new coins were called "tinsel" money, the white coating of which wore away after a few weeks in circulation. Children played with it in the street.[58]

As inflation proceeded and the distribution of income and wealth became more and more skewed, riots broke out. The houses of exchange dealers were stormed in Brandenburg and Halberstadt, and in February 1622 a riot in Magdeburg involved several hundred people, leaving 16 dead and 200 wounded. In Cracow crowds clashed with the municipal council in 1622 and 1623, largely over money matters. Some cities in Saxony forbade gatherings for fear of demonstrations after crowds stormed houses in various places in 1621.[59] Most of the historians commenting on these demonstrations observe that the crowds blamed the exchangers and minters rather than the nobles, princes, and cities that established scores of new mints and leased still more.

The impact of the *Kipper- und Wipperzeit* on mosaic Germany is a matter of some debate. In one view, so much of the population was engaged in the natural economy, living with little need to earn or spend money, and so few had fixed incomes, despite some mention of "widows and orphans," that the debasement and inflation did not hurt many people. Officials, it is claimed, were able to keep pace by graft and corruption.[60] A similar view is that the economic and demographic catastrophe of the Thirty Years' War is, if not a myth, at least exaggerated.[61] An economist who does not work with primary sources is in no position to judge the devastation of either the debasement or the war, but can

58. Redlich, *Die deutsche Inflationen,* 14; Schöttle, "Münz- und Geldgeschichte," 86; Bogucka, "Monetary Crisis," 146; Schöttle, "Die grosse deutsche Geldkrise," 47, 52; and Langer, *Kulturgeschichte,* 30.

59. Redlich, *Die deutsche Inflation,* 36; Langer, *Kulturgeschichte,* 119; Bogucka, "Monetary Crisis," 146; and Wuttke, "Zur Kipper- und Wipperzeit in Kursachsen," 150.

60. Van Klaveren, *General Economic History,* 165; and Wuttke, "Zur Kipper- und Wipperzeit in Kursachsen," 97–98.

61. Parker, *Thirty Years' War,* chap. 7, part 2, esp. 214; and Steinberg, "Thirty Years' War," 1060.

call attention to one view that the former was far worse than the latter— in fact comparable with the devastation of the Black Death.[62] Support for this view comes from Macaulay's *History of England,* in a passage dealing with the wave of clipping that led to the recoinage of 1696.

> Yet it may well be doubted whether all the misery which has been inflicted on the English nation in a quarter of a century by bad Kings, bad Ministers, bad Parliaments and bad Judges, was equal to the misery caused in a single year by bad crowns and bad shillings.[63]

Or, as one Guibert de Nogent (1053–1124) remarked on the medieval debasement of Bishop Gaudri II of Laon, France: "No hostility, no plunderings, no burnings have done worse damage to this province. . . ."[64]

The Path Toward Stabilization

The breakdown in both trade and the acceptance of *Kippergeld* became so complete that various steps were taken, albeit slowly and ineffectually at first, to bring the currency crisis under control. The first attempt was in Lower Saxony in 1619; despite the spread of the Thirty Years' War, there was talk of stabilization but no action. In February 1620 the Wurtemberg authorities sought to join Electoral Pfalz, Baden, Ulm, Augsburg, Strassburg, and other units in a minting union. But because the majority of the cities and states involved were geographically separated by intervening governments that did not join, the attempt failed. Then in March 1620 the treaty of Ulm among Augsburg, Nuremberg, Frankfurt, Strassburg, and Ulm sought to establish new minting rules and to produce a 31-batzen piece equal to 2 florins, 4 kreuzer as the equivalent of a Reichstaler. Ulm used the occasion to accelerate its minting.[65] The same five cities tried to join with northern German cities in the endeavor, but without result.

Action, when it came, began in the north with the Hanseatic cities. Hamburg and Lübeck concluded a mint treaty in 1618. They were joined in January 1620 by the Duke of Mecklenberg in the Lower Saxon Circle and by the city of Bremen in agreement with Wismar. The Reichstaler was set at 42 schillings (equal to groschen), but raised in April to 48. The

---

62. Gaettens, *Geschichte des Inflationen,* 94.
63. Macaulay, *History of England,* vol. 4, 186.
64. Quoted in Bisson, *Conservation of Coinage,* 3.
65. Schöttle, "Münz- und Geldgeschichte," 84–85.

Kreistag at Luneberg in April 1621 set up a commission on the minting question. It reported back belatedly in 1623 with recommendations that, once adopted, constituted the decisive act in ending the *Kipperzeit* in the Lower Saxon Circle.[66]

The Upper Saxon Circle came along only in 1623, but in one fell swoop rather than step by step. The gradual model, which was followed by the Swabian, Franconian, and Bavarian circles, was termed on one occasion by Schöttle a "gigantic error" and later "unwise."[67] Many mints in Upper Saxony had stopped producing *Kippergeld* in 1622 and 1623 because its passers could no longer get people to accept it. In June 1623, the Elector of Saxony brought together the various official boards and asked them five questions about currency policy. The commission reported the next day in a memorandum of 26 pages that recommended returning to the Imperial Ordinance of 1559 and setting the Reichstaler at 24 groschen. In the following days the Elector ordered a recoinage on that basis and the reinstitution of the mint trials, which has been allowed to lapse for five years.[68]

Shaw states that a great imperial deputation of all the circles was convened in 1623 to establish the final return to the Augsburg Ordinance of 1559, but this is not treated in the German literature I have consulted. The value of 1 florin, 30 kreuzer to the Reichstaler lasted with minor exceptions as the standard until the Zinnaïsche standard of 1 florin, 45 kreuzer, established in 1669 in an attempt to stabilize the currency once more, well after the end of the war. There was then a still further depreciation in the Leipzig standard of 1690 to 2 florins, or 120 kreuzer.[69]

It is of some interest that Ulm produced new copper coins while the stabilization was being worked out on a silver basis, and that in the Upper Saxon Circle a limited amount of credit money began to circulate after *Kippergeld* could no longer be placed—an important step, Wuttke claimed, in the development of German monetary relations.[70] These steps toward providing some sort of circulating medium after all subsidiary coins had vanished and high-denomination coins were hoarded are evocative of the Rentenmark established in the fall of 1923 before the creation of the Reichsmark under the Dawes Plan the next year.

---

66. Gaettens, *Geschichte des Inflationen*, 91.
67. Schöttle, "Die grosse deutsche Geldkrise," 53; and Schöttle, "Münz- und Geldgeschichte," 92.
68. Gaettens, *Geschichte des Inflationen*, 92–93.
69. Shaw, *History of Currency*, 106, 199, 200.
70. Schöttle, "Münz- und Geldgeschichte," 93; and Wuttke, "Zur Kipper- und Wipperzeit in Kursachsen," 153.

A Comparison with the German Inflations of the Twentieth Century

The debasement/inflation of 1619 to 1623 came in for renewed study in Germany after the inflations of 1919 to 1923 and 1939 to 1948. One telling difference noted by Gaettens is that the inflation of three centuries earlier got under way before the outbreak and especially before the spread of the Thirty Years' War, and stabilization took place early in the war rather than well after it.[71] Although the institutions of 1618 and 1918 were vastly different, central authority was weak in both cases: in the former because of the organization of the Holy Roman Empire, in the latter because of the strength of warring "distributional coalitions," to use Olson's phrase—Junkers, peasants, industrialists, laborers, and civil servants—all pulling in separate directions and determined to fend off some appropriate share of the burden of reconstruction and reparations.[72] The path to monetary reform after the more damaging World War II was smoothed both by the destruction of those vested interests in the Nazi period and during the war and by the existence of the authority of the occupying powers, which ultimately produced the stabilization of the monetary reform of 1948—despite the widespread myth that this was the work of Ludwig Erhard.

One more comparison is worth making between the *Kipper- und Wipperzeit* and the positions taken after World Wars I and II: it concerns the question of debt. This is widely discussed in the literature on the earlier inflationary episode; it is generally agreed that the muddling through that ensued was not satisfactory. Princes, nobles, and ecclesiastics who had been paid rents or interest in debased money lost, as did all manner of states that similarly received money in taxes and dues. Ordinary people who turned in their debased money for recoinage and got back in new coin only its metallic value also lost heavily. So did those whose debts had been repaid in debased money. New debts contracted during the inflation provoked the difficult question of what money was required for the payment of interest and repayment of principal. An earlier rule of 1572—a period of far milder inflation—stated that debts should be repaid in the currency in which they had been contracted, and there was a wave of pressure for reinstituting such a rule. The issue animated churchmen and jurists as well as business people, lenders, and borrowers. Redlich charges that the Elector of Saxony, who insisted on new money for his *Kippergeld* loans, was either feathering his own nest

---

71. Gaettens, *Geschichte des Inflationen*, 91.
72. Olson, "Some Questions about the Weimar Republic."

or drunk. In any case, the invasion of Electoral Saxony in the Thirty Years' War made any payment of debt by the impoverished populace impossible.[73] In general, different circles and the states and cities within them worked out different solutions over a period of years stretching well beyond the 1648 Treaty of Westphalia. The Swabian Circle laid down a rule as early as March 1622 calling for creditors to get back when they invested—good money for good, bad for bad—following not the letter of the law but the dictates of Christian love. There were many exceptions to the 1622 rule, especially where official fiscal interests were affected, and the authorities were still struggling with the issue three decades later when it was decreed that all debts remaining from the period were to be cut in half. Kassel in Hesse promulgated an effective and equitable solution set out in detail by Redlich over three pages.[74] One distinction was drawn between debts contracted in money and in goods. Authorities and courts were overwhelmed for years. The comparison holds, of course, not only with the period after the inflation of 1919 to 1923, when holders of property and those who had repaid debt gained substantially whereas wealth in the form of money and government debt was wiped out, but also with the *Lastenausgleich* associated with the Monetary Reform of 1948 after World War II, which together reduced all fixed claims to wealth by 90 percent and imposed a mortgage of 50 percent on real property.

Conclusion

Let me try to draw some conclusions from the foregoing. To the five known methods of propagating international financial crises—(1) gold and short-term capital movements (or money flows); (2) price changes in internationally traded goods and assets; (3) trade flows; (4) long-term capital movements, including their sudden halt; and (5) pure psychology—we can add currency debasement that spreads abroad following Gresham's Law, though this may perhaps be regarded as a special case of money flows.[75]

There is also considerable support for the view that 1619 to 1623 was a watershed in the economic development of Germany, as the entire first half of the century was for Europe as a whole. It is striking how

73. Redlich, *Die deutsche Inflation*, 57.
74. Schöttle, "Münz- und Geldgeschichte," 98–100; and Redlich, *Die deutsche Inflation*, 58–61.
75. Kindleberger, "International Aspects of Financial Crises."

many economic series are broken then—stopping short of 1620, starting only in 1624, or showing wide gaps in the data for those years (for example, in the exchange rate of Piacenza on Nuremberg, but not Frankfurt). Note also the number of missing observations in Elsas's price series for Germany.[76] Bookkeeping in the imperial city of Nördlingen broke down during the hyperinflation and took years to recover.[77] Of greater importance was the shift from old banks such as the Welsers of Nuremberg, which went bankrupt in 1614, and the Neapolitan Bank of the Holy Spirit, which stopped growing in 1622 after a brilliant expansion from 1600,[78] to new deposit banks, which hastened the development of the bills-of-exchange network.

Another issue, which has a bearing on a banking question of today, is the stability of free competition in the creation of money. Roland Vaubel and Friedrich Hayek in Europe and George Selgin, Richard Timberlake, Lawrence White, and Leland Yeager in the United States advocate abandoning monetary controls and opening the business of issuing money to anyone who chooses to enter it. This policy assumes an inverse of Gresham's Law: that the public will perceive which firms issue good money and bank with them alone. This surely happens at the peak of a debasement or overissue, when money becomes so bad as to be worthless and substitutes are found. But free minting, which occurred when the controls of the Holy Roman Empire—coin-testing days, oaths of mint masters and their journeymen, oaths of the official assayers, agreements of the separate circles and the monetary controls within them—all broke down, suggests that some control is necessary. The fallacy of composition worked against a simultaneous and universal movement toward restraint, each circle free-riding in a fashion that prevents production of the public good of monetary stability in the absence of effective central government. Various appeals to the Elector of Saxony were made for help in the currency disorder, but he did not see what he could do. No single *Stand* could produce order. The only possible means was a general Imperial Assembly, but the Elector's proposal for such a meeting would not work. The weakness of the Empire lay exposed to all eyes. And the Elector realized that he could not produce order by himself.[79]

Centralized effective control might not be necessary in a world

---

76. Hoskins, "Harvest Fluctuations"; Posthumus, *Nederlandische Prijsgeschiedenis;* Silva, *Banque et crédit en Italie*, vol. 2, 149–52, 187; and Elsas, *Geschichte der Preise.*

77. Friedrichs, *Urban Society in an Age of War,* 148.

78. Spooner, *Monetary Movements in France,* 65.

79. Wuttke, "Zur Kipper- und Wipperzeit in Kursachsen," 137, 154.

populated by economic men—rational, intelligent, and with access to cheap information—but history reveals that the world is not like that. By revealed historical preference, some controls are needed to protect the vulnerable underclasses, and in a world in which some people at various levels of authority are greedy and perhaps unprincipled, strong, honest, central control is necessary. The breakdown of wildcat banking in Michigan in the 1830s, I understand, is blamed by the advocates of free banking on government: they claim that if the bankers had been left alone free banking would have worked. This counterfactual strikes me as absurd. In addition to the millions of vulnerable in the world are perhaps hundreds of thousands of the guileful—persons ready to exploit the unwary—and including even those assigned to protect the unsophisticated. The *Kipper- und Wipperzeit* was blamed at the time on the minters who violated their oaths or on the exchangers and smugglers of good coin out and bad coin in. Source after source, however, recognizes that the real responsibility lay with the nobles, princes, city officials, high church officials, and even the Emperor.

Monetary regulation, as the press has constantly reminded us in the 1980s and early 1990s, can never be completely effective; nor can it be safely abandoned. The tension between regulators and regulated, and between regulators and their watchdogs, is inevitably continuous.

References

Attman, Artur, *American Bullion in the European World Trade, 1600–1800* (Goteborg, 1986).

Barbour, Violet, *Capitalism and Amsterdam in the Seventeenth Century* (paperback edn., Ann Arbor, MI, 1966).

Bernholz, Peter, "Currency Competition, Inflation, Gresham's Law and Exchange Rate," *Journal of Institutional and Theoretical Economics,* 145 (Sept. 1989), 469–88.

Bisson, Thomas N., *Conservation of Coinage: Monetary Exploitation and Its Restraint in France, Catalonia and Aragon, c 1000–1225 A.D.* (Oxford, 1979).

Bogucka, Maria, "The Monetary Crisis of the XVIIth Century and Its Social and Psychological Consequences in Poland," *Journal of European Economic History,* 4 (Spring 1975), 137–52.

Braudel, Fernand, *The Structure of Everyday Life,* vol. 1 of *Civilization & Capitalism, 15th–18th Century* (New York, 1986).

Braudel, Fernand, *The Wheels of Commerce,* vol. 2 of *Civilization & Capitalism, 15th–18th Century* (New York, 1986).

Chaudhuri, K. M., *The English East India Company: The Study of an Early Joint-Stock Company, 1600–1640* (London, 1965).

de Roover, *Gresham on Foreign Exchange: An Essay on Early English Mercantilism* (Cambridge, MA, 1949).

dtv (Deutscher Taschenbuch Verlag), *Atlas zur Weltgeschichte, Karten und Chronologischer Abriss*, vol. 1, *Von den Anfägen bis zur Franzöischen Revolution* (Munich, 1964).

de Vries, Jan, *The Economy of Europe in the Age of Crisis, 1600–1750* (New York, 1976).

Ehrenberg, Richard, *Capital and Finance in the Age of the Renaissance: A Study of the Fuggers*, translated from the 1898 German edn. (New York, 1928).

Einaudi, Luigi, "The Theory of Imaginary Money from Charlemagne to the French Revolution," translated from the Italian of 1936, in F. C. Lane and J. C. Riersma, eds., *Enterprise and Secular Change* (Homewood, IL, 1953), 229–61.

Ellis, Howard E., *German Monetary Theory, 1905–1933* (Cambridge, MA, 1934).

Elsas, M. J., *Umriss einer Geschichte der Preise und Löhne in Deutschland*, 3 vols. (Leiden, 1936, 1940, 1949).

Feaveryear, Sir Albert, *The Pound Sterling: A History of British Money*, 2nd edn., rev. by E. Victor Morgan (Oxford, 1963).

Friedrichs, Christopher R., *Urban Society in an Age of War: Nördlingen, 1580–1720* (Princeton, 1979).

Gaettens, Richard, *Geschichte des Inflationen*, 2nd edn. (Minden, 1986).

Glamann, Kristof, "European Trade, 1500–1750," in Carlo M. Cipolla, ed., *The Fontana Economic History of Europe: The Sixteenth and Seventeenth Centuries* (Glasgow, 1974), 427–526.

Gould, J. S., "The Trade Depression of the Early 1620s," *Economic History Review*, 2d series, 7 (Aug. 1954), 81–90.

Heckscher, Eli F., *An Economic History of Sweden*, translated by Göran Ohlin (Cambridge, MA, 1954).

Henning, Friederich-Wilhelm, *Das vorindustrielle Deutschland, 800 bis 1800* (Paderborn, 1974).

Hobsbawm, E. J., "The Crisis of the Seventeenth Century," in Trevor Aston, ed., *Crisis in Europe, 1560–1660: Essays from Past and Present* (London, 1965), 5–58.

Hoskins, W. G., "Harvest Fluctuations and English Economic History, 1480–1619," *Agricultural History Review*, 12 (Summer 1964), 28–46.

Hoszowski, St., *Les prix à Lwow (XVIè-XVIIe siècles)*, translated from the Polish (Paris, 1954).

Judge, A. V., "Phillip Burlamachi: A Financier of the Thirty Years' War," *Economica*, 6 (Nov. 1926), 285–300.

Kellenbenz, Hermann, *Sephardim an der unteren Elbe: Ihre wirtschaftliche und politische Bedeutung von Ende des 16. bis zum Beginn des 18. Jahrhunderts* (Wiesbaden, 1958).

Kindleberger, C. P., "International Propagation of Financial Crises: The Experience of 1886–1893," in C. P. Kindleberger, *Keynesianism vs. Monetarism and Other Essays in Financial History* (London, 1985), 226–39.

Kindleberger, C. P., *Manias, Panics and Crashes: A History of Financial Crises,* 2d ed. (New York, 1989).

Kindleberger, C. P., "The Panic of 1873," in Eugene N. White, ed., *Crashes and Panics: The Lessons from History* (Homewood, IL, 1990), 69–84.

Kindleberger, C. P., "Spenders and Hoarders: The World Distribution of Spanish American Silver, 1550–1750," in C. P. Kindleberger, *Historical Economics: Art or Science?* (Berkeley, CA, 1990), 35–85.

Kindleberger, C. P., "International (and Interregional) Aspects of Financial Crises" in Martin Feldstein, ed., *The Risk of Economic Crisis* (Chicago: University of Chicago Press, 1991), 128–32.

Klíma, Arnošt, "Inflation in Bohemia in the Early Stage of the 17th Century," in Michael Flinn, ed., *Seventh International Economic History Congress* (Edinburgh, 1978), 375–86.

Langer, Herbert, *Kulturgeschichte des 30 jähriges Krieges* (Leipzig, 1978).

Macauley, Thomas Babington, *History of England from the Accession of James II,* vol. 4 (London, 1948).

Olson, Mancur, "Some Questions about the Weimar Republic and Possible Parallels in the Developed Democracies Today," in Peter Koslowski, ed., *Individual Liberty and Democratic Decision-Making* (Tübingen, 1987), 127–41.

Opel, J. C., "Deutsche Finanznoth beim Beginn der dreissigjährische Krieges," *Historische Zeitschrift,* 16 (1966), 213–68.

Parker, Geoffrey, "The Emergence of Modern Finance in Europe, 1500–1730," in Carlo M. Cipolla, ed., *The Fontana Economic History of Europe: The Sixteenth and Seventeenth Centuries* (Glasgow, 1974), 529–94.

Parker, Geoffrey, *The Thirty Years' War,* rev. ed. (London, 1987).

Phelps Brown, E. H., and Sheila V. Hopkins, "Seven Centuries of the Prices of Consumables Compared with Builders' Wage-Rates," *Economica,* n.s. 23, 92 (Nov. 1956), 296–314.

Posthumus, N.W., *Nederlandische Prijsgeschiednis,* 2 vols. (Leiden, 1943).

Rapp, Richard T., *Industry and Economic Decline in Seventeenth-Century Venice* (Cambridge, MA, 1976).

Redlich, Fritz, *De Praeda Militari: Looting and Booty, 1500–1815, Beihefte 39 to Vierteljahrschrift für Sozial- und Wirtschaftsgeschichte,* 1956.

Redlich, Fritz, *Die deutsche Inflation des frühen 17. Jahrhunderts in der zeitgenössischen Literatur: Die Kipper und Wipper* (Cologne, 1972).

Romano, Ruggerio, "Italy in the Crisis of the Seventeenth Century," in Peter Earle, ed., *Essays in European Economic History, 1500–1800* (Oxford, 1974), 185–98.

Schöttle, Gustav, "Die grosse deutsche Geldkrise von 1620–23 und ihr Verlauf in Oberschwaben," in *Würtembergische Vierteljahrshefte für Landesgeschichte,* N.F., 30 (1921), 36–57.

Schöttle, Gustav, "Münz- und Geldgeschichte in ihren Zusammenhang mit der jenigen Schwabens," in *Würtembergische Vierteljahrshefte für Landesgeschichte,* N.F., 31 (1922–24), 54–128.

Shaw, William A., *The History of Currency* (London, 1895).

Shaw, William A., "The Monetary Movements of 1600–21 in Holland and Germany," in *Transactions of the Royal Historical Society,* n.s., 9 (1895), 189–213.

Silva, Jose-Gentil da, *Banque et crédit en Italie au XVIIe siècle,* 2 vols. (Paris, 1969).

Smith, Adam, *The Wealth of Nations,* Cannan ed. (New York, 1937).

Spooner, Frank C., *The International Economy and Monetary Movements in France, 1493–1725* (Cambridge, MA, 1972).

Steinberg, Siegfried Henry, "The Thirty Years' War: Economic Life," in *Encyclopedia Britannica,* 14th ed. (1968), vol. 21 (Soelman-Timmins), 1060.

Stuart, James Montgomery, *The History of Free Trade in Tuscany, with Remarks on Its Progress in the Rest of Italy* (London, 1876).

Supple, Barry E., "Thomas Mun and the Commercial Crisis, 1623" *Bulletin of the Institute of Historical Research,* 27 (May 1954), 91–94.

Supple, Barry E., "Currency and Commerce in the Early Seventeenth Century," *Economic History Review,* 2d ser., 10 (May 1957), 239–55.

Supple, Barry E., *Commercial Crisis and Change in England, 1600–1642* (Cambridge, 1959).

Thirsk, Joan, and J. P. Cooper, eds., *Seventeenth-Century Economic Documents* (Oxford, 1972).

Tilly, Richard, *Financial Institutions and Industrialization in the Rhineland, 1815–1870* (Madison, WI, 1966).

Trevor-Roper, H. R., "The General Crisis of the Seventeenth Century," in Trevor Aston, ed., *Crisis in Europe, 1560–1660: Essays from Past and Present* (London, 1965), 59–75.

van der Wee, Herman, "Industrial Dynamics and the Process of Urbanization and De-urbanization in the Low Countries from the Late Middle Ages to the Eighteenth Century: A Synthesis," in Herman van der Wee, ed., *The Rise and Decline of Urban Industries in Italy and the Low Countries (Late Middle Ages-Early Modern Times)* (Leuven, 1988), 307–81.

van Klavaren, Jacob, *General Economic History, 100–1760: From the Roman Empire to the Industrial Revolution* (Munich, 1969).

Vilar, Pierre, *A History of Gold and Money, 1450–1920,* translated from the 1969 Spanish original (London, 1976).

Wilson, Charles, *The Transformation of Europe, 1558–1648* (Berkeley, 1976).

Wolowski, Louis, *La question monétaire,* 3d ed. (Paris, 1869).

Wuttke, Robert, "Zur Kipper- und Wipperzeit in Kursachsen," in *Neue Archiv für Sachsiche Geschichte und Alterstumkunde,* 15 (1916), 119–56.

CHAPTER 15

The Great Disorder by Gerald D. Feldman:
A Review Article

Among the big unsettled questions of modern history and economic history, four loom large—the industrial revolution, the French Revolution, the German inflation of the 1920s, and the world depression of the 1930s. All are still studied, debated, giving rise to many theories, mostly mono-causal and conflicting. More may be on the way, for example the inflation of the 1980s and the stagnation of the early 1990s. But Gerald Feldman has written a big book that must be taken into account in any discussion of the German inflation, big in many senses, 1,000 pages of double-column print (triple columns in the index), 4.48 pounds in weight at my local supermarket, and covering in the order of the subtitle the politics, economics, and sociology of this pathological episode. Specialists in any one discipline may find their own discipline relatively neglected, especially economists who tend to want more theory, as D. C. Coleman indicates, who asserts that theories are what economists make, while historians need evidence (1960, 8). The evidence here is prodigious: forty-nine tables, two-thirds that number of photographs and illustrations, eighty-five pages of endnotes, twenty-four pages of bibliography, and a forty-two-page index, the work of fifteen years of study of the subject and forty-three earlier publications of Feldman—books, articles, and edited work, some with colleagues, mostly his own. The feast is rich; some economists and economic historians may find it too rich for ready digestion.

Feldman is aware of his problem in combining contradictory modes of analysis, but believes it necessary. Partly in a reaction to the work of Carl-Ludwig Holtfrerich, whose *The German Inflation, 1914–1923* (1989) concludes that the results of the inflation on balance were favorable in giving Germany years of investment and full employment in a largely

Review of *The Great Disorder: Politics, Economics and Society in the German Inflation, 1914–1924,* by Gerald D. Feldman (New York and Oxford: Oxford University Press, 1993).

Reprinted from *Journal of Economic Literature* 32, no. 3 (September 1994): 1216–28.

depressed world and ridding it of private foreign and all internal debt, he asserts:

> What has been missing in the investigations of the German inflation has been a detailed narration and analysis of the role and interaction of business and political leaders, on the one hand, and social organizations and structures on the other. The goal of this book, therefore, is to explore politics and society in Germany in their domestic, and very importantly in their international context from the onset of the First World War to the stabilization. (11)

The narrative form of the discussion—in seventeen chapters, each on the average fifty pages in length, with, again on the average, 150 footnotes directing one to extensive archives and private papers along with contemporary writing and secondary literature—divides the treatment chronologically and omits tables and treatment of individual institutions covering large sections of the period, and especially the years from 1921 to 1924. The account is divided into six parts: the war and reconstruction; the crisis from November 1918 to the Kapp (right-wing and failed) putsch of April 1920; relative stability to May 1921, when the London Ultimatum fixing reparations at 132 million gold marks was issued and reluctantly accepted; trotting to galloping inflation leading to the assassination of Walther Rathenau, the industrialist-politician and foreign minister, in June 1922; the buildup to hyperinflation in the second half of 1922 and 1923; followed by the *Rentenmark,* the Dawes Plan, and stabilization. Those who need longer statistical series are referred, beyond the classic studies of Frank D. Graham (1930) and Costantino Bresciani-Turroni (1937) to, among others, Holtfrerich (1986) and Steven Webb (1989).

I

Three competing but not necessarily mutually exclusive theories seek to explain inflation in Germany, and perhaps elsewhere: the monetary, the balance-of-payments, and the structural. The monetary theory was propounded for the German experience by many German economists, bankers and even industrialists, by the British expert, Sir John Bradbury, whose plan for its correction was on the table for a time, and by Bresciani-Turroni, who served as an Italian member of the Reparations Commission in Berlin. Its formulation is sometimes general and monocausal, as in Milton Friedman's repeated statement in *Money Mischief*

(1992): "Inflation is always and everywhere a *monetary* phenomenon" (emphasis in the original).

The balance-of-payments theory was pleasing to German politicians and officials, who blamed the inflation on reparations. In this view, reparation payments led to exchange depreciation, which raised domestic prices and wages, calling on the central bank to issue more money to prevent economic collapse. The two accounts are sometimes combined in succession. Initial exchange depreciation in 1919, coming not from reparations but from heavy industry paying off its Swedish debt for iron ore bought during the war, led to inflation so long as the mark was undervalued. With bull speculation in the currency as foreigners bought marks in anticipation of a return to par, the currency became overvalued, and the source of inflation, after a period of stabilization, turned to the domestic side. At a late stage, with capital, both foreign and German, fleeing the country when the hopes of revaluation were lost following Rathenau's assassination, undervaluation led again, but was closely followed by internal money creation. Feldman insists that the beginning of hyperinflation in July 1922 originated largely with the Reichsbank's discount of commercial bills on a rapidly rising scale, along with its continued discount of treasury bills to finance the Reich deficit.

The structural theory of inflation seeks to go deeper, and regards money creation and capital flight as symptoms rather than causes. One variation is the wage-push theory put forward by Karsten Laursen and Jørgen Pedersen (1964). More generally, it applies in a society in which "distributional coalitions," to use the phrase of Mancur Olson (1982), or interest groups in society, try to avoid bearing an undue, or large, or in some instances any share of a burden placed on a society—in the German case, the costs of war, reconstruction, and reparations. Feldman likens the process to the game of Old Maid—in German *schwartze Peter*—in which players try to rid themselves of the Queen of Spades (in the case of Old Maid) by passing it on to the next person.

Among the Germans who embraced the balance-of-payments theory were Karl Helfferich, an economist who had been Finance Minister at the end of the war, and Rudolph von Havenstein, president of the Reichsbank. Along with many politicians, they maintained that stabilization could not be undertaken until the Germans knew what the reparations bill would be, and that it was payable, perhaps, with a large international loan. Lacking a loan, the need was for a moratorium on reparation payments in sizable amount until economic recovery had been assured. French hopes rested on German borrowing from abroad to pay reparations—"commercializing the debt," much as foreign subscriptions to the Thier *rentes* in 1871–72 had enabled the French to pay off the Franco-Prussian indemnity ahead of schedule. But no amount for reparation payments was given until May 1921, and then in the form of an ultimatum that the Germans agreed to with the greatest misgivings and foreboding. The Socialist government pursued a "policy of fulfillment," trying to pay reparations without much hope that it would succeed.

Feldman asserts that the London Ultimatum was a British creation, an attempt to reduce the total bill without fully informing the French and British publics. Twelve billion and thirty-eight billion of gold marks would be paid through the issue of A and B bonds between July 1 and November 1, 1921, while the remaining eighty-two billion of C bonds would not be due until the Germans had covered interest and sinking funds under the A and B bonds (339). Some optimistic Germans believed that the Allies would demand only the fifty billion gold marks, and not the rest, an amount that Germany had offered, which experts like Carl Melchior and Max Warburg of the Warburg Bank in Hamburg thought feasible, and which was not exorbitantly far above the forty billion gold marks of John Maynard Keynes's polemical *Economic Consequence of the Peace* (1919). But if the London Ultimatum misled the French and the British publics, it deceived most Germans as well. It was accepted by the Reichstag only 220–173 (343). The assassination of Matthias Erzberger, the finance minister, in August 1921, after a vitriolic attack on his character by Helfferich, further contributed to the decline in the mark, which went from the sixties to the dollar in the first five months of 1921 to 84 in August and 105 in September (5, table 1). "Fulfillment" continued as a policy, but it became a tactic, not a conviction (452).

Reparations posed a number of vicious circles in the minds of participants on both sides. Domestic stabilization had to wait until the reparations issue was settled; on the other hand, reparations could not be fixed with assurance until some stability had been gained on the domestic monetary and fiscal fronts. To pay reparations in the short run, Germany needed loans, but bankers refused to lend until a reparations settlement was reached. Inside Germany, Joseph Wirth and Wilhelm Cuno, successively chancellors, and Havenstein of the Reichsbank maintained that outside assistance was the first need, while Julius Hirsch, economics minister, Rudolf Hilferding, finance minister, and Moritz Bonn, an economist and widely used expert, thought that internal stabilization came ahead of external (466). Foreign exchange collected from exports and speculative capital inflows, together with the gold of the Reichsbank, were available alternatively for reparations, and for imports of food and raw materials—in the last case, including steam coal for the *Reichsbahn* (German railroad system) to replace the coking coal shipped as reparations to France and Belgium. In addition, Havenstein of the Reichsbank was determined to hold on to his gold of roughly one billion marks as a "last reserve," much as admirals were reported to be reluctant to expose a "fleet in being" to the risks of naval battle.

On the domestic front, there were many who argued with Hirsch, Hilferding, and Bonn, that the Reichsbank should stop or at least slow down discounting Treasury bills. The list included many distinguished economists in private life who believed in the quantity theory of money— Walter Eucken, Ludwig Mises, Karl Schlesinger, Alfred Lansburgh, Ludwig Pohle, and L. Albert Hahn (402). A few, including the Reichsbank vice-president, Otto Georg von Gläskapp, advocated higher discount rates (640). It is shocking to modern economists who observe interest on long-term bonds rising and falling with hints of price levels moving up or down, that the Reichsbank's discount rate was set at 5 percent through 1920, 1921, and July 1922, before being raised by slow steps to 12 percent in January 1923, 18 percent in April, 30 percent in August, and 90 percent in September and October as stabilization finally began to bite (Holtfrerich 1989, 73, table 23; only the 1922 and 1923 figures are provided by Feldman in 590, table 27).

As already indicated, Feldman blames the hyperinflation from July 1922 on the Reichsbank discount of commercial bills. It can be argued, however, that the refusal of the International Bankers' Committee on June 12 and the assassination of Rathenau on the 24th turned the speculative capital flow from inward to outward, leading to undervaluation of the mark and a push to inflation from this source. The dollar rose from 272 marks on June 1 to 318 on June 12, 355 on June 24, and 374 on the last day of the month. In addition, if one insists on the internal cause, it is easy to get misled by the fact that table 26 (585) on commercial discounts of the Reichsbank is in millions of paper marks, whereas the preceding table 25 on treasury bills and the percentage of them held outside the Reichsbank is in billions. The increase in T-bills discounted by the Reichsbank between July and December comes to 1,076 billion, whereas that of commercial bills discounted is 434 million for the same period. Pride (or shame) of place should go to the treasury.

It is thoroughly upsetting to a modern economist, to be sure, that the Reichsbank encouraged the discounting of commercial bills on the real-bills theory that tripped up the Bank of England at the time of the bullion controversy in the 1810s, by holding the discount rate at 8 and 10 percent when commercial banks were earning 30 to 50 percent on their lending. The rest of Germany was learning the necessity of valorizing or indexing prices, income, and taxes. It is surprising, perhaps shocking, that the Reichsbank was so unsophisticated and slow.

Valorization proceeded at different paces for different groups, if for few with market capacity as slowly as the Reichsbank. The lags were critical to the inflationary process. Payroll taxes were collected for wages and salaries by employers, who held the money to pay the treasury quarterly with depreciated monies. Property owners, including industrial corporations and farmers, paid taxes not as income was earned, the system applied to the working class, but belatedly, after making up the profit accounts and often after disputes with the tax authorities, again with cheaper money. Multiples applied to specific customs duties and export taxes lagged well behind the depreciation of the mark. The highly decentralized system of German finance inherited from 1871 and little modified by Karl Helfferich, the finance minister during much of the war, was finally reformed by Matthias Erzberger, finance minister, in 1920, but still left gaps in timing that contributed to the Reich's rising deficit.

Another massive contributor to the deficit was the bloated civil service of the Reich and the states, and the workforce of the nationalized railway system. Feeble attempts to reduce numbers failed until the heroic efforts of Gustav Stresemann and Luther in later 1923 with the help of emergency powers to govern by decree. Civil servants, railroad workers, and coal miners were the privileged groups in the labor force, whose threatened strikes, and in one case actual strike, reduced government to impotence (579). While labor clung to the eight-hour day, industry, including especially Hugo Stinnes of the iron and steel concern, opposed it with a ferocity that verged on the paranoid. Industrialists also felt strongly about the need to reduce the civil service in numbers and to privatize the *Reichsbahn* (railroad system) for the same purpose.

II

Structural theory regards the falling exchange rate and rapidly rising money supply as symptoms, not causes. Feldman is eloquent on the divisions within German society, and the conflicting agenda of various groups. Labor had won the eight-hour day in the revolution of November 9, 1918, after campaigning for it since the 1890s, and was determined to keep it. Civil servants and the railroad workers had good jobs at good pay and were determined to use their political clout—in ways that would please public-choice theorists—to stay not too far behind, even with, or if possible ahead of the rising cost of living. At one late stage, the civil service managed to win an arrangement under which it was prepaid its wages quarterly on a schedule that anticipated the rate of inflation, a victory that outraged the private sector, not least doctors, lawyers, and writers, who were reduced to eating meat only once a week (679-80). Socialists demanded a capital levy, or "appropriation of real values," to force property owners to share the burdens of the lost war. All classes, in fact, felt disadvantaged (193). In a mixed metaphor, an American reporter in November 1923 wrote that the German people were "at one another's throats like a pack of wolves instead of standing man to man by the ship and forgeting their petty quarrels" (773).

Disagreements ran within as well as between classes and factors of production, and of course between creditors and debtors. Bankers disagreed with industrialists, industrialists of the Ruhr and Rhineland with those of Berlin. Processors of iron and steel in the machinery industry felt imposed upon by producers of iron and steel, while those among the latter that were not vertically integrated blamed their troubles on the coal mines. States such as Bavaria, Saxony, and Thuringia, along with the Rhineland with its particular problem of occupation, threatened at the end to secede. Manufacturers were accused by wholesalers of profiteering, whether individually or through their many cartels, while retailers, who daily faced the angry consumer, insisted that the fault lay with the wholesaler.

Particularly badly off were the professional classes—lawyers, doctors, authors who quarreled with publishers, actors with stars and directors. The *Mittelstand*, which translates poorly as "the middle class," including along with the professions of teachers and intellectuals, such other groups as shopkeepers, felt particularly aggrieved. In professors' houses, leather chair sets were cut up to make shoes, curtain linings ripped out for clothing (528–34).

In his book, Holtfrerich argues forcefully that the distribution of income and wealth was rendered more equitable by the inflation (1986, 272–73, 277, tables 57–60). Feldman agrees that unskilled workers gained at the expense of skilled, and both sets of workers gained on that part of the *Mittelstand,* consisting of small rentiers, pensioneers, and disabled with their losses in money and money claims (613–14). Academic readers will be particularly moved by the section of chapter 12 on "The Distress of the Intellectual Workers," with tables 21 A and B showing the real wage of a higher official, adjusted for normal expenditure, falling below one-half of that of an unskilled worker in April and July 1922, and only slightly higher, at 55 percent, in October of that year (549). *Privatdozent,* equivalent perhaps to an American assistant professor, were the worst off (547), except for students, who were hungry much of the time (779).

III

Debtor relationships in hyperinflation produced all sorts of social tension and stress. Most of the difficulty was domestic; some involved debts owed by German concerns, including governmental bodies, to foreigners. In a section of chapter 12 entitled "Mark for Mark," the question was addressed whether a paper mark of a given period would satisfy a debt contracted earlier in gold marks or marks of a higher dollar value. The issue posed an agonizing problem for the law, and German judges for a long time ruled that a mark was a mark, and that debts of any kind, including bonds and mortgages, with and without a gold clause, could be paid off within the terms of the particular contract, by paper marks regardless of the extent of depreciation. The same issue had arisen three centuries earlier in the debasement of metallic coins under the Holy Roman Empire at the outset of the Thirty Years' War, with similar messy results (Kindleberger 1991, 169–70). Late in 1923, however, a Supreme Court in Leipzig ruled in favor of a defendant who was being sued for refusing to accept paper marks to pay off a mortgage on property in a former German colony in Southwest Africa. The judgment was rendered on the grounds of equity and good faith, and opened up a series of suits, mostly settled by arbitration, with creditors who had been paid off in paper marks seeking some revaluation of the debt (812 ff). Settlements ranged from 5 to 50 percent in gold marks, with most concentrating at about 15 percent. No adjustment was made for Reich debt, despite the gold clause, nor were ways found to compensate pensioners, war widows, or disabled veterans. The disorderly experience paved the way for the *Lastenausgleich* (equalization of war losses) that followed the monetary reform of 1948 after World War II. All money claims were reduced by 90 percent, and then a 50 percent mortgage was imposed on real assets—the capital levy so much wanted by Socialists in 1920–23.

IV

Like the biographies of Karl Helfferich (Williamson, 1971) and Matthias Erzberger (Epstein, 1959), Feldman's book is loaded with words that lie outside the usual economic lexicon—hate, fury, rage, putsch, along with the assassinations of Erzberger and Rathenau, each after vicious verbal attacks on him by Helfferich, himself "the most hated man in Germany" (Williamson 1971, 342). Feldman further records threats of assassination against a Prussian police official, who, in his antiprofiteering campaign, used cartoons by the left-wing artist, Käthe Kollwitz, which were thought to stir up class hatred (246); rumors of assassination attempts by the right wing against Chancellor Joseph Wirth (483); and threats against Stresemann, who served as chancellor and later as foreign minister (706).

Labor, agriculture, and industry were each strongly conscious of their class or factor interest. Government was weak (69). In a telling aside, Feldman writes that Rudolf Hilferding, the Socialist finance minister, "persistently transcended class interests in his quest for a solution to the nation's problems, a characteristic he shared with Stresemann" (718), and presumably with no one else. Feldman is enthusiastic about Erzberger, the Centrist finance minister of 1919 and 1920: "Energetic, ebullient, resourceful and optimistic . . ." who forced through plans for tax reform of his predecessors and officials "with a vigor, skill and insistence rarely found, not only in the Weimar Republic, but also in government anywhere in modern history" (160). He equally lavishes close to hyperbolic praise on Stresemann, who with Hans Luther put through the transformation to the stabilized *Rentenmark*—authorship of which is contested by or shared among Helfferich, Luther, and Hjalmar Schacht—calling Stresemann "one of the great political figures of the twentieth century" (698). "The real success of the stabilization was less the so-called miracle of the *Rentenmark* [but see p. 698 "there are no miracles in history"] than the political successes of the Stresemann government, which were then consolidated under his successor, Wilhelm Marx" (754).

One economist who comes off well is Moritz Bonn, whose analysis was realistic, recognizing that the French had to be paid something because they were in bad fiscal shape and depended on receiving reparations, perhaps, in his judgment, one billion gold marks a year while working out a long-term arrangement. Bonn worried about stabilizing the mark early, lest foreign speculators take their profits or accept their losses, leading to a massive outflow of foreign capital. Like others, he wanted a foreign loan but primarily to gain time for recovery when a generous and feasible settlement of the reparation could be made (400–402). Unlike most leading industrialists, bankers, politicians, and diplomats, who gambled in terms of "fantasies" (Stinnes) or rigid conceptions, Bonn was a realist who argued that Germany should show empathy for the mentality of the rest of the world, not quibble over a few billion, more or less, and seek to trade a longer moratorium for a larger reparations program (506–7). But Feldman recognizes that the longer the moratorium and the greater the German recovery it allowed, the greater the chance that Germany in the end, in a stronger bargaining position, would have insisted on renegotiating reparations downward.

Hugo Stinnes, the right-wing industrialist, takes up a large amount of Feldman's attention. Feldman is now writing a biography of Stinnes, possibly to reconcile his conflicted view of this powerful personality:

> the living embodiment of Germany's inflationary reconstruction . . . [who] has gone down in history as the classic example of inflationary empire builder as well as one of Germany's "destroyers" . . . Stinnes has been vilified as having the worst characteristics ascribed to German industrialists—self-serving opportunism, arrogance, reactionary authoritarianism and social indifference. . . . His approach to problems, both economic and political, was determined by an almost obsessive concentration on what he deemed to be the economic logic of the situation. . . . He was uniquely optimistic and self-confident, traits seldom found in so great a measure among the rather sour and dour colleagues in the Ruhr. (284–85)

Lloyd George, on meeting him at Spa, said afterward that he had met "a real Hun" (314). In a speech on November 9, 1922, he insisted that labor work a ten-hour day without overtime pay and wanted abolition of all German controls and subsidies, withdrawal of Allied troops occupying the Rhineland, and the granting of most-favored-nation treatment to Germany by the Allies (487).

There were rare occasions when left and right or labor and industry drew together. One was a meeting of Stinnes and Rathenau that took place on June 23, 1921, at the house of the U.S. Ambassador Alanson Houghton, when Stinnes joined a dinner party at 10:30 in the evening and went back to his hotel with Rathenau, where they talked until four o'clock in the morning. It was a fateful occasion: Helferrich had unleashed a venomous attack on Rathenau in the Reichstag during the day; Rathenau was murdered on June 24 in the late morning. In their talks, Rathenau told Stinnes he thought 50 billion gold marks were feasible for reparations and agreed that controls should be ended and greater productivity drawn from the German labor force (447–49). Rathenau could get together with Stinnes better than other Socialist leaders, perhaps, for while he was a Socialist and Jewish, he was also a monarchist and as an erstwhile industrialist, as official of the A.E.G., or German General Electric Company, he was fairly conservative and even somewhat anti-Semitic (450).

France, and especially Raymond Poincaré, have been blamed for taking tough positions of German reparations. Feldman holds that this is mistaken and that the opening of the French archives has shown that much of the difficulty in fact came from the British, especially Lloyd

George, until his ministry fell in 1922. "The Germans, aided and abetted by the duplicitous British . . . undermined and aborted French efforts to secure a peaceful and satisfactory solution" (309). The British were particularly upset by German reparations paid to France and Belgium in coal that competed with their exports of coking coal, and the depreciated exchange rate that produced exchange dumping (327).

A theme that runs through the book is the German fear of foreign controls such as were imposed on Austria when that country sought a loan from the League of Nations. At the evening with Ambassador Houghton and Rathenau, Stinnes, accused of fostering inflation, hotly denied that he wanted to see the "Austrianization of Germany" (477). After all, Germany was a great power (456). There are several references in the narrative to the *assignats* of the French revolution, the previous canonical instance of hyperinflation (see index), and one to the inflationary debasement of the coinage in the Thirty Years' War. As it became clear in the fall of 1923 that something had to be done to halt the inflation, there were threats of revolution, a failed putsch by Adolph Hitler in Bavaria, and thought of a "Directory," in parallel to that of the French Revolution. The group consisted of a general, Hans von Seeckt; an experienced bureaucrat, politician, and ambassador, Otto Wiedfeldt; and an industrialist from the Stinnes firm, Friederich Minoux, whom Stinnes was not sure he trusted (742). The general lacked Napoleonic qualities, however, Hitler was jailed, and Stresemann and Luther rode out the squall.

V

Perhaps of greatest interest to the student of Germany after World War II are the many differences from the highly successful monetary reform of 1948. This involved one plan, formulated by Gerhard Colm, Joseph Dodge, and Raymond Goldsmith after consulting forty German experts: a conversion of money and all money claims above a small minimum, 10 *deutsche marks* for 100 *Reichsmarks,* and a capital levy of 50 percent on all real property in the form of a mortgage given to a fund for the equalization of war losses (*Lastenausgleich*). When a capital levy was finally agreed upon in late 1923 it came to 5 percent, readily converted to income tax. The fundamental difference, however, was the absence of conflict among interests. It is sometimes held that foreign occupation made German acceptance of the 1948 reform so easy, but this overlooks that the American secretary of war, Kenneth Royall, refused to agree to the capital levy for Germany on ideological grounds. The *Lastenausgleich* was thus left for the new, weak German government to impose on its countrymen. A case could possibly be made that the failure of the Potsdam scheme for reparations after World War II made monetary reform and burden sharing far easier than a quarter-century earlier. I have doubts. The burdens of reconstruction and coping with the influx of refugees were far larger in the second case, and after recovery Germany voluntarily undertook an extensive program of reparations to Israel that was easily borne. Waves of undervaluation of the mark certainly contributed substantially to the earlier inflation, but those in 1922 and 1923 were related more to capital flight than to reparations. The argument is even made that American speculators in marks in effect "paid reparations" to Germany (Schuker 1988). No, the difference lay, in my judgment, in the crushing of major economic and political interests during the Nazi period and in unambiguous defeat in the war. Large-scale agriculture had been obliterated by the westward movement of the eastern frontier to the Oder-Neisse line, small agriculture and trade unions by Nazi suppression, industry and the civil service rendered ineffective by loss of prestige in losing a war under a shameful regime.

VI

In discussing this article, the editor, after a quick perusal of the book, said he missed the abundance of anecdotes associated with the inflation. Feldman does not completely approve of this approach, which characterizes, for example, a book of readings edited by Fritz K. Ringer, *The German Inflation of 1923* (1969), which he also faults for the temporal inaccuracy of its title. Anecdotes, he holds, fail to explicate the inflation in all its variation and complexity (9). Nonetheless, there is a series of stories of an insightful sort scattered throughout the book. Prohibited from exporting its product, a shoe factory found the price control imposed on it left no room for profit, but continued to manufacture shoes and store but not sell them, until it acquired an inventory of a million pairs (237). Fritz Haber, the Nobel laureate in chemistry, hoping to alleviate the damage to German science of the inflation, set out to solve the reparations problem by extracting gold from sea water (514–15). A popular anecdote concerned a rope manufacturer whose sales kept rising but failed to cover the cost of renewing his stock of hemp. He became successively a millionaire and a billionaire, continuously unable to buy as much hemp as he was using, until at last he had only enough hemp to make a single rope, with which he hanged himself (568). A business traveller to Italy found, on returning, that the valorization of the railroad fare required more marks than he had on his person. Asking what he should do, he was invited to hang his watch on a board in the station, along with a number of other watches (803).

There is little doubt that the Reichsbank was a weak reed, despite its vaunted autonomy. It yielded to the government's demand to discount enormous amounts of treasury bills on the ground that if it did not, the state would be bankrupted and the economy would collapse, perhaps in civil war. Feldman seems to accept but not analyze this contention. Moreover, when it was called upon to support the mark, the Reichsbank did so hesitantly and passively, without attempting a "squeeze" of the speculators such as that in France in March and April 1924, which put the speculators (temporarily) to flight (Philippe 1931). Havenstein's lack of understanding with respect to the real-bills doctrine, and to the appropriate policy on the discount rate in periods of inflation has already been noted. Hilferding regarded the Reichsbank with contempt (692). The question remains whether, given the fissures in German society, a strong central banker—Benjamin Strong, Emile Moreau (of the Bank of France), Montagu Norman, or more realistically, Hjalmar Schacht—would have performed very differently.

Particularly fatuous were Havenstein's professions of pride over his success in printing mark notes of higher and higher denominations and larger and larger numbers, so as to prevent the gold value of currency in circulation from declining faster. In addition to the Reich Printing Office, eight-four private printing establishments were directly involved, with forty-eight others assisting. Thirty paper companies were involved and twenty-nine galvanized-plate manufacturers who delivered the plates for denominations that finally reached as high as one trillion marks. In addition, states, cities, and firms printed *Notgeld* (emergency money), like the Clearing House certificates issued in U.S. financial crises under the National Bank Act that traded only locally. Despite my admiration for German efficiency, I have difficulty in believing the Reichsbank's figures for the exact amount of currency in circulation: 2,504,956 trillion marks in October 1923, 496,585,346 trillion at the end of December (785).

VII

The Great Disorder poses a question for social scientists as to the differences between economics and history, including with economics in this instance, economic history. The issue was encountered in World War II in the Research and Analysis Division of the Office of Strategic Services, as to which discipline contributed more to intelligence useful for the pursuit of the war. A book on the subject records that the economists were disdainful of the historians as gatherers of facts without much theory, while the historians were wont to criticize the economists as sometimes (frequently?) too ready to theorize without a sufficient body of fact (Katz 1989). I happen to believe in Evans's Law—Robley Evans is a physicist at M.I.T. of my generation—that "everything is more complicated than most people think." However, one has the feeling on finishing the book that the chronological order mixing economics, politics, and sociology year by year makes understanding the entire episode more difficult than need be the case. Feldman's analysis differs in significant ways from that of Holtfrerich, and may well be superior, but like a typical German sentence, it is so long and involved that as one gets deep into it, one begins to forget the start before getting to the end. At the same time, after plowing through these pages, it is hard for me to hold with Anthony Downes, Gary Becker, and George Stigler that politics and sociology are simply lesser branches of microeconomics.

I am persuaded that Feldman is entirely right in stressing the structural theory of inflation. The best technical economic plan in the world in 1920 to 1923 would not have forestalled inflation, given the impossibility of achieving agreement on it when the vested interests were so dug in on minimizing their shares of the burden of war, reconstruction, and reparations. At the same time, Feldman leaves open the monetarist case in failing to demonstrate why the Reichsbank would have brought on state bankruptcy and civil war if it had failed to accommodate the treasury. The issue of whether there was an alternative available arises again in the controversy over Bruening's policy of deflation from 1930 to 1932, which has given rise to an enormous literature. (For a summary, see Baron Jürgen von Kruedener 1990, and especially the papers by Knut Borchardt and Holtferich). Unfortunately for our discipline, we cannot run either experiment again with critical changes.

On the fundamental question of whether the social trauma produced by World War I and the inflation was responsible for the rise of Hitler in 1933 and World War II, Feldman understandably hedges. Germany gained in economic and financial terms from the inflation—the capital inflow, the reconstruction and the erasure of debt—but it lost heavily in political and social terms (837–38). Feldman quotes Stefan Zweig that nothing made the German people so furious with hate and ripe for Hitler as the inflation (858), but between 1923 and 1933 there was a world depression in which Germany suffered dreadfully again. Like that from the *assignats* to Napoleon, the line from the inflation to Nazi takeover was indirect.

While the chronological and highly complex treatment makes it hard for a reader trying to trace a single idea or institution through these pages, the index is superb and should be used. Remarkable also are the translations from German into English, so difficult to do well, as Mark Twain has indicated, but which in this case are beautifully fluent. It would have been helpful to have a list of abbreviations, especially when one or two are missing from the index, for example, VdA, which is not under "V", but which I finally encountered under Association of Employer Organizations. Students will hanker for a *Reader's Digest* Book Condensation or Cliff Notes.

And yet the book is mandatory reading for social scientists of all kinds, and not only monetarists and historians dealing with twentieth-century Germany. I commend it especially to officials in developing countries, if they can spare the time. The process will not be repeated. Colm is quoted as saying in 1931 that, if Germany were to undergo another inflation, it would leap over the early stages of 1921 and 1922 and go directly to 1923 (853), presumably because all groups would have absorbed the lesson about the need for valorization or indexation. Nonetheless, one can learn a great deal from it about pathological societal conditions. Not all readers will lay the book down in complete agreement with Feldman's theory of structural inflation, but they should be ready to forego mono-causality in favor of recognizing the complexity of our world.

REFERENCES

Bresciani-Turroni, Costantino. *The Economics of Inflation: A Study of Currency Depreciation in Post-War Germany, 1914–1923.* London: Allen and Unwin, 1937.
Coleman, D. C. "Editor's Introduction." In D. C. Coleman, ed., 1969, *Revisions in Mercantilism,* pp. 1–18. London: Methuen.
Epstein, Klaus. *Matthias Erzberger and the Dilemma of German Democracy.* Princeton, NJ: Princeton University Press, 1959.
Friedman, Milton. *Money Mischief: Episodes in Monetary History.* New York: Harcourt Brace Jovanovich, 1992.
Graham, Frank D. *Exchange, Prices and Production in Hyper-Inflation: Germany, 1920–1923.* Princeton, NJ: Princeton University Press, 1930.
Holtfrerich, Carl-Ludwig. *The German Inflation, 1914–1923.* Berlin and New York: De Gruyter, 1986.
Katz, Barry M. *Foreign Intelligence: Research and Analysis in the Office of Strategic Services, 1942–1945.* Cambridge, MA: Harvard University Press, 1989.
Keynes, John Maynard. *Economic Consequences of the Peace.* London: Macmillan, 1919.
Kindleberger, Charles P. "The Economic Crisis of 1619–1622." *Journal of Economic History 51,* no. 1 (March 1991): 149–75.

Laursen, Karsten and Pedersen, Jørgen. *The German Inflation, 1919–23*. Amsterdam: North-Holland, 1964.

Olson, Mancur. *The Rise and Decline of Nations: Economic Growth, Stagflation and Social Rigidities*. New Haven, CT: Yale University Press, 1982.

Philippe, Raymond. *Le drâme financier de 1924–1928*. Paris: Gallimard, 1931.

Ringer, Fritz K. ed. *The German Inflation of 1923*. New York: Oxford University Press, 1969.

Schuker, Stephen A. *American "Reparations" to Germany, 1919–33: Implications for the Third-World Debt Crisis*. Princeton Studies in International Finance, no. 61 (July). Princeton, NJ: International Finance Section, 1988.

Von Kruedener, Baron Jürgen, ed. *Economic Crisis and Political Collapse: The Weimar Republic, 1924–1933*. New York: Oxford, Munich: Berg, 1990.

Webb, Steven B. *Hyperinflation and Stabilization in Weimar Germany*. New York and Oxford: Oxford University Press, 1989.

Williamson, John. *Karl Helfferich, 1872–1924: Economist, Financier, Politician*. Princeton, NJ: Princeton University Press, 1971.

CHAPTER 16

Review of Michael North, *Geldumlauf und Wirtschaftskonjunktür im südlichen Ostseeraum an der Wende zur Neuzeit* (1440–1570)

This study of monetary conditions in the Wendish Monetary Union before the arrival in Europe of the flood of Spanish silver from the New World divides naturally into two parts. The first deals with coins in circulation in the Eastern Hanseatic area, the second with whether the price revolution of the sixteenth century was a monetary phenomenon or a response to the rise in population after the Black Death.

The first four chapters, on the circulation of money, were fascinating to this economist, untutored in numismatic research. In June 1984 a treasure of 395 gold and 22,000 silver coins was found under the ground floor of a house in Lübeck, the largest find for its time in Germany, though similar to others in the South Netherlands and Jutland. Some gold and large silver coins are shown in colored plates, but the primary interest lies in comparing the coins by denomination, type, place of origin (with maps), and date with other fifteenth- and sixteenth-century finds. The treasure, hidden between 1533 and 1537, proved to be a merchant's hoard, or working capital, as the house had been used as a warehouse. Other finds were single gold coins, possibly given as christening or wedding presents, ecclesiastical treasures, tax collections, and Gresham's-Law hoards.

The interest of the numerous comparisons may be shown best perhaps by reproducing Table 14 (63), comparing the mint location of the number of coins of the Lübeck treasure with the 53 other discoveries in Northern Europe, 29 from the fifteenth century and 24 from the sixteenth (Table 16.1).

The table shows the growing internationalization of circulation of

Review of Michael North's *Geldumlauf und Wirtschaftskonjunktur im südlichen Ostseeraum an der Wende zur Neuzeit* (1440–1570) (Sigmoringen: Jan Thorbecke Verlag, 1990). Reprinted from *Journal of Economic History* 51, no. 4 (December 1991): 966–67. Copyright © The Economic History Association. Reprinted with the permission of Cambridge University Press.

the larger coins. Small silver coins—95 percent from the Wendish area—circulated more narrowly. The minting site of a coin may not indicate whence it came to Lübeck. Spanish and Portuguese coins often came from the South Netherlands (104). Coin dating also may be misleading, as some mints used an old die over a span of years (79). In the first half of the book, the author skillfully integrates a wide knowledge of archival records from such sources as the Hamburg Chamber, the Schooner Shippers of Hamburg, and tax records that list coins into the evidence from the finds.

The rest of the book addresses whether the depression of the fifteenth century and the price revolution of the sixteenth were monetary in origin or came from the real economy, in particular the decline in population due to the Black Death and its subsequent sharp recovery at a rate that produced a "bullion famine." Money losses from wear and tear in circulation and "fluctuating losses" from the melting pot, hoarding, and losses at sea pull down the money supply at rates ranging up to 5 percent a year and call for continual replenishment. Increases in velocity to overcome losses increase wear and tear. As is well known, the Hanseatic cities were backward in using bills of exchange and book entries, which were available from the Italians, to help overcome the bullion famine.

North tries to estimate the balance of payments of Lübeck from bilateral balances. The city lost precious metals to the east and north and acquired them to a degree from southern Germany and the west (Antwerp and Bruges). Gradually, however, the city was being displaced as an entrepôt center by Amsterdam.

TABLE 16.1.   Summary of Gold and Large Silver Money Circulation Based on Mint Location (In percentages)

Mint Location	Fifteenth Century	Sixteenth Century	Lübeck Treasure
Northern Germany-Northern Europe	37.1	27.0	26.3
Upper and Lower Saxony	0.8	4.6	4.4
Hesse, Rhineland, Westphalia	34.6	21.4	19.2
Franconia, Bavaria, Austria	2.8	13.3	10.9
Upper Rhine, Schwabia	4.3	4.2	5.7
Bohemia, Hungary	0.9	3.9	9.2
Netherlands	16.3	7.7	14.4
England, France	3.2	6.3	3.2
Mediterranean	—	10.8	6.7
Total	100	100	100

Population rebound, stronger in cities than in the countryside, accounted for the higher price rise of grain than of wages and craft output, supporting the real-economy side of the debate. The chapter on business fluctuations contains a large number of diagrams of price series over the period. Those for grain rose most sharply from about 1525; wages, herring, and craft output rose much less. Oxen, lamb, and geese, dependent on purchased fodder, fell in price in the short run through increased slaughtering.

The first portion of the book on the Lübeck treasure is as engrossing as a detective story. The rest is highly competent and useful in sifting through an enormous amount of literature, if less riveting.

Index